H. L Chamberlain, Houston Chamberlain

Judah and Israel

H. L Chamberlain, Houston Chamberlain

Judah and Israel

ISBN/EAN: 9783337101886

Printed in Europe, USA, Canada, Australia, Japan

Cover: Foto ©Lupo / pixelio.de

More available books at **www.hansebooks.com**

JUDAH AND ISRAEL;

OR,

THE KINGDOM OF THE GOD OF HEAVEN
(Dan. 2--14)
AS IT IS NOW:

AND

THE KINGDOM OF THE SON OF DAVID
(Dan. 7--13, 14)
AS IT WILL BE.

Being a Careful Study and Comparison of all the Prominent Passages of Scripture bearing upon the Coming of the Messiah, the Setting Up of His Kingdom, and other Correlative Subjects: and a Plain, Consistent, and Common Sense Interpretation of the Same.

SAN FRANCISCO:
THE BANCROFT COMPANY, PUBLISHERS,
1888.

DEDICATION.

To the Lord Jesus, the Christ, and the Holy Spirit, my constant companions and instructors in all holy things, without whose leading and enlightment this book could never have been written, to whom be glory forever and forever,

This book is joyfully dedicated by

'Jezreel.'

Original of the British Coat of Arms, 2000 years old.
Page 112.

PREFACE.

A SPECIAL PLEA TO THE READER.

It has been said that a book without a preface is generally not worth the reading. Now, as we believe this book, by virtue of the subjects treated, is eminently worth the reading by every man and woman who love the appearing of our Lord, we must needs have a preface ; first, to show why this book exists ; second, what is the plan and purpose of the book.

(*a*) The very unsatisfactory conclusions of all the theories we have read or heard for forty years past, respecting the character, continuance, and final results of Christ's kingdom on earth, have led us to search the scriptures carefully and patiently, guided, as we believe, by the Holy Spirit, for a solution of the prophetic record that would be in harmony with God's revealed plans, consistent with itself, and a fair and natural interpretation of all the scripture bearing upon this subject. It must also agree with the "signs of the times" which, after all, are the best interpreters of prophecy ; for, if the events predicted agree perfectly with the realised facts all along the line to the present, we are sure of our position and there *can* be no other solution. Christ himself has given us the key-note. "Ye can discern the face of the sky, but can ye not discern the signs of the times?"

(*b*) We trust we have shown in these pages that there is a perfect and very simple plan of God for the government of this world and, though the details may be intricate and not always within our grasp because of our want of knowledge in certain particulars, the general features of that plan have been so far revealed as to be seen and understood by all earnest and patient students of the word, who are willing to be led by the Spirit.

All prophecy has one central thought, purpose, and object, around which every single vision or prophetic utterance clusters and revolves more or less remote. As long as astronomers stood on the earth to view our planetary system, they saw confusion where only harmony and regularity of motion were to be expected, some going one way and some another, but when one thought to stand on the sun, he found the fault had been in himself and not in the heavenly bodies; he, with others, had taken a wrong point of vision. So with the prophecies of the Bible; if we do not get the proper point of vision all is confusion and contradiction.

Prophecy has, moreover, another phase in that much of it is formed into an enigma or puzzle to which there is one solution, and only one. Every part of the puzzle must fit into its proper place and in no other, and all parts must be there. To say that there is no plan or method connecting the whole, and that each part is independent of every other part, and has no special relation to the whole nor to all the parts, is to charge God with folly in presenting a revelation to intelligent men, to which it is impossible to find a solution, and so it becomes no revelation at all; just as if the heavenly bodies were independent of each other, and each planet was running on its own hook. Yet this is the theory of many pious and learned souls who have undertaken to give us an interpretation of symbolic prophecy. Men may not always be able to find the key, since God has that in his own keeping, and gives it to whom and at what time he will. His choices in the past have not always been in the line of "natural selection," or "scientific methods," but, as a *general* thing, they have proved correct. I cannot now call to mind any *mistakes*. Those who hunger and thirst after the knowledge of God and are willing to abide His time, will always be satisfied.

That the true interpretation of the prophetic record lies along the lines we have indicated in this volume, we *are absolutely certain,* because it fills *all* the required *conditions.* Whether we have been able to present the truth in such a way as to enlist and convince all Christian readers, is quite another thing, for the power of the truth depends almost wholly on the attitude one assumes toward it.

If you are a true "*Berean*" you will search the scriptures daily to see if these things *are* so; not, if they are *not* so. This is the attitude you expect of unbelievers, and we have a right, therefore, to ask the same of you. To have stopped to refute these various theories would be an endless task. We have, therefore, refrained as much as possible from even alluding to them, resting satisfied to present the truth as we feel assured the Spirit has given it to us, and to leave results with God.

We have been solicited often to submit these strange interpretations to some learned divines for their indorsement. As well might Paul have been asked to submit to the Sanhedrim, at Jerusalem, his letters to the churches. Our blessed Lord was asked by his brethren to get the sanction of the Doctors of the law before going out to the people, but he chose rather to keep away from Jerusalem and let the people receive him on his merits and not by popular favor and applause. The Spirit indicates the same to me.

If, after careful study of the scriptures—not the commentaries—you are convinced the puzzle is not solved by a fitting in of all the parts in their natural order, then reject it; if, on the other hand, you find that all the conditions and requirements of the scriptures are met, then accept it as the only interpretation possible, and, having the courage of your convictions, *proclaim* them, for you have no time to spare.

Far be it from me by these remarks to disparage the learning of the schools. They have done too much for the world and are being used of God to-day altogether too largely to be set aside with a sneer. One only proclaims his own ignorance by so doing. In all matters of fact, historical and antiquarian research and philological enquiry, they are invaluable aids to scriptural study and cannot be too highly prized, but in the interpretation of prophecy, especially symbolic prophecy, where God evidently holds the key, it must be evident that mere learning in any man, however holy he may be, is not going to solve the puzzle, many instances of which will appear as we proceed. Yet both the puzzle and those that have attempted its solution have answered God's purpose hitherto, and kept alive the interest of the Christian world in these sublime utterances respecting the latter day glory of the Church on earth.

One of the most notable results of learning in its influence upon scholars, especially Christian scholars, has been to create a feeling of modesty in the expression of opinions and to lead them to defer to the learning of others: so much so, that in numerous instances even gross errors in the domain of scientific enquiry, having the endorsement of some great name, have gone unchallenged round the world. Especially has this been the case in respect of the symbolic prophecies of Daniel, Zecheriah and John, and the Christian Church seems to have settled down into a chronic acceptance of certain interpretations, at once absurd and contradictory, with no one to lift a voice against them. In peace and security the Church sleeps on at the very threshold of fiery trials and judgments, waiting for the learning of the schools to inform her when she may expect the coming of her Lord. That is precisely what they did in Christ's time eighteen hundred years ago.

Christ sent out invitations to the wedding when he

was about to leave the earth. Long ages have passed and the Bridegroom, waiting to receive his Kingdom,[1] tarries, and "while he tarried they all slumbered and slept." Forty years ago the herald went forth with the cry, "Behold, the Bridegroom cometh, go ye out to meet him," yet we know it not, or, worse still, we heed it not.

This book is sent forth under God to call your attention, dear Christian reader, once more to the fact of the near approach of Christ to take his Kingdom and to receive his bride, not to *Celestial* joys through the portals of death or the resurrection, but to the joyous festivities of the marriage supper in "the new heavens and the new earth." It is written in language and style easily to be understood, and though a large number of scripture passages are quoted, there are plenty more left in the same line requiring your prayerful attention. We have confined the passages quoted strictly to the subject of the chapters in which they are found, and have not, as is so often the case, taken any passage that suited our purpose wheresoever we could find it.

What is here written is only suggestive: the exhaustive part is left with the Christian reader ; and it will carry you through the whole range of scripture with intense interest and delight, as new beauties are unfolded in the simplicity, harmony, surpassing conciseness, and wealth of expression of that wonderful book called "The Word of God." Any departures from the text of the authorised version will be found in the Revised ver-

---
[1] Psalms 110-I.

sion. That the spirit of God may guide you into all truth, and inspire you with fresh zeal to labor for the coming of the Kingdom, is the sincere prayer of

"JEZREEL."

San Francisco, May, 1887.

Summary of Contents.

CHAPTER.
- I. Signs of the Times.
- II. The Father and the Son: twofold character of the plan.
- III. Israel and Judah; subsidiary agents in the plan.
- IV. Israel in Europe, "a multitude of nations;" "the tall cedar planted by great waters."
- V. Spiritual Israel in the New World; the tender twig "planted upon an high mountain."
- VI. The God-appointed name—America.
- VII. Material endowments of the land.
- VIII. "The God of Heaven shall set up a kingdom."
- IX. The moral and political characteristics of the kingdom.
- X. Death blow to Papacy and Imperialism; pivotal point of the ages.
- XI. Fiery trials and judgments for cleansing the kingdom.
- XII. Binding the Dragon for a "thousand years."
- XIII. "Behold, He cometh with clouds" to take the kingdom.
- XIV. The millennial glory.
- XV. The New Jerusalem.
- XVI. The release of the Dragon; Christ's personal coming in judgment.

General Index.

CHAPTER I. (Page 1.)
SIGNS OF THE TIMES.

Momentous Times—The French Soldier—Discontent of the Masses—The Divine Right of Kings—Chess-board of Europe—Overthrow of Imperialism—Armies of Europe—Depleting Process—Empire of Turkey—Ceding of Cyprus—England's Ally—Russia's Motives—The Holy City—Impending Ruin—Immigration—Demands of Atheists—The Liquor Curse—Statistics of Crime—Political Corruption—The Mormon Problem—Divorce—Desecration of the Sabbath—Christian Science—The Bright Side—Christian Activity—Moral Reform—Brewers' Prayer—Fields White to Harvest—Religious Statistics—Student Missionaries—Church Building—Spirit's Presence—"Sinews of War"—Intellectual Activity—Pangs of a New Birth—Poetry.

CHAPTER II. (Page 39.)
THE FATHER AND THE SON; TWO-FOLD CHARACTER OF THE PLAN.

Indifference to Prophecy—Material things of the World—Conflicting Theories—First Advent—Uncertain Predictions—Time of the Papacy—Second Advent Theories—God's Plan—The Garden—Disobedience—Promise of Restoration—Justice takes its Course—No Pardon—Offer of the Innocent—The Greek Magistrate—Way of Transgression hard—Blood Sacrifices—Their Inadequacy

—Necessity for Change—Judgment given to the Son—The Great Commission—Love Wins Love—Christ's Kingdom not of the World—Takes time for Success—Victory over Death—Worked out under present Conditions Otherwise Redemption ends—Poetry.

CHAPTER III. (Page 59.)

JUDAH AND ISRAEL; SUBSIDIARY AGENTS IN THE PLAN.

Influence of the Hebrew Race—Two Lines—Each with Shepherding Power—One Kingly and Spiritual—The other Political and Martial—Ancestors of the Hebrews—Departure from Egypt—In the Wilderness—Life in Canaan—Consolidation under David—Promise of endless Reign—Elements of Decay—Secession of Ten Tribes—Ultimate Union—Judah's Defection—Return from Babylon—The Temple Rebuilt—Convulsions in the Kingdom—The last Prophet—Advent of Messiah—Fall of Jerusalem—End of Judah's Mission—Israel's Kingdom—Effects of Idolatry—Captivity—Israel Hidden—Their Resurrection—A New People—New Religion—Place of Exile—Ezekiel's Vision—Assyria Conquered—Scythians and Sacæ—Rock Temple Inscriptions—In the far East.

CHAPTER IV. (Page 99.)

ISRAEL IN EUROPE, A MULTITUDE OF NATIONS; THE TALL CEDAR PLANTED BY GREAT WATERS.

The Western Migration—Sources of Information—Inducements to leave Armenia—Inscription proofs—Scythians and Sacæ—Derivation of Sacæ—Early occupation of Europe—On the Euxine—Cup of Indignation—Rome Conquered—Character of Conquerors—Influence upon Southern Nations—Progress North and West—Pushing the People—Saxon supremacy—Engels of Engel-land—Entrance into Britain—Fragments of History—Saxon Influence

—The Northmen in Normandy—Great Imitators—Mutual Benefits
—William in England—Norman Influence—Israel resumes her
Name—Retrospection—Is this the End—David's Throne—The
latter-day Temple—Spiritual Israel its Builder.

CHAPTER V. (Page 119.)

SPIRITUAL ISRAEL IN THE NEW WORLD; THE TENDER TWIG "PLANTED UPON AN HIGH MOUNTAIN."

Critical point—Facts and Prophecy One—Conditions Imposed—Thus far Fulfilled—Early days of the Puritans—They remove to Holland—Sufferings in Starting—They remove to Leyden—Twelve years quiet Residence—Will move to America—Last affecting Meetings—On board the *Speedwell* for Southampton—Joined by the *Mayflower*—At Sea and putting Back—Final Departure—On the Broad Ocean—Consideration of New Heavens and New Earth—Old interpretations Rejected—Proofs of Symbolic character—An Oriental Book—Use of Symbols—One Spirit for the Whole—Destruction of Matter not Recognised—Moral and Political changes—The Sea a Home of Monsters—Sea and Abyss Interchangeable—No more Sea—What John Saw—Pilgrims introduced to the New World—New Heavens—A little one Enlarged.

CHAPTER VI. (Page 139.)

THE GOD-APPOINTED NAME AMERICA.

Scripture use of "High Mountain"—Inappropriateness of the Term—Not a Symbol—Solving the Problem—Doubtful derivation of Name, America—Its true meaning—Was it known to Columbus—No mention of it—Expectations of Columbus—Indians' supply of Gold—The Americ Range of Mountains—Name still Retained—Popularised by Sailors—First Publisher of the Name—Vespuchy not Entitled to the Honor—Contrary to all Rule in Bestowing

Names—No Chance to Deny the Honor—Columbus unable to Correct it—Superior advantage of New Derivation—Relieves Vespuchy's Name of a Charge—An Aboriginal Name—Americ or Amerique is American.

CHAPTER VII. (Page 156.)

MATERIAL ENDOWMENTS OF THE LAND.

Israel's "Place of their Own"—Oppressors far Removed—Ensign set up—Judah obeying the Call—Russia and France aiding—Material Blessings Promised—Palestine Devoid of Them—Spain the Discoverer—But does not Hold it—Vastness of the Domain Adaptability to Population—A Home for All—Free of Wild Beasts—Yet Abounding in Forests—Old Wastes to be Occupied—A place of Broad Rivers and Streams—Mineral Resources—World's Granary—National Wealth—Recent gains—Half a World Unknown—A large and fat Pasture.

CHAPTER VIII. (Page 171.)

THE GOD OF HEAVEN SHALL SET UP A KINGDOM.

Colonial Growth—Paternity of Kings—A new Birth Promised—A very Peculiar one—Nature Reversed—Bible idea of things Begun—Gregorian Calendar supersedes the Julian—Lunar time for Israel—Reasons given—Cup of Indignation—After-pangs of a Nation's Birth—Character of the Stripling—A Political kingdom "In the Days of these Kings"—Cut out of the Mountain—Antagonistic to Imperialism—Therefore Republican—Only two kinds—Cannot exist Harmoniously—Must Destroy all Opposition—Principles Involved—Political Israel God's Battle axe—Spiritual Israel a Theocratic Republic.

INDEX. xiii

CHAPTER IX. (Page 191.)

THE MORAL AND POLITICAL CHARACTERISTICS OF THE KINGDOM.

The Vision of Ezekiel—Division of Canaan—Levi Reinstated—Thirteen Divisions—The Sons of Zadoc—Service to the Nation—The Sanctuary in the Midst—The Second Gathering—Choice of one Head—A New Covenant—A New Name—One Language—Married to the Land—A Land of Homes—Number of Farmers—Investment in Farms—General Intelligence—Blind see and the Deaf Hear—First Asylum—Happy Children—Security of Highways—The One Religious Festival of Thanksgiving—Passover and Pentecost of no Significance—The Chinese Named—The Ethiopians in Chains—Control of Commerce—Nobility of Europe as Real Estate owners—Our Sea-board Safe—Perpetual Peace Assured—Clear cut Outline.

CHAPTER X. (Page 212.)

DEATH-BLOW TO PAPACY AND IMPERIALISM; PIVOTAL POINT OF THE AGES.

The Mystery of the Ages—Duration of the 1260 years—Rise of Papacy—Early Edicts—Valentian and Theodosius—Code of Justinian—Exarchate of Ravenna—Pepin of France—Uncertainty of Dates—The Apocalypse in its proper Divisions—Conditions Imposed—Gloom of the Church—Condition of Europe in 18th Century—The Wesleys and Whitefield—The Great Awakening—The Church in America—The Two Witnesses—The Bible a Sealed Book—Rome's Hatred of it—French Revolution—Churches Despoiled—Bible and Mass Books burned—Goddess of Reason Worshiped—God Dethroned—Dead in the Streets of Sodom—The great Earthquake—Carlyle's Description—Work of the Guillotine—Priests Destroyed—Edge of the Abyss—King and Queen Beheaded—The Pope a Prisoner—Death in Exile—Resurrection of the Witnesses—The Shout of the Angels—End of the Mystery—The Judgment upon the Beast.

CHAPTER XI. (Page 245.)
FIERY TRIALS AND JUDGMENTS FOR CLEANSING THE KINGDOM.

Judgment not Ended—Tares in the Wheat—Vials of Wrath—The Sixth Plague—The great Earthquake—Cleansing the Land and the Temple—Rewards of Iniquity—Survival of the Fittest—The Judgment of the Sword—God's Deliverance—Unpalatable Methods—God's Noble Army—Enormity of the Crime—Not a question of Expediency—Desperate Character of the Foe—Covetousness—Robbing the Poor—Divorce and Mormonism—Sabbath Desecration—Example of our Rulers—The Church largely Responsible—Opposition of Infidels—Their Demands—Christian Organisation—Foretaste of Trials—Hiding from the Storm—Judgment to the Line—What will you Answer.

CHAPTER XII. (Page 267.)
BINDING THE DRAGON FOR A THOUSAND YEARS.

An Accepted Theory—A Pleasant One—Rule of Interpretation—The Six Factors—Uniform Values to Symbols—Beasts out of the Sea—War in Heaven—Zecheriah's Vision—Satan in Person not there—Israel versus Imperialism—Key, Chain and Abyss, as Symbols—Substance of the Vision—The Last Conflict—Delayed for a Purpose—Elements of the Conflict—The Dragon Quiescent for a long Period.

CHAPTER XIII. (Page 278.)
BEHOLD HE COMETH WITH CLOUDS TO TAKE THE KINGDOM.

Graphic Descriptions—Efforts to Solve the Puzzle—God's purpose Answered—Intent of John's Vision—Grace not Limited—

The Tables Turned—The true Victory—God's Conflict with the Nations—The Great Trumpet—Gathering the Elect—Apathy of the Church Every eye shall See Him The Consumption Decreed A Fountain Opened He cometh with Clouds The Ascension at Olivet His like Return Clouds as Symbols Their Values—His Coming to the Churches of Asia—God's Moral epochs Quiet Affairs—One of Ancient Days One Like a Son of Man—A Willing Offering—The Midnight Cry—Expectation of the Marvelous The Marriage Supper.

CHAPTER XIV. (Page 301.)

THE MILLENNIAL GLORY.

Christ on the Throne Paul's Vision—Conflict and Sorrow Hitherto—Reduced Physical Powers Plan to Save the Race Those best Fitted to live—Smile of Heaven upon them A Purer Atmosphere—No more curses heard Present Developments Considered Advancement by Evolution Nothing Irruptive Victory by Faith Teachings of the Church Increasing Faith An easy Victory—Holiness unto the Lord—Dawning of better Days The first Resurrection "Healing of the Nations" Bruising the Serpent's head The whole Creation Groaneth—Victory over Death Tears from off all Faces New beauties Perceived—No end to the Prospect—Unappreciated Blessings Brief Mention—Regaining lost Energy—The true Interpretation.

CHAPTER XV. (Page 324.)

THE NEW JERUSALEM.

A literal Reading—Its Absurdity Shown Beauty of the Symbolism—Value of the Symbol The Language of Gems Well known to the Ancients—Expressive of Spiritual Truths The Living Temple—God Magnified The Branch of the Lord—The

Prospect before Us The Tables turned on Satan Angels Ascending and Descending The Holy City already Descended—But few now Walking its Streets—More Welcomed- Countless Hosts of the Future.

CHAPTER XVI.   (Page 334.)

THE RELEASE OF THE DRAGON; CHRIST'S PERSONAL COMING IN JUDGMENT.

Satan loosed from his Prison—No more Satan now than Before Natural Division of the Apocalypse Scriptural Explanations— End of the Thousand Years A Limited Time Reappearance of the Dragon Renewal of the old War From the same old Quarter Consigned to the Abyss from which he came—Age of Christ's reign not Limited by a Thousand Years An Endless Reign An exhausted Earth Then cometh the End —Judgment of the Finally Impenitent Descent of the Lord Himself The Earth reserved unto Fire Resurrection of the Saints- Instantaneous Change— Ever with the Lord No return to Earth An Incorruptible Body All power Relegated to the Father.

CHAPTER I.

SIGNS OF THE TIMES.

"And when he was demanded of the Pharisees when the kingdom of God should come, he answered them and said, the kingdom of God cometh not with outward show. Neither shall they say, lo here! or, lo there! for behold the kingdom of God is among you." (LUKE 17-20, 21).

"Behold the fig tree, and all the trees; when they now shoot forth ye see and know of your own selves that Summer is now nigh at hand. So likewise ye, when ye see all these things come to pass, know ye that the kingdom of God is nigh at hand." (LUKE 21-29, 30).

That we are living in peculiar and even momentous times no one will for a moment dispute. They are times which find no parallel in any age of the world's history of which we know. As the telegraph and the press bring to us daily and even hourly the quick-beating pulsations of the world, they seem to tell us that the moral and political forces of the earth are putting themselves in array for a struggle of such mighty proportions that old earth herself promises to "reel to and fro like a drunken man" under the heavy tread of men, angels, and demons, combatants for victory or death.

The exhuberant exclamation of the soldier of Napoleon's army when crossing the Alps seems likely to be realised. Looking back from a lofty height whence he could see the immense army filing and defiling up the mountain sides, surrounded on every hand by lofty peaks and overhanging crags, he could contain himself no longer, but stepping aside from his comrades he shouted in thunder tones: ATTENTION, THE UNIVERSE!! *Wheel by kingdoms!* What was thus spoken in extatic rapture seems on the eve of fulfillment as we behold in the old world the marshalling of forces never before dreamed of for number and gigantic armament, and hear the low rumbling of distant armies taking their appointed places for the last great conflict of the ages.

On all sides the murmurings of discontent, the deep undertone of the wailing masses, bubbling, seething, and often boiling into open outbreak, give premonition of the coming storm. Nothing but force, based upon the old idea that "might makes right," keeps these pent up waters from bursting their barriers and engulfing thrones and dominions in one common maelstrom of destruction. Only He who now restrains will continue to restrain until the cup of indignation is full, "*to execute upon them the judgments written.*"

"The divine right of kings" has proved a costly and burdensome pageant and the people have begun to trace many of the burdens of life to this cause, which imposes oppressive taxation upon the untitled masses for its support, for the benefit of the privileged few. Police surveillance consequent upon this condition of things, besides entailing immense cost, weighs like an incubus upon free thought respecting this huge assumption of a by-gone age, and they desire to have done with it at once and forever.

As these burdens become more and more oppressive and irksome, those who can flee from them without too great a sacrifice will be driven to this and other lands where greater freedom may be enjoyed and where life may be made more productive of happiness.

The political chess-board of Europe is just now one of mighty significance for the future well being of the world. Premising, without argument, a reign of peace just previous to and for long ages after the coming of Christ to take his kingdom, which was prefigured by the seven years of peace and the shutting of the Roman temple of Janus on the occasion of Christ's first advent, let us see, as briefly as may be, some of the "signs of the times" which we perceive foreshadowed in scripture and realised in our days, for a permanent peace, upon the exhaustion and final overthrow of the powers that to-day represent old Imperial Rome, which gave her power and her seat of empire to the Papacy for the persecution of the saints and the destruction of the church of God.

That these powers are to be overthrown and Imperialism be cast into the "abyss" for a "thousand years" or co-existent with the reign of Christ on earth, is clearly written in the scriptures, as we hope to prove in coming chapters. What we may say here of the "signs of the times" pointing to this end is simply a matter of private judgment and may be taken for what it is worth as a standpoint from which to watch these movements and see the unfolding of God's plan for the overthrow of the nations that have given their power to the "beast" for ages past, as saith the prophet:

"Therefore wait ye upon me, saith the Lord, until the day that I rise up to the prey: for my determination is to gather the nations, that I may assemble the kingdoms, to pour upon them mine indignation, even all my fierce anger: for all the earth shall be devoured with the fire of my jealousy." (Zeph. 3-8).

"And the angel thrust in his sickle into the earth, and cast it into the great wine-press of the wrath of God." (Rev. 14-19).

"For THEN will I turn to the people a pure language, that they may call upon the name of the Lord to serve him with one consent." (Zeph. 3-9).

The destruction of Imperialism and the Papacy seems to be an absolute pre-requisite of Christ's reign of peace on the earth, since they are diametrically opposed, the one to the other, and cannot exist in peace together. Between them there has always been, and there will always be antagonism until one or the other is destroyed. To this end, the powers that to-day represent the old Roman imperialism are being exhausted by the tremendous cost of their standing armies and navies. Ten millions of men drawn from the active fields of productive industry, and ready at thirty days' notice to take the field, are a sight never before seen, and a burden which the nations cannot long maintain without bankruptcy.

Russia alone is able, on an emergency, to put five millions of men in the field, and these are being drilled for that *possible* emergency. What towering accumulations of debt are being entailed by these exhaustive preparations in the European kingdoms! Since the Franco-German war of 1870 France has accumulated a debt of seven billions of dollars, and her annual deficit now, with all her returning trade and industries, is two hundred millions of francs. Many writers, seeing this state of things, are declaring that war is the only safety-valve for the preservation of the nations.

Since the Russo-Turkish war, Russia has borrowed an average of one hundred millions of dollars annually, and her debt is now ten times more than it was in the Crimean war. There is now no market for her bonds either in England or Germany, and she is seeking in France for a new loan, with very indifferent success.

Instead, however, of disarming and settling down to the peaceful avocations of life, they are constantly augmenting their forces and armaments under a fearful foreboding of something (they hardly know what) for which they seem impelled to prepare as by an unseen, all-powerful, irresistible force. Yet they cannot precipitate the battle if they would, until this depleting process has done its work almost to the point of ruin, and the command goes forth: "Thrust in thy sickle and reap; for the time has come for thee to reap; for the harvest of the earth"—the Roman political and ecclesiastical world—"is ripe." (REV. 14–15).

This depleting process must continue, therefore, to a point just previous to complete exhaustion, so that when the final defeat comes, it may be so crushing, so ruinous, that long ages of peace will be gladly accepted for recuperation. In the meantime, the principles of arbitration for all international disputes will have so far prevailed as to make it very nearly impossible for any nation to inaugurate a war on any such pretexts as have heretofore prevailed. Add to this that many of the questions now at issue will be settled forever by this very war, and it is plain to be seen that inferior questions will not be worth the powder for a resort to arms between any of the great powers, who will also take upon themselves the task of settling in an amicable way all disputes between second and third-rate nations. Should any serious disputes arise between the two great powers themselves, which seem difficult of settlement, the United States will, doubtless, act the part of peacemaker and give righteous judgment.

We shall, therefore, hear of "wars and rumors of wars," but the end is not yet, though removed by only a few years. The "septennate" war-measure of Germany, recently passed, may possibly help us in our calculations. But that the defeat is to be final and overwhelming to the representatives of Roman imperialism and the papal hierarchy, is clear and unmistakable, as may be gathered from Eze. 38th and 39th chapters, and Rev. 16–16 to 20, and corroborated by the "signs of the times."

The same process of depletion that characterises the representatives of imperial power is also going on in the Empire of Turkey; but the process in her case is modified somewhat by the prophetic record which declares that her end shall be like the drying up of a river by cutting off all the streams of supply, rather than by revolution and a final disastrous conflict as with the greater powers. (REV. 16–12). This process has been going on since 1826, when Greece cut loose from the Tartarian grasp of Turkey and set up for herself. Next followed Egypt, bringing her victorious forces, in 1833, to the very gates of the Bosphorus and the Imperial City. But for the intervention of England, and the withdrawal of the support of France, the Empire would undoubtedly have fallen. But God had decreed otherwise. She recovered lost provinces by conceding much to Egypt, who continued to acknowledge suzerainty by paying tribute until 1866, when much larger concessions were peaceably effected, and in 1872 Egypt became entirely independent of the Porte.

In the Russo-Turkish war of 1876, nearly all the European territory of Turkey was wrested from her, for, while the two parties to the conflict were facing each other in martial array, four or five of her principal provinces slipped away and set up housekeeping for themselves, leaving to her only the territory south of the Balkans, including Macedonia. It is a very notable fact, and one worthy of record, that in all that war, continuing for a period of three years, not a notable or decisive battle was fought at any point. The siege of Plevna came the nearest to anything decisive, and that was simply a starvation process, and that ended the war; yet Turkey had at various points and in the field from 250,000 to 300,000 men, eating out her vitals.

To add to her discomfiture and final ruin, England must needs assume to be the "mutual friend" at the Berlin conference in the person of Disraeli, and, by the most consummate assurance, with the acquiescence of Germany, compelled Russia to accept and Turkey to pay a *money* indemnity, which of all things she could *least* spare, instead of a *land* indemnity in Asiatic-Turkey, which of all things she could *best* spare, and what above all earthly possessions Russia *most* desired. Two little ports on the west side of the Black Sea were all she was allowed to receive. This deep wound to her pride, and defeat of her pet scheme of conquest in that direction have caused her more chagrin and deep seated hatred of England than all other causes combined, and, if we mistake not, will transfer the battle ground of the final conflict from Europe to Asia. Let us see.

To add, if possible, still further to the discomfiture of Russia, and to show the far-reaching sagacity and prescience of England's Prime Minister, Disraeli, a private bargain was made with the Porte, outside of the Berlin conference while it was still in session, by which the island of Cyprus was ceded to England,[1] and a "protectorate" accorded to her over the whole of Asia-Minor. This was a most important concession, both in its relations with Syria and Palestine on the mainland, and as a barrier for the Suez Canal and Egypt. Europe was for a moment astonished at the audacity of

---

[1] Recently confirmed and ratified.

the scheme, and its significance—as related to India
with its vast populations—as a military rendezvous, in
case of need, by way of the canal. A more consummate
piece of political jugglery and impudence throughout the
whole transaction, was never before witnessed in modern
times, for who does not know that a "protectorate,"
with England, means nothing more than final occupation
and acquisition, when the "sick man of Europe" becomes comatose or expires and his estate is divided.

Thus a Jew of the house of Judah leads political
Israel of the house of Joseph (as we hope to prove in
its proper place) to the possession of her old time
inheritance, under the guiding hand of Him who "moves
in a mysterious way, his wonders to perform." Truly,
Joseph is fulfilling his mission, for "his horns are like
the horns of unicorns; with them he shall push the
people together to the ends of the earth; and they are
the ten thousands of Ephraim, and they are the thousands of Manasseh." (DEUT. 33-17).

"The signs of the times," corroborated by scripture,
point also to Germany as the ally of England in the
great conflict, when she shall have accomplished her
great life purpose of a consolidated Empire of German
speaking people. This must now be at the expense of
Austria who will be compensated, very probably, by
the division of European Turkey, if not by the incor-
poration of the Balkan provinces into a confederacy of
of Schlavic peoples. Then, "Euphrates" being dried
up "that the way of the kings from the sun rising

might be prepared," these two nations, England and Germany, will be compelled to join hands for a life or death struggle with the Northern Bear for world wide supremacy. Other southern nations, remnants of the old-time kingdoms, will probably join Russia for the righting of their special grievances, or for some hope of gain.

That England and Germany are financially better prepared for this struggle than any of the other nations of Europe, seems to be a well established fact. That they will come out of it victorious and retain their supremacy, no one will deny who is at all acquainted with the Bible and historical records; see Gen. 22-17 : Jer. 51-19, 20, 21. The "manifest destiny" of political Israel, represented principally in these two nations, is impelling them towards old-world empire, "*that in Isaac and his seed all the nations of the earth may be blessed.*" The union of these two factors in the world's destiny, with any other of the northern Teutonic nations who may choose to fall into line, is not yet, but the progress of events in the near future will compel it.

The impelling motive of Russia, however, for the world's empire is born of a very different spirit, and partakes largely of an insatiable desire and lust of imperial power as with old Rome, and the underlying impulse is the same in both—the spirit of all evil.

England's interference, therefore, with her pet scheme of conquest in the direction of Asia Minor, Jerusalem and other sacred places of the Holy Land, a southern capital and kingdom, and a southern naval outlet, have secured for her an ill-disguised hatred that only waits the divine permit to hurl itself with superhuman vengeance on whatever stands in her way.

Another object had in view by Russia in her schemes of aggrandisement is the consolidation of the scattered and divided members of the Eastern or Greek church, numbering in all nearly ninety millions, under one political, and, perhaps, spiritual head, with the "holy city" as a capital with all its hallowed associations and inspiring history clustering around it. The "holy city" is the ultimate objective point of Russia's desires, whatever may be her present operations and outlook, all signs pointing to the acquisition of Constantinople as the end of her aspirations to the contrary notwithstanding. These have only been a feint to deceive the European powers or blind them as to her real purpose. In the division of what is left of Turkey in Europe, doubtless, Greece would largely share, since a promise to that effect was given by England at the Berlin Conference and not yet realised. Of course Albania and Macedonia would naturally fall to her, and Austria might take the rest.

At the close of the Russo-Turkish war, both Germany and Russia hinted to Austria that she was at liberty to help herself to what provinces she desired, but she didn't seem to take the hint. At last she was told outright by Bismarck to help herself, but such unwonted generosity was unappreciated. She must have felt that sometime an equivalent would be required of her which she might not be willing to give. It will be required of her when the time comes, all the same, with or without equivalent territory, and the requirement will be the half of her kingdom, with its back-bone—the German speaking people with their territory.

In this scheme of a southern capital at Jerusalem it is possible, and to me seems probable that the western Papal church, which has an equal interest in the holy places of "Jerusalem," may find sufficient inducements looking to the re-establishment of her coveted temporal power, to lead her to lay aside, for the time being at least, some of her assumptions in order that the "deadly wound" may be healed. There have been many and mutual excommunications by the Eastern and Western churches in all ages up to the time of Leo X. in 1054, A. D. Then the separation was final, and the ostensible cause of its finality was the introduction by the Latin or Western church of two words—*filioque*—into the creed. It was this addition which was, and still remains, the permanent cause of separation.[1]

This profound theological question, so all-important to the parties in dispute was, simply, whether the Holy Spirit proceeded from the Father *alone*, which the Greek church holds, or *conjointly* from the Father *and the Son* —filioque—as the Western church holds. This, and the assumption of papal supremacy have kept these two churches apart since the fifth century, when the Latin

---
[1] Ency. Britt.

church may be said to have commenced its career as an independent church. It may be counted among the probabilities that these differences may be laid aside for an all-absorbing purpose by mutual concessions. In this lies the ruin of the Latin church, for the impending calamity that will overtake the "Prince of Rosh, Mesheck, and Tubal," in his championship of the Latin nations, will bring remediless ruin and utter annihilation to that church as a *Roman, ecclesiastical, hierarchy!*[1]

"And a mighty angel took up a stone like a great millstone and cast it into the sea, saying: 'Thus with violence shall Babylon be thrown down.'" (Rev. 18-21).

"Behold, I am against thee, O Gog, chief prince of Rosh, Mesheck, and Tubal, * * * and I will plead against him with pestilence and blood; and I will rain upon him and upon his bands, and upon the many people that are with him, * * * Persia, Cush, and Put, * * * an overflowing rain, and great hailstones, fire and brimstone, * * * and I will turn thee back, and will leave but the sixth part of thee." (Eze. 38-3, 5, 22).

"So the house of Israel shall know that I am the Lord their God from that day and forward." (39-22).

But now having portrayed what seems to us the trend of events, and some of the underlying causes of the coming political conflict of Europe in the not distant future, let us turn our attention to our own beloved land and see what are the "signs of the times" for us. If the contest in the old world is for the supremacy of imperialism

---

[1] Since writing the above I have been pleased to see that a political writer in *The Nineteenth Century* magazine of London, for May, takes, from a purely political standpoint, the very results I have assumed, save in respect of the Papacy and Russia's designs on Asia and Palestine; of these he says nothing, but proceeds to show, conclusively, why England should cultivate closer relations with Germany,—and *she will.*

under the instigation of Satan, as against constitutional government represented by England or (as we assume) *political* Israel, then we may naturally expect that the same spirit of all evil will force the conflict with *spiritual* Israel, on this side the water, on *moral* questions. This is precisely what is going on to-day.

The tremendous strain upon the resources of Europe, caused by these huge preparations for war and the resulting taxation, has, for many years past, been sending to our shores immense numbers of all classes of people— good, bad, and indifferent. Such an influx of foreign element into the midst of a peaceful people is unprecedented in the history of the world. In any country but ours it would produce the wildest alarm, if not revolution and bloodshed. The peculiar nature of our institutions, and the wonderful provision which God has made in domain and resources, enable us to receive and assimilate these vast multitudes, and millions upon millions more who have yet to come, provided they are all industrious and law-abiding citizens. Unfortunately, a large proportion of them are imbued to a greater or less extent with the socialist, nihilist, and anarchist views of the middle and lower classes of European life. Finding the restrictions of the old world too exacting for their peace and safety, many leaders and other prominent men among them have come over to this country to plant here their noxious theories, and develop their plots for the overthrow of society.

Not satisfied with the fullest freedom of thought and

opinion, they have determined that any public recognition by the Government of the Christian religion, above the Muhammadan or Heathen religions, is a usurpation of privilege and power, and inimical to the spirit of liberty. Their vaunted love of liberty is simply a love of license by which every man hopes to do according to his own sweet will. Of late years they have associated with the Atheists and Infidels of the country, and together they are making of Congress in the most open and unblushing manner the following demands, which are placed at the head of their paper, *The Boston Index*. (1) We demand that churches and other ecclesiastical property shall no longer be exempt from just taxation; (2) that chaplains in all institutions aided by public funds, be discontinued, (3) and all religious services abolished; (4) that the Bible, as a text-book or as a book of worship in public schools, be prohibited; (5) that the appointment of religious festivals and fasts by President or Governors shall wholly cease; (6) that the judicial oath in all departments of government be abolished, and simple affiirmation substituted; (7) that all laws enforcing Sunday as the Sabbath shall be repealed; (8) that all laws enforcing "Christian morality" be repealed; (9) no privilege conceded to Christianity or any special religion; (10) that government shall be founded and administered on a *purely secular* basis.

They are organizing in every considerable town and city for the accomplishment of their purpose, founding their demands upon the fact that God is not distinctly recognised in the Constitution and, therefore, government has no right to favor the Christian religion above any others. They wholly ignore the fact that all our institutions were founded and built up on the Christian *sentiment* of the people, which had its roots deep-laid in the word of God. Such is the "*liberal*" Christianity of infidels. France tried that kind of Christianity to her sorrow and we want none of it, yet Christian ministers are found favoring the secular idea of government, of which the above is the natural and logical conclusion. Does not the public conscience need to be aroused on this and kindred topics that threatened dangers may be avoided ?

Then we must add to these the liquor dealers of the country, to a very large extent foreigners who, for the huge gains of their traffic, bid defiance to the laws and hesitate not to make threats against the lives and property of those who oppose them in their nefarious business. They carry out their threats too, as four instances of cold-blooded, premeditated murder of late will testify. They are necessarily hand in hand with the classes we have already mentioned, because one spirit from Tartarus animates them all, and they find in each other their best friends and patrons. The vile and maddening compounds constituting their stock in trade inflame the the passions, deaden the moral perceptions, destroy the body, and steal away the honest earnings of vast numbers who otherwise would be sober, industrious and thrifty citizens. Careful estimates from census reports place the direct amount spent for liquors in this country at the enormous figures of seven hundred and fifty millions of dollars, and the resultant expenses will swell the amount five hundred millions more. The direct expense is distributed among fourteen million five hundred thousand drinkers at a cost per capita of nearly fifty dollars. Of this vast number of drinkers, sixty thousand go annually to a drunkard's grave, their places to be filled by the long line of followers pressing on behind, from the boy who takes his wine at his father's table or the young man at his "club," to the bloated and ruined soul just ready to drop over into perdition. But for this cursed habit of drink men would be able to tide over times of depression. Vast numbers would own their homes for themselves, and would be less liable to join the godless, inflamed and turbulent classes whose shibboleth is, "Death to the bondholder."

But the cost of liquor drinking is not alone in money. If that was all the cost, it might be endured, but it costs immensely in other directions, and entails injuries and heart-aches that are quite beyond all figures to compute. "Four-fifths of the inmates of our jails, prisons, penitentiaries, and reformatories are brought there, directly or indirectly, by strong drink. There are five hundred thousand of these whisky *criminals* in the United States to-day. Every institution that is open for their reception is full of them, and the number is rapidly increasing. Then there are eight hundred thousand idiots, insane persons, helpless inebriates and paupers in the poor-houses and charitable institutions of the country, costing the taxpayers one hundred millions of dollars. But this is not all. Most of the criminality which costs the public so much money, is directly traceable to this one parent vice of drinking. This is not all. "No pen but the Recording Angel's is able truthfully to portray the sorrow that is inflicted upon loving hearts by this infernal habit of drinking stimulants. No class is so high in the social scale that it is not dragged down by it, and no class is so poor and degraded that it is not made more inhuman and miserable by it. Science shows how vice of any kind vitiates the blood and, although it may skip one generation, it is sure to crop out farther down the stream. A dead drunkard often reaches out his hand from the grave, and with his skeleton fingers palsies the brain of his descendents and sends them, like so many jabbering idiots, to the insane asylum to be supported by charity. The liquor traffic must be characterised as an unmixed curse, viewed from any standpoint whatever, and as such it does not pay."

Surely Paul's description of certain classes in his day will apply with redoubled emphasis in these "latter days."

"**Filled with all unrighteousness, fornication, wickedness. covetousness, maliciousness; full of envy, murder, debate, deceit, malignity; back-biters, haters of God, despiteful, proud, boasters. INVENTORS OF EVIL THINGS,**" (bombs and infernal machines?) "**disobedient to parents, without understanding, covenant breakers, without natural affection, implacable, unmerciful.**" (Rom. 1-29, 31).

How true to the character of many of these self-styled

"lovers of liberty." Said one of these, a "prison bird," at an ovation given to him in New York, in a fierce tirade against the press, addressing its reporters, "You ought to be hung! and when Anarchy prevails you will be hung in a batch. You are marked men." Commenting upon this the next day, one of the city papers said these true words. "They never cease to mouth about liberty, and name their organ 'Freiheit,' but all the time they mean liberty for themselves and subjection and death for all who dare to differ with them in opinion. They are a lot of loafing, lazy tyrants, usually drunken and always filthy either in person or in speech." These, then, are the people whom the spirit of all evil has moved to come over here to demolish, if possible, our God-given institutions, and bring upon us the judgments of Heaven. "Hell from beneath is moved for thee to meet thee at thy coming," O thou son of David, King of Peace! The powers of darkness seem bent on holding high carnival over the destruction of all we hold dear on earth, and carrying us back to the darkest days of the Bastile and the Guillotine.

But there are large numbers of people in every large community who have no sympathy with either of the above classes; men of standing, of education, of benevolent instincts, and of social position, who declare with emphasis that there is no need of the Church, and the God of the Bible. They think science and education are sufficient to lift men up and make them better. More education and culture they want, and less church and less religion. But men are *not* lifted up and made better by these means alone, but in this nineteenth century, when popular education prevails everywhere, especially in these United States, and every means are afforded for culture and enlightenment, we are apparently growing worse and worse, just as the word of God eighteen centuries ago said we should.

"This know, also, that in the last days erilous times shall come; for men shall be lovers of themselves, boasters, blasphemers, fierce, despisers of those that are good, traitors, headstrong, puffed up, lovers of pleasure more than lovers of God, having a form of godliness but denying the power thereof: from such turn away. For of this sort are they which creep into houses, and lead captive silly women laden with sins, led away with divers lusts, ever learning and never able to come to a knowledge of the truth." (2 Tim. 3-1 to 7 inclusive).

See yourselves reflected, men of the world, in this faithful portraiture, and say to which class you belong. Your position on certain moral questions which are sure to come up in the near future for your decision, will show you precisely where you belong in spite of yourselves if you are not willing to own it now, for this is not the end of it;

"But evil men and seducers shall wax WORSE and WORSE, deceiving and being deceived" (Ver. 13), "and mens' hearts shall fail them for fear of those things that are coming on the earth." (Lu. 21-26).

If, as it is said, "figures don't lie," we are presenting a curious spectacle to the Christian philanthropist, as well as to the world at large, when it is shown that in every thousand of the population in England two die every year of strong drink; in Scotland, three; Ireland, two; France, two; Switzerland, three; Sweden, six; and in New York State, *twelve*, and in many other States a much larger proportion. The ratio of murders per million of inhabitants has been in England. 711; in Ireland, 883; in France, 796; in Germany. 887: in the United States, 2,260.[1] We have become nearly as bad as Italy and Spain, those hot-beds of crime.

Is it not a "sign of the times" that a contest of no mean proportions is upon us for which the mightiest energies of the nation will be taxed for our preservation? Yet the strange spectacle is presented to our eyes, of ministers of the gospel, doctors of divinity even, elders, deacons, and many of the rank and file of the church militant, who are voting and speaking in a way that tends to the continuance of the saloon nuisance. and are hailed with acclamations as "men of sense," men of "liberal ideas," while they lay it to their souls with flattering unction that they are endeavoring to *suppress* the loathsome pest. Why then do the saloonists claim them as friends? Is it not a sure evidence that the "deceiver" is abroad in the land and deceiving "the very elect?" If God is pledged to rain upon his old-time cohorts in the old world a "horrible tempest," think you not the same doom awaits the hosts of Satan in this land, albeit, it may be by a different process? Nor are these all the evils that threaten to engulf us. by any means.

Closely connected with and growing out of this inordinate love of money, is the festering corruption of political life in its connection with the saloon. which

---

[1] Joseph Cook in 'Boston Lectures.'

virtuous men recognise as a threatening danger to the Republic. In support of this statement we cannot do better than append the following testimony of an eminant public man.[1] Among other things he said:—

"The corrupt use of money is, in my judgment, one of the most dangerous evils which now threaten the future of the Republic. It is the blighting, festering source of many of the other evils of which we complain. It is sapping the very foundations of public confidence and respect for law, by polluting the sources of political power. It stalks with brazen face into our legislative halls, and with scarcely a pretense of concealment dictates our laws. It too often corrupts the press, and changes the truth into a lie. It is the ready and well-known instrument by which the will of the people is thwarted in a thousand ways. It is the efficient means by which individual wealth and corporate power aggrandise themselves at the expense of the people, and by which giant evils maintain their hold upon society. Let it be generally understood and acquiesced in that elections depend not upon the free will of the people, but that their results are purchased with money, or whisky, and the end of free institutions is not far off.

Upon the ruins of Judah is written "Idolatry;" of Greece and Rome, "Sensuality;" of Spain, "Avarice;" and upon the ruins of the Great Republic will be written "Corruption," unless there be virtue enough in the

---

[1] Hon. William Windom, formerly United States Senator from Minnesota, in a public Fourth of July address at Woodstock, Conn.

people to rescue it from the bottomless abyss toward which its steps are tending. Combine and aggregate all the other corrupting agencies and influences of our times, and they are dwarfed beside the Liquor Power. Indeed, but few of the other methods of corruption are complete without it. I know of no other agency which openly proclaims its right and its purpose to control elections, and to prevent the passage of distasteful laws by the use of money.

In most of our cities the drinking saloon is the central power around which politics revolve, and which dictates candidates and party policies. Even in our National elections it sometimes exercises a controlling influence and decides Presidential contests. By the peculiar relation of political parties, New York has become a pivotal State. The saloons rule the city, the city rules the State, and the State decides what shall be the ruling power of the Republic. We are, therefore, to all intents and purposes, a rum-ruled nation."

The "Mormon problem" is acknowledged by all good men to be a blot upon our fair escutcheon, and one not only difficult to deal with, but one which threatens to spread its baleful influence through all our Western Territories. Religious zeal in error limits itself by no scruples in the accomplishment of its purposes and, under the inspiration of Satan, can do a deal of harm. This is plainly seen by their boast that "Congress can make no law through which the Mormons cannot drive a six-mule team." They have no regard whatever for an oath made to the Government on the plea that, in its violation, they are only lying to the "Gentile God," and not to the Mormon (Adon) God.

Great things are expected of the new Edmunds-Tucker bill that has become a law, which provides for the disfranchisement of women, the dissolution of the Corporation of the "Church of Jesus Christ of Latter Day Saints," and the test oath as a qualification for voting, which provides that no man "who directly or indirectly counsels, advises, aids or abets, the practice of polygamy" shall be entitled to vote. "This oath the Mormons are taking by wholesale, on the plea that, as the church organisation is annulled, there is no such corporation, and therefore an oath not to aid or abet a practice which has been declared illegal as a doctrine of a corporation, is entirely consistent and can be broken without perjury."

In order to defeat this Bill they are organising Womens' Mission Societies, whose aim is to send women throughout the Territory "preaching polygamy, and urging the brethren to hold fast to their covenants. All these things are making the law of none effect. Polygamy is practiced now quite as much as before, in spite of the continued prosecutions, and fanaticism is rampant. A six month's term in the penitentiary has become only a martyr's crown. What the end is to be we cannot tell." We recognize it as a "sign of the times" calling for the judgments of God if we do not cleanse the land of this gross pollution.

Closely allied with this in criminal enormity is our own lax law of divorce, which serves only as a pretext for legalised whoredom, and this the Mormons, with bitter irony, throw in our teeth when we talk to them of their system of plural marriages, and they certainly have the better of the argument as things now stand. In this matter we distance all competitors the world over, to our shame and disgrace and the evil is constantly increasing. In every thousand marriages in 1880, there were of divorces and separations, in England, two ; Scotland, three ; France, nine, and in godly, erudite, Massachusetts, *forty-five*. Many other States show a far worse record, and the scenes witnessed and the testimony often heard in divorce courts in connection, are of the most shameless kind and frequently too vile to be printed in the secular press. I have known church members to swear to "desertion" as the cause of divorce when the wife was boarding in the next house to her husband's and her board was paid by him. Yet the Church gave both of them letters of dismission—under protest too—to other churches as "members in good and regular standing," because "that was the easiest way to get rid of them." For shame! to palm off such members on other denominations for such a reason. Thank God, a truer conviction is taking possession of the Church and she is uttering her voice against the unholy practice and, we trust, will shortly clear her skirts of such foul stains. It is entered here as a " sign of the times," that Satan is moving his cohorts all along the line for the final struggle, knowing that he has but a short time and is now come to the " last ditch."

The general desecration of the Sabbath and its debasement to purposes of gain or pleasure by a vast majority of the people, is another of the lines on which the spirit of all evil is working for the ruin of the people and the Government. It proved to be the rock on which Israel of old struck and went down, and nothing but the divine interposition can save us, unless we restore the Sabbath to its pristine simplicity as a day wherein thou shalt

"**Turn away thy foot from doing THY pleasure on my holy day; and call the Sabbath a delight, and the holy of the Lord honorable; and shalt honor it, not doing THINE OWN ways, nor finding THINE OWN pleasure, nor speaking THINE OWN words; then will I make thee to ride on the high places of the earth"** etc. (Isa. 58-13).

It is a shameful fact that Christians are largely responsible for the introduction of the Sunday trains—as we learn by the report of the Massachusetts Sabbath Committee—to aid them in reaching their accustomed places of worship in the city from their suburban homes.

Still further to desecrate the day, Satan prompts the people to ask for their mail on this sacred day and thus the Government, to accommodate the people, becomes the greatest desecrator of all by compelling many thousands of clerks to be at the office to distribute the mail. Many professed Christians make no scruple of getting their mail and reading it all. Thus they bring secular affairs into the very sanctuary of God and work out their plans for gain on the morrow. We are fast coming into the Sabbath of Paris, and were it not for the promises of God, we should believe into an inheritance of Paris' doom. Pierre Joseph Proudhon, the communist and atheist, says of the French Sunday: "Sunday in the towns is a day of rest without motive or end: an occasion of display for the women and children; of consumption in the restaurants and wine shops; of degrading idleness; of surfeit and debauchery. The workmen make merry, the grisettes dance, the soldier tipples, the tradesman alone is busy." "Thus by a disorder which cries to Heaven for vengeance, the holy day is the day of the week most profaned." This closing reflection is by Abbe Gaume, a priest of the Catholic Church, on this horrible state of affairs. California can almost rival it.

With this greed of gain and pleasure and this wholesale trampling on the laws of a Holy and Just God, is it any wonder that the foundations of principle are undermined? the outcroppings of which are seen in defalcations, and swindling schemes, and robbing of the public treasury, and embezzlements, and fleecing of the widow and fatherless, and perversion of justice, and blood. Surely we are in the midst of the "last days," or "the consummation of the age," when Christ said the tares shall be gathered out from the wheat and cast into the fire. Nothing can save the land from this doom but a *complete reformation* like that of Nineveh.

Without stopping to dwell upon "Spiritualism" as one of the "signs" that Satan is moving all his forces to meet the corresponding developments of Christian activity through the Divine Spirit, we desire to call attention to the last, most subtle and effective delusion of the Devil in what is called Christian (?) Science or Mind Cure. As always, heretofore, since the days of Jannes and Jambres in Moses' time, Satan imitates the real thing and produces *like results* with only this slight (?) difference in the last "craze:" "All power is given unto *me*," says Christ, "in heaven and in earth." But Satan says "*Mind* rules matter, *mind* controls all things and, hence, one finds in *one's own self* all the power necessary to heal all bodily ailments, and to "say to this mountain be thou removed and cast into the sea and it shall be done." O, my dear Saviour, they have no place for you now in the world, to soothe its sorrows and lift its burdens, and for whose advent we thought the "whole creation was groaning and travailing in pain together until now!" No invitation will be extended to you now by these to come and take your inherited and richly-won throne! They have found a panacea for all ills and all burdens—SELF.

With all the warnings which have been given to you. dear brother. sister, how is it that you cannot discern the "signs of the times," and see that "these are the *spirits of devils working miracles*, which go forth to the kings of the whole inhabited earth," to gather them to the battle of *that great day* when your "*refuge of lies*" will be swept away, and your *agreement with hell* shall be disannulled." I beseech you. "touch not the unclean thing lest you be defiled." and your names blotted out from "the book of life."

Having now set forth the *dark* back-ground of the "signs of the times," the dark side of the "pillar of cloud to the Egyptians." let us see if there is any light in "the pillar of fire to Israel" to guide us in our journeyings toward the promised land. the gift of the "God of Heaven." that *is to be* the "kingdom of His dear Son."

If we have seen surprising activity among the hosts of Satan, there is equal, if not greater, activity and exertion among the followers of King Jesus. Certainly no age since the Apostles' has begun to see such splendid efforts "all along the line" as are being made to-day, and we want it to be impressed as with a pen of iron upon the mind of every man. woman and child that this activity began at the very commencement of this century nearly ninety years ago. You will see the significance we attach to that time, as we proceed, as the pivotal point of the ages.

If the Nihilists and Atheists are seeking to destroy the foundations of society. they have compelled the Christians also to organise for its preservation. especially to preserve our Republican institutions and religious privileges as they were bequeathed to us by our fathers. with this notable addition: instead of depending for good rulers and legislators on the moral and religious sentiment of the people—always a variable quantity—as did our fathers. the foremost Christians of the country have organised the Moral Reform Association of Philadelphia for the special purpose of effecting such a change in the organic law of the land as will recognise the word of God to be the true basis of all legislation, God as the rightful source of all authority to rule, and Jesus Christ, His Son, as the rightful heir of the kingdom in this and all lands, as saith the prophet Isaiah:

> "O Zion, that bringest good tidings, get thee up into the high mountain; O Jerusalem, that bringest good tidings, lift u thy voice with strength; lift it up, be not afraid; say unto the cities of Judah, 'BEHOLD YOUR GOD'!"

To this end the Association is sending out lecturers in every part of the land and instructing the people in respect to the claims of God's law and the rights of the King. At the same time they are doing valiant service in the line of better Sabbath observance, and the utter annihilation of the drink traffic. It is gratifying to know that the people are giving earnest attention to this subject, and heartily endorsing the movement as soon as they understand its aims. Of a truth, light is beaming upon us from the "pillar," and many of the first minds of the country are becoming enlisted in the cause and writing for it, though the full significance of the movement cannot as yet be fully and generally understood.

Thoughtful men, and women too, are waking up to the fact that many and great perils threaten our American institutions and Christian civilisation.[1] As a result of this widespread conviction, born of the Spirit of God,

---

[1] See the call of the Evangelical Alliance for 1887.

there has never been a time so pregnant with mighty issues. The spirit of organisation has taken possession of men, especially in the line of all benevolent and Christian effort: for men *feel* what they cannot as yet clearly see, that the great battle of the ages between the powers of darkness and those of light is upon us, and the issue must be met. Christ is marshalling his forces for the mighty struggle, out of which Spiritual Israel shall come purified, refined and strengthened, both in graces and in numbers.

"**For the weapons of our warfare are not carnal but spiritual and mighty through God to the pulling down of strongholds.**" (2 Cor. 10-5).

"**For He is FAITHFUL and TRUE and in righteousness He doth judge and make war: and He is clothed in a vesture dipped in blood; and his name is called, 'THE WORD OF GOD'; and they were slain with the sword of Him that sat upon the Horse, which sword proceedeth OUT OF HIS MOUTH.**" (Rev. 19-11, 12, 21).

All enemies must, therefore, "in this manner be killed." This characterises the warfare as a moral one and the victory certain.

Thus we see on every hand such a searching of the word of God to know the mind of the Spirit; such a longing and striving after " holiness unto the Lord " and, though at present the cloud of promise be no bigger than a man's hand, yet it gives promise of better things to come, even such an outpouring of the spirit that " there shall not be room enough to receive it." Bibles are being multiplied by the million and carried even to the most out-of-the-way places to the very doors of the people, and personal conversations had with them respecting their souls' salvation. Millions upon millions of children and youth are gathered every Sabbath in this and other lands for the study of this word of God in a lesson common to the world.

The ablest men of the age are searching the fountains of knowledge for material to prove, to elucidate and fortify the word of God and make it what it is intended to be, a "household word" in every family.

Some eighty-four Bible societies with their various auxiliaries in all lands, are publishing the Bible in three hundred and fifty-four different languages and dialects, and scattering them broadcast throughout the land and the world. Does it look as though "twenty years will see the Bible an obsolete book?"

Never before have so many prayers been offered up daily and hourly, "Thy kingdom come, O Lord, thy will be done *in earth* as in heaven." For a week in every year the world is circled with united prayer, as Saturn with his rings, while angels and archangels send back the glad response, "Peace on earth, good will to men." Moreover, there has never been since the apostolic days, such answers to prayer as are witnessed daily throughout this land; and the promise seems already fulfilled,

"**Before they call I will answer, and while they are yet speaking I will hear.**" (Isaiah 64-24).

Before this mighty power of faith and prayer the hoary headed faiths and philosophies of the world are tottering to their foundations. Says a recent writer in his report of the work in India and Ceylon:[1] "The godless are more wicked, for education has torn from them the last fibre of religious or temple restraint; the thoughtful and moral are perplexed or desperate; they are watching in suspense for the next change, or are holding fast to that which they have ceased to believe, clinging to the last plank of a shipwrecked faith." What a striking reproduction of the social condition of the falling Roman, Pagan faith during the first centuries of the Christian era. Why, even Satan himself, in his desperation, is instructing his followers to seize this mighty weapon of prayer for the support of his tottering kingdom; and at a recent convention of "brewmasters" at Chicago, the President rose and said:

"It is the usual thing to open large assemblies and conventions with prayer, and it therefore behooves us to conform to the established usage. As no member of any denomination (?) is present, I take upon myself the onerous task, which I think should conform with the disposition of this assemblage."

He then with fervor and solemn unction poured forth a prayer commencing thus:

"O, God! .Thou hast not only provided the water for our use, but, also, to the end that our bodies may be strengthened and our souls rejoiced, thou hast granted us other and pleasanter beverages. especially beer." * * *

"Brewers, as we are the instruments of the Heavenly

---

[1] Rev. E. E. Jenkins, in Methodist Times, London.

will, let us *pray earnestly* that the greatness of this gift be not misapplied. To that end let us pray for good beer and plenty of it, and let us earnestly resolve from this time on to brew no other."

If this is not offering "strange fire" on the altar, we fail to see what is, and the same doom awaits them. But let us resume.

Never before have the fields been so "white to the harvest" all over the world—with which every Christian should be familiar—and never before have so many laborers been sent forth by the Lord of the harvest for the ingathering of the fruits unto life eternal. The bonds of the Levitical priesthood have been burst asunder that we might become a "kingdom of priests and an holy nation." (Ex. 19-6). Volumes would fail to tell the wonderful story, and a few facts, only, must suffice. To say nothing of the large numbers of lay Evangelists and "Bible readers" of this country whom the Lord has sent *in haste* into the vineyard, and the larger numbers who have gone out from the Holiness Associations; and the ten thousand officers of the 'Salvation Army' in this country and in England, all supplementing the churches and reaching out after 'the masses' with redemption's glad story, we come to the missionary work of the world which now includes fifty organised American societies with an annual income of $4,420.613, and fifty European societies with an income of $5,303.237. In the employ of these societies there is a total of 2,275 ordained missionaries, 2,162 women, 2,243 ordained native helpers and 644,584 communicants in churches. besides 1.750.000 evangelised adherents in attendance. These totals show a gain over the preceding year of $659.350 of income, 25 ordained missionaries, 70 lay missionaries, 140 women, 133 ordained natives. 8.637 native helpers and 26,137 communicants.

A most remarkable movement has grown out of a meeting of two graduates of Princeton College (sons of missionaries in India) with Mr. Moody's Northfield Conference, from which they started out to visit the various colleges of the land to interest the students, if possible, in foreign missionary work, and the result has been, thus far, fully *two thousand* students have pledged themselves to the work of evangelising the world. Glory be to His dear name! Add to this the wonderful work that has sprung up in the English and Scotch Universities in the same direction and under the same divine impulse, and it is not difficult to see the "signs of the times." Many of these English students go out at their own expense, having consecrated themselves and their all to 'Him who redeemed them from the curse of the law.' Please do not forget that the first organised Missionary Association was founded in 1792 — "The Baptist Society for the Propagating of the Gospel in Heathendom"—and in 1795, "The London Missionary Society," when the dawn of missionary enterprise was concurrent with a blessed revival of piety and effort.

No longer are we required to go three times a year to Jerusalem to worship and offer sacrifices, for Christ is become our Passover for all mankind and for all time, in any place or temple where fervent souls meet for His worship. In a recent year, prior to 1876, there were built and dedicated three Christian churches for every working day in the year, *one for every three hours*, nearly, and every year brings new demands and new supplies. For four years preceding 1880 the average was more than *ten* each day.

The temple with its rent vail has passed away never more to rear its golden towers to the sky, for Christ has taught that the human heart, redeemed and cleansed of all impurity, is the only fit dwelling place on this earth of the Holy Spirit—the 'Shekina' of God.

"**Know ye not that YE are the temple of God and that the Spirit of God dwelleth in you?**" (1 Cor. 3-16).

"**And it shall come to pass afterward that I will pour out my spirit upon all flesh; and your SONS and your DAUGHTERS shall prophesy.**" (Joel 2-28).

As a fulfillment of this gracious promise we have to-day as never before, since the day of Pentecost and Apostolic times, such wonderful manifestations of the Spirit's presence in all parts of the land and of the world. News is borne on every breeze of a mighty awakening of men's minds for the reception of the truth. Never, *never* before, have gentle women been led forth as by the mighty hand of God "to the help of the Lord, the help of the Lord against the mighty." It fires the soul with a divine, an all-consuming enthusiasm, as we read and see what work these godly, Christian women are doing for the cleansing of the land of its foul corruptions. "This is the Lord's doing: it is marvellous in our eyes." (Ps. 118-23).

But not alone to the 'advance guard' of Christ's followers is committed this regeneration into a new life. Men of all shades of belief, as if moved by an unperceived, impelling power, are pouring out their money in lavish streams to supply the 'sinews of war' for this simultaneous advance. The history of the world—excepting, possibly, the age of the Crusades, and that was but a blind, religious zeal for a sentiment—shows nothing of the kind in the past for the lifting up of humanity and for the relief of distress irrespective of age, religion or race. No sooner does the cry of distress and misfortune come than relief is furnished till they cry "stop!" Freighted ships are sent to distant lands and an alien race, to feed the hungry and clothe the naked. Sorrow and suffering make the whole world akin by the mighty power of that love which knew no north, no south, no east, no west, heaven-born and Godlike. But not a tithe is now given of what will yet be consecrated to the Lord for the enlargement of His kingdom. But the good work does not stop here.

Never before has human thought been so stimulated to multiply the rewards of human industry, and while it has multiplied, *eleven* times over, the combined producing power of the world, the wages of labor have been increased *fifteen* times. Nature's laboratory and laws are being ransacked as never before to add to man's comfort and supply his needs. As the forests disappear under accumulated demands, vast fields of coal stored for countless ages are opened up and brought to our very doors. Steam, light, electricity and even the air itself are made to bend beneath the controlling hand of man, and minister to his will, while each new development, each new leaf turned in Nature's book, only opens up still greater wonders as among the possibilities of Nature's ponderous volume.

What mean these mighty upheavals of spiritual, moral and intellectual forces if they be not premonitory signs of the consummation of the age? They are the pangs of a new birth that shall introduce a reign of righteousness, joy and peace for ever. The increase, by more than one hundred per cent. in modern times of "earthquakes in divers places" gives evidence of the truth of the record, and that nature herself sympathises with man in his mighty efforts to roll off the incubus of the ages and stand forth a free man.

"The whole creation groaneth and travaileth in pain together until now, waiting for the adoption, to-wit, the redemption of our body" (from the power of sin) and "the manifestation of the Sons of God." (Rom. 8-22, 23, 19).

" Mine eyes have seen the glory of the coming of the Lord :
He is trampling out the vintage where the grapes of wrath are
        stored ;
He hath loosed the fateful lightning of his terrible swift sword,
        His truth is marching on !

" I have read a fiery gospel writ in burnished rows of steel ;
As ye deal with my contemners, so with you my grace shall deal.
Let the Hero, born of woman, crush the Serpent with his heel,
        Since God is marching on !

"He has sounded forth the 'trumpet' that shall never call retreat ;
He is sifting out the hearts of men before His judgment seat ;
O, be swift my soul to answer him, be jubilant my feet,
      Our God is marching on !

"In the beauty of the lilies, Christ was born across the sea,
With a glory in his bosom that transfigures you and me :
As he died to make men holy, let us live to make men free.
      While God is marching on !"

CHAPTER II.

THE FATHER AND THE SON.—TWOFOLD CHARACTER OF THE PLAN.

"And I will put enmity between thee and the woman, and between thy seed and her seed ; it shall bruise thy head and thou shalt bruise his heel." (Gen. 3-15).

"Which is now made manifest by the appearing of our Saviour, Jesus Christ, who hath abolished death and brought life and immortality to light through the gospel." (2 Tim. 1-10).

"And the God of Peace shall bruise Satan under your feet shortly." (Rom. 16-20).

It is a matter of great regret that there exists such a widespread indifference in the Christian church to prophecies respecting what is commonly called the 'second advent.' When spoken to on the subject the reply usually is, "We know nothing about the subject and have no particular desire to know about it, it is all so obscure. If we are prepared for death we shall be prepared for his coming." Just as though Christ did not know what he was talking about when he warned us over and over again to watch for *his coming*, not for death.

The scriptures nowhere speak of preparation for such an event as being a sufficient preparation for his coming, but they teach that a joyful expectancy of and preparation for his coming provides for all contingencies, since the greater always includes the less. By so much as the marriage feast with all its joyous festivities surpasses the mere preparation for it, does a full and clear conception of Christ's coming and "the glory that should follow," as well as of our present relations to it, surpass any personal preparation for death, or any vague expectation of a distant coming.

After all of Christ's warnings in ten or twelve different places, and the warnings of the Apostles to the same effect, do you suppose God has left us without any definite knowledge of that stupendous and all absorbing event, or that He has left us entirely in the dark respecting that which was the delightful theme of contemplation and utterance by prophets, priests and kings, as well as of the Apostles of the Lord Jesus? May it not be rather that we have failed to see the glorious vision because of our lack of interest in and neglect of the prophecies respecting it?

Christ especially warns us against falling into a

condition of indifference in regard to this subject, lest we begin to say within ourselves "My Lord delayeth his coming" and thus grow careless, worldly, unscrupulous and selfish. Inasmuch, then, as the appearing of our Lord is set forth in the scriptures as the great hope of the ages, "What manner of persons ought we to be in all holy conversation and godliness:" * * * "and *so much the more* as ye see the day approaching."

If Satan presents the material things of the world as his strongest strategic point from which to assail us and draw us from our allegiance to Christ, we are presented in the scriptures with the material interests and glory of Christ's earthly kingdom sufficiently to interest and satisfy all hearts and keep them true to him.

I know of no more absorbing study than to get first a plan of the campaign for the recovery of the world, and then to watch the unfolding of the plan—especially since "the mystery of God is finished"—and see by what "stately steppings" God is moving on to that point when He will give the kingdom to His dear Son, to the utter and complete discomfiture of Satan and all his hosts. It fills my soul with unutterable joy as I see that day hastening, and watch the events that are unmistakably pointing to it.

But you probably will reply to me, "There have been so many and such conflicting theories among the wisest and best of men respecting the coming of Christ, that I think it best for me to walk in 'the good old way' and let them all alone; by so doing I cannot go far astray."

Let me ask you, did the coming of many pretenders before the time of Christ absolve a single soul from his duty to compare with the sacred record the claims of all who appeared? That would have settled the question at once, provided they were well acquainted with the record. If the many pious Jews of Christ's time had been familiar with the prophetic record, do you think the learned Doctors of the Law could have settled the question of his coming so easily when they uttered their wonderful (?) argument, "Look and see, for out of Gallilee ariseth no prophet"?

We say then, be familiar with the record; be patient; compare scripture with scripture, and by the teachings of the Spirit you will find untold comfort in the thought of His coming, and that you may greatly help in preparing the way for him.

But there are many on the other hand who are intensely interested in this subject but who, from looking at one class of scripture only, or one phase of the subject only, have been led to believe in a coming so at variance with the plan of God that my heart is pained to witness the unhappy results that have followed such wild and exciting theories, though apparently supported by a very considerable array of scripture. Paul was obliged to warn the Thessalonians not to be deceived into a belief of the near coming of Christ in person in his day, and we need in our day to be warned that all theories which make the coming of Christ a *personal* one at this time or in the near future with all its attendant phenomena, are contrary to scripture, antagonistic to the plan of God, and derogatory to the mission of Christ.

If there was any event of ancient times likely to be foretold with any certainty as to the time of its occurrence, that event would have been the birth of the promised Messiah. That event was foretold in precise and clear terms thus :

"From the going forth of the commandment to build and restore Jerusalem, unto Messiah the Prince, shall be seven weeks, and three score and two weeks. And after three score and two weeks shall Messiah be cut off." (Dan. 9-25. 26).

One would think this prophecy to be so definite that no one could mistake the time, yet they did, although there was a general *expectancy* of the near approach of the time for his coming. Thirty years elapsed after the expiration of the date given, before it was announced that Messiah had come, whereas a belief had grown up that he would come suddenly at the appointed time, in full grown manhood from some mysterious source, like Minerva from the head of Jove full armored and complete. They had become accustomed to look at *one phase* only of his character as a Prince and, not taking the trouble to become familiar with *all* the scripture concerning him they completely failed, with few notable exceptions, of perceiving his presence among them.

Again, the time though apparently so definite was yet very uncertain, for there were four separate edicts to build Jerusalem covering a period of nearly one hundred years. God never intended the prophecy to give them any more than a general expectancy of the event, until after men had compared His character and claims with the divine record, and if the two tallied exactly they could *then* reckon back four hundred and ninety years and find corroborative evidence to a day of the truthfulness of Christ's assumptions. That is God's way of telling the grand events of His Government for the purpose at once of keeping them from the knowledge of the world, and to keep the interest of His own people alive to the scripture record, and to the "signs of the times" until the events foretold are *complete,* or so near complete (*as at the present time*) that wicked men cannot forestall or overturn them. Shall we repeat the blunder of the Jews? Then we must examine carefully the interpretations given in this book and compare them with the scripture record, for we are in a worse dilemma than were ever the Jews respecting the time of Christ's coming, as well as the character of it and the results to flow from ignoring it.

All the times which have been heretofore set for the coming of Christ and the setting up of the kingdom have been based upon the various historical dates given for the commencement of the Papacy and the corresponding continuance of the twelve hundred and sixty years of John's and Daniel's visions. In this case there are two hundred and twenty-two years between said first and last dates. The same difficulty is repeated in this prediction as in that of the decrees to build and restore Jerusalem. Who shall determine which is the right date from which to commence the duration of the papacy? That point will be determined in a scriptural manner in a future chapter. At present it is introduced to show how absurd it is, after the example of former times to undertake to fathom "the times and the seasons" *from that end of the line.* It is absolutely impossible.

Of course each "expounder of the mysteries" can suit either of the supposable dates to any preconceived theory he may happen to have, and since Christ has not come yet, the Advent has been advanced from the time of Wm. Miller, about forty years ago, all along till the present. Many are still expecting his coming in the dim future, for those historical dates will not end until 2016 A. D.

Thoroughly disgusted with these attempts to limit the Almighty by such uncertain dates, the more thoughtful expounders of the Word have now settled down to the conviction that Christ's coming is now at any time *imminent* and are holding themselves ready for it. But here again they are divided, on account of certain irreconcilable passages of scripture, into two classes called respectively pre-millennial and post-millennial theorists. Within these two bodies of expectants there are all shades of belief and almost no belief at all. It is our hope to reconcile all these divergencies on a scriptural and common sense basis.

We might go on and show in quite a number of particulars wherein we are repeating the very mistakes of the

Jews in Christ's time, by which they deluded themselves and their descendents to this day into the belief that his first advent is still in the dim future. But we think sufficient has been said respecting the time, and in allusions to some of their fallacies to insure a fair and unbiased hearing to the close of this examination of what the Bible really says respecting Christ's second coming and kindred events.

And now, dear reader, if you are prepared to follow us with an unbiased mind, let us begin at the very beginning of God's word and see if we can find out His plan in the government of this world, for it is all important for a proper consideration of this whole subject that we commence right. It is on this starting point that the whole arrangement of scripture hangs and around which it revolves. If we can settle definitely the object and outlines of the campaign for the control of the world we shall readily perceive how naturally the details find their appointed place under the guiding hand of God for a sure and decisive victory.

Hardly was man comfortably located in the garden of Eden with his new help-mate, before we find that both had disobeyed the divine command at the instigation of Satan in the person of the serpent. The eyes of the guilty pair had indeed been opened to behold good and evil, but the dangerous experience had cost them their innocence and purity, for they "hid themselves from the presence of the Lord God among the trees of the garden." (Gen. 3-8). Separation and estrangement had come, where before were loving obedience and companionship; shame and confusion had taken the place of manly dignity and womanly modesty.

In this strange position into which this happy family had come in its social relations with their Creator, there is but one course to pursue. Justice must take its course. The law had been fairly proclaimed and had been deliberately disobeyed. The consequences involved in the penalty were distinctly understood so far as they needed to be, but the word of the Serpent had been trusted rather than that of the Creator. The Garden is no more a happy home to them under the protection and companionship of the Father, but the wide world becomes their home and they must make their own roof and their own bed as best they can and where they may choose. They can no more eat at a free table with the Father's blessing, without a care or thought of trouble, but must provide for themselves out of ground *"cursed for thy sake; in sorrow shalt thou eat of it all the days of thy life. Thorns and thistles shall it bring forth to thee, and thou shalt eat the herb of the field"* until they and their seed after them shall have learned by bitter experience the horrible nature of the service into which they have deliberately entered and shall re-enter the service of their Benefactor whose allegiance they have so shamefully abandoned. "Let the decree be entered."

Everyone understands that the Civil Judge has no choice in the matter of pardons. His only duty being to see that the law is vindicated and the proper penalty imposed. So the Immaculate Judge of all the earth, being the executor of his own laws, must of necessity make the law honorable and magnify it, by seeing to it that no sinner escapes the penalty. Any other course would destroy his government. He can only proclaim the law, "Obey and live, disobey and die." The rewards of a life of obedience can be proclaimed as an incentive, and the terrors of the penalties of broken law can be sounded out as a preventive. But, alas, it is found that the offspring of the guilty pair have partaken of the taint and follow in the steps of the parents.

Only two courses are left open to God, either to pass sentence of death upon every human being, or some one innocent of any crime must voluntarily offer himself to suffer for the guilty. But where can the man be found without sin and willing to die? Nowhere. In this emergency God himself in the person of his Son "in his great love wherewith he loved us," declared "I will give my life for guilty man and, by the power of infinite love, will draw him from the service of Satan to myself." Thus Justice will be satisfied and the law will be magnified and made honorable.

It is related of a Greek magistrate that his only son was once brought before him charged with a crime, the penalty for which was the loss of both eyes. He was tried, convicted and sentenced. The multitude waited in anxious suspense to see if the judge would permit the sentence to be executed upon his own son. His fatherly heart yearned to save his son, but as judge the vindication of the law was of more value than many sons. To magnify the law and make it honorable he consented to lose one of his own eyes for that of his son, and thus preserve one for himself and one for his guilty boy.

But man has become obstinate and self-willed by his disobedience and will not yield to even a greater evidence of the Father's love until he has learned that the way and service of Satan is a very hard one. Thus he will obtain an impelling motive as well as a drawing one to return to his former obedience and allegiance to God. More than this, for he will try every scheme that the ingenuity of Satan can suggest to him to remedy the effects of his disobedience until, sick of sin and sick of his own efforts to redeem himself, he at last yields himself a willing and cheerful subject of his Benefactor and King.

To give ample time for these vain efforts and, at the same time, to give opportunity to any who might wish to return to his allegiance on the strength of a *proclamation* of the proposed sacrifice on the part of God, there was instituted the law of blood sacrifices pointing to the one great sacrifice which would be made "in the fullness of time," under the conditions of the promise given at the beginning, "The seed of the woman shall bruise the serpent's head." Here then we have the origin and reason of the ceremonial law, which was the very best that Divine Justice could devise under the circumstances— a system of rewards and punishments based upon a perfect sacrifice made, virtually, "from the foundation of the world."

But this law proved entirely inadequate to man's needs, because punishment is shown to be impossible as a reformatory measure, and rewards are not a sufficient inducement, to any great extent, to lead men away from sin. To arrive at all these conclusions has taken long ages of time, but the lessons are *for* all time and need never to be repeated. It has become evident, moreover, that the full power of the divine-human sacrifice, and another law than that of rewards and punishments and a slain lamb, must be tried if the allegiance of the world is ever to be regained to God; and to that we now turn.

We have seen how utterly impossible it was for God, in his character as lawgiver and judge, to regain the lost allegiance or obedience of man—for that is really the prime object of all His efforts—out of which come as a *result* man's happiness and salvation, since obedience always *precedes* salvation. Thence came the necessity for a change in the mode of operations, and for another person than the Lawgiver to effect a reconciliation between man and his maker. Thus we learn the reason that henceforth "all judgment is committed to the Son," and *He* shall decide when judgment shall be executed upon the wicked, when the barren fig-tree shall be cut down, and when the law shall take its course that "every man may die for his own iniquity."

This, then, is the "Great Commission" of the Son— to regain the love and allegiance of the world, which God the lawgiver had lost, and present it to the Father, blood-washed and redeemed to an eternal sonship.¹ Surely he has undertaken a mighty task, but Love is all-powerful and will come off victorious. Love will certainly answer to love, where all the power of punishment would prove unavailing. To regain this love Christ comes to earth in human form and is obedient in all things ; "tempted in all points like as we are yet without sin;" endears the people to himself by acts of love ; suffers the jeers and insults of the rabble at the instigation of those whose hypocrisy he had condemned; voluntarily offers his life to prove his love for man and prays, in cruel agony, "Father forgive them for they know not what they do."

The great lesson is taught that love can only be gained by love, and we are enabled to understand what he means when he says, "And I, if I be lifted up, will *draw* all men unto me." No force, no compulsion, no terrors of the law even, except as a horrible nightmare of the past, will be used to accomplish his purpose. Everything, from a single soul to a kingdom of people, must come under this universal rule of willing, cheerful, loving obedience as a pre-requisite of citizenship in the new kingdom. Here lies the distinguishing characteristic of Christ's kingdom as separate and distinctive from the government of the world under the Lawgiver. This distinction must constantly be borne in mind. Each is working on different lines and by different modes of action to accomplish a common object. The prophecy

¹ 1 Cor. 15-28.

of this crops out emphatically in Daniel's vision, and more or less distinct in other parts. A failure to observe this distinction lies at the root of half the trouble in interpretation.

Christ says, "my kingdom is not of this world." It is not fashioned nor built up after the manner of the kingdoms of this world by usurpation and the sword and bloodshed, nor governed by their principles of action. It is not built up by force of arms in the acquisition of territory, the inhabitants being willing or unwilling. But in the government of the world, and in the shaping and creating of kingdoms, God controls and directs *all these means* as is his inalienable right. Hence we find Him saying to the Son,

"Sit thou at my right hand until I MAKE thine enemies thy footstool. (Ps. 110-1). I will overturn, overturn, overturn, and it shall be no more, until He come whose right it is ; and I WILL GIVE IT TO HIM." (Eze. 21-27). "Thy people SHALL be willing in the day of thy power." "The Lord at thy right hand shall strike through kings in the day of his wrath." (Ps. 110- 3, 5).

These and many other passages show that God controls all moral and material forces for the accomplishment of his purposes, as Christ controls and directs all spiritual agencies for the accomplishment of his. By these means God is making even "the wrath of man to praise him" and working for the establishment of the "throne of the house of David," while Christ is working in the domain of individual human souls to bring them into loving relationship with himself. Both are operating for the self-same ultimate object—though by dif-

THE TWOFOLD PLAN. 53

ferent routes and lines of action—the loving allegiance of mankind.

But this work of love on the part of Christ takes time, and cannot in anywise be forced. "For he must reign till He hath put *all enemies* under his feet. The last enemy that shall be destroyed is death. For *He hath* put all things under his feet." (1 Cor. 15-25, 26, 27), and in his own person has given an earnest of what he purposes to do for *all his disciples*, if we will only *obey orders* and give him time.

But how is death to be destroyed? Is it to be by one grand holocaust of death and destruction to saint and sinner? It is only begging the question to say the saints will not die but will be quickened. They are taken from the present sphere of action by the use of Omnipotent power in the burning of the world and placed beyond the influence of Satan and death, and that virtually leaves Satan in possession of the field before the work of salvation is hardly begun. No! no! A thousand times, no! Such is not God's plan, and no such purpose can be found in the Bible except by distortion and wretched misapplication of scripture truth.

The victory, to be worthy of Christ and to show the power of divine love and an indwelling Spirit, must be a moral and spiritual victory, and to this all scripture agrees. Hosea, when speaking only of the resurrection of Israel as distinguished from Judah, from their graves among the nations, uses this emphatic language, " I will ransom them from the grave; I will redeem them from death : O Death, I will be thy plagues; O grave, I will be thy destruction ; repentance shall be hid from mine eyes." (Chap. 12–14). The vision of Ezekiel (chap. 37) concerning the "dry bones" is kindred to that of Hosea. But Isaiah is more particular and emphasises the character of the victory as pertaining to individual man—to spiritual Israel.

"**He will swallow up death in victory; and the Lord God shall wipe away tears from off all faces; and the rebuke of his people shall he take away from off all the earth.** (Chap 25-8). **"And I will rejoice in Jerusalem and joy in my people; and the voice of crying shall no more be heard in her, nor the voice of weeping."** (Chap. 65-19).

Paul says, "The sting of death is *sin.*" (1 Cor. 15–56); now, if the blood of Jesus Christ cleanses from *all sin*, where is the sting of death ? and if the power of death is destroyed through the resurrection of Christ (Rom. 6–9), is not our victory complete ?

Death may now say as did Julian the apostate, " O Gallilean, thou hast conquered !" for death is counted an enemy, with all the rest of hell's forces, and must be conquered in the same manner as they. " For this is the victory that overcometh the world, *i. e.*, the flesh, the devil, and the grave, " even your *faith.*" "And the God of peace shall bruise Satan under your feet shortly." (Rom. 16–20). Anything less than this is unworthy of Christ and shows weakness somewhere, and anything more than this argues defeat, which cannot for a moment be admitted. If the Father at this stage of the conflict must needs exercise omnipotent power for the destruction

THE TWOFOLD PLAN. 55

of the world, or even for a radical change from present conditions, and the withdrawal of death's victims by quickening or otherwise into the celestial state, it argues inability to overcome these enemies by the operation of forces now in the field. Hence we conclude that the victory, to be worthy of the wisdom and power of God in Christ, must be worked out *on the present plane of conditions*, since it was on that plane that the battle was lost in the beginning. Nothing short of this will fill the measure of the divine plan as clearly revealed in the scriptures. It took four thousand years to carry man to the bottom of the hill of moral and physical degeneracy (and it is always much easier to go down hill than up). Shall we not allow an equal time at least for man to rise to the best possibilities of his nature before we cut him off from this sphere of action? Let us "give the man a chance!" Do not be so eager, my dear "advent" brother, to bring down fire from heaven on poor sinners, lest we hear the Master saying to us, "ye know not what manner of spirit ye are of." "For I came not to judge the world, but to *save* the world."

There is one more consideration which ought to have great weight with us in determining the character and duration of Christ's kingdom on the earth, and it is this: when Christ was on the earth he said to his disciples, "Nevertheless I tell you the truth: it is expedient for you that I go away; for if I go not away the Comforter *will not* come to you, but if I depart, I will send him unto you." (Jno. 16-7). The logic of this statement must certainly be that the personal coming of Christ will *end* the work of redemption, whether we suppose him to come before or after the millennium. This truth is self-evident and needs no argument.

If Christ's kingdom on earth is both a spiritual and (through his saints) a temporal one, by a giving to him of the "kingdom which the God of heaven" sets up. composed largely of his own followers, how clear and beautiful is the prospect for the fulfillment of all the glorious promises of God's word which otherwise are dark and inexplicable.

We have need to modify somewhat our modern ideas of what the scriptures term "The kingdom of heaven," "The kingdom of God," as used by Christ and his disciples. In the one hundred and thirty-five places in which these phrases occur, in no instance do they refer primarily to Heaven the abode of the saints, but rather to that condition of the soul in its relations with God which fits it to be the recipient of all that comes to us as a gift of God through Christ of pardon, purity, love, and joy in the Holy Spirit. This condition of our spiritual nature gives us the victory over our surroundings and lifts us into a new atmosphere and kingdom. If this is accomplished here in the flesh we may have a blessed assurance that we are fitted for companionship with the saints and all holy beings in Heaven, for which other terms are used in the Gospels when speaking of or referring to it.

The next thought in connection with this phraseology

THE TWOFOLD PLAN. 57

is that it contains not only the idea of the King ruling in us and reigning over us, but of a *realm* in which to reign ; over which Christ shall have equally rightful sway through the cheerful obedience of the subjects of the realm, and into which shall be gathered all the richest material gifts of God's marvellous bounty for an endless reign of righteousness under the *Son of David*, Prince of God. These two ideas of inward joy and physical blessings permeate the whole body of Old Testament scriptures as fine gold permeates rich quartz rock. Christ gave practical expression to these views by releasing bound souls, healing the sick, feeding the multitudes and stilling the tempest. Thus by his life here he proved himself to be the very embodiment of all there is to be obtained by the establishment of the "kingdom of heaven" on earth. By an indwelling presence through the reception of His spirit we are enabled to perceive the "things of the kingdom" which to others are withheld by grossness of life, and unwillingness to yield to the demands of the Spirit.

"**And it shall come to pass in that day that the light shall not be clear, nor dark : but it shall be one day which shall be known to the Lord, not day, nor night; but it shall come to pass that at EVENING time it shall be LIGHT. (Zec. 14-6, 7)**
"**For out of Zion shall go forth the law, and the word of the Lord from Jerusalem." (Isa. 2-3 : Micah 4-1, 2).**
And the nations of them which are saved shall walk in the light of it; and the kings of the earth do bring their glory and honor into it." (Rev. 21-24.)

From these passages it appears evident that the reign of Christ on earth is to be one of constantly increasing light and beauty from its inception to its close in the glorious evening of time. No clouds nor darkness in the spiritual horizon of that day when Christ shall have enabled us to rise victorious over all enemies, when tears shall be wiped away from all faces, and death shall have lost all his terrors. The ages of the millennium will give ample time to prove the wonderful superiority of Christ's kingdom over every other form of government the world has ever seen. "The Sun of Righteousness shall arise with healing in his wings, and the leaves of the tree shall be for the healing of the nations. "Happy is that people that is in such a case: yea. happy is that people whose God is the Lord."

> " Hark ! hark, my soul ; Angelic songs are swelling
> O'er earth's green fields, and ocean's wave-beat shore ;
> How sweet the truth those blessed strains are telling
> Of that new life when sin shall be no more.
>
> Onward we go, for still we hear them singing,
> ' Come, weary souls, for Jesus bids you come ;'
> And through the dark, its echoes sweetly ringing,
> 'The music of the Gospel leads us home.'
>
> Far, far away, like bells at evening pealing,
> The voice of Jesus sounds o'er land and sea,
> And laden souls by thousands meekly stealing,
> Kind Shepherd, turn their weary steps to Thee."

CHAPTER III.

ISRAEL AND JUDAH, SUBSIDIARY AGENTS IN THE PLAN.

" And I will make of thee—*Abraham*—a great nation ; and I will bless thee and make thy name great : and I will bless them that bless thee and curse them that curse thee ; and in thee shall all the families of the earth be blessed. And I will make a *multitude* of nations of thee, and kings shall come out of thee. And thy seed shall possess the gate of his enemies." (Gen. 12-2, 3 : 17-6 : 22-17).

" And in thee—*Isaac*—and in thy seed shall all the nations of the earth be blessed." (Gen. 26-4).

" Let the people serve thee—*Jacob*—and nations bow down unto thee : be lord over thy brethren, and let thy mother's sons bow down unto thee ; cursed be every one that curseth thee, and blessed be he that blesseth thee. Be fruitful and multiply ; a nation and a *company* of nations shall be of thee, and kings shall come out of thy loins." (Gen. 27-29: 35-11). " And ye shall be unto me a kingdom of priests and an holy nation." (Ex. 19-6.)

Judah, thou art he whom thy brethren shall praise : thy hand shall be in the neck of thine enemies ; thy father's children shall bow down before thee. The sceptre shall not depart from Judah, nor a lawgiver from between his feet until *Shiloh* come : and unto him shall the gathering of the people be. (Gen. 49-8, 10).

Joseph is a fruitful bough, even a fruitful bough by a well, whose branches run over the wall : the archers have sorely grieved him and shot at him, and hated him ; but his bough abode in strength, and the arms of his hands were made strong by the hands of the mighty God of Jacob ; from thence is the *Shepherd* the *Stone* of Israel. The blessings of thy father have prevailed above the blessings of my progenitors 'unto the utmost bounds of the everlasting hills : they shall be on the head of *Joseph*, and on the crown of the head of him that was separate from his brethren. (Gen. 49-22, to 26).

"Blessed of the Lord be his land for the precious things of heaven, for the dew, and for the deep that croucheth beneath, and for the precious fruits brought forth by the sun, and for the precious things put forth by the moon, and for the chief things of the ancient mountains, and for the precious things of the lasting hills, and for the precious things of the earth and the fullness thereof, and for the good-will of him that dwelt in the bush : let the blessing come upon the head of *Joseph*, and upon the top of the head of him that was separate from his brethren. His glory is like the firstling of his bullock, and his horns are the horns of unicorns : with them he shall *push* the people together to the *ends of the earth ;* and they are the ten thousands of Ephraim and they are the thousands of Manasseh." (Deut. 33-13 to 17).

In these verses, for the most part from the book where things are born, we have a series of most remarkable prophecies concerning a people—then yet to come —whose influence on the world through all time should be most beneficent in saving the race of men from utter degradation and ruin and, as we learn further on, who should eventually reorganise society on a different basis for an almost endless reign of peace, prosperity and happiness. At the same time they should be throughout their career a most marvellous fulfillment of the divine purposes foretold at the very commencement to Abraham (at a time when he had no offspring and no prospect of any), and confirmed with stronger emphasis and particularity to Isaac and Jacob and the offspring following. On the word of Jehovah it is promised that they should become a multitude of nations with many kings, presumably for each of the company of nations; that these nations in conflict with their enemies should be victorious; that his people should be divided into two lines, each of which should have gathering power, one a royal line without break until the coming of *Shiloh* —the Messiah—who should gather the people to himself, in whom they should find a "*place of rest.*"

It was declared that the other line should also have gathering power in "the Shepherd—the *Stone* of Israel;" that his domain should extend to "the utmost bound of the everlasting hills;" that his special mission should be to push his way, and the people before him, with an ever conquering hand to the ends of the earth for the accomplishment of the divine purpose; that his tree should be "planted in a good soil and by great waters," that it might bring forth branches, and that it might bear fruit, that it might be a goodly vine:" that the earth should be exceeding fruitful, and that the everlasting hills should minister to his wealth in all material riches.

These promises have never been fulfilled (so far as the Church knows at this present time), save those pertaining to Judah; and they were never forfeited in the curse pronounced upon those who crucified the Messiah, for Joseph was not a participant. They have never been abrogated, but are in full force to-day. It is our purpose to show that they have been and are being fulfilled under our very eyes and we know it not.

We propose therefore to trace in brief these two lines

to their historical finality, and bring them together again into one, as declared by later prophets should be the case, and then place the prophetic record beside them to see if we can find sufficient agreement between the historical facts and the record, to warrant the conclusions of this book.

The ancestors of the Hebrews were nomads of the desert with their flocks and herds, wandering up and down the country as the seasons advanced and receded and the needs of the flocks demanded. This pastoral nature was inborn, for so had their fathers done before them for generations. When therefore God commenced the fulfillment of his promises by permitting Joseph to be sold into Egypt, that Jacob and his sons might be drawn by the strength of the father's yearning love for his long lost boy to leave the home and nomad life of his ancestors, it seems to have been His settled purpose to keep them there until by long years of apprenticeship, servitude, and suffering, they might become weaned of their nomadic life, fused together into one homogeneous body, and prepared for national life as the peculiar people of God through all coming ages.

Two hundred and fifteen years of actual life in Egypt have the desired effect, and now their cry of distress, on account of grinding oppression, brings deliverance by reason of the stupendous miracles wrought at the hands of Moses, who was ordained of God a lawgiver and leader, out of their cruel house of bondage. They are let go in haste, laden with presents asked—backsheesh

—not "borrowed" of the Egyptians. They are led through the sea out into the wilderness of Sinai, "that we may sacrifice unto the Lord our God; and we know not with what we must serve the Lord until we come thither." (Ex. 10-26). In the wilderness they sojourn forty years until the effects of the servitude have died out and a younger, more courageous and more obedient people are prepared to enter into the promised possession of Canaan.

Four hundred years of somewhat disjointed tribal life in their new home, with varying fortune in respect to their relations with the idolatrous peoples left in the land contrary to explicit commands of God, bring us down to the reign of David, whose wise and heroic reign brings all the tribes into one consolidated, homogeneous, nationality. The promise to Judah for the "*chief prince* (though the birthright was Jeseph's[1]"), is confirmed in the house of David for an eternal heir and kingship. Solomon knits the kingdom more firmly together by the building of the Temple and the centralisation of religious worship, as well as by the phenomenal prosperity of his reign which enriched all classes of his people.

But the elements of decay were already at work, and under Rehoboam the son of Solomon a demand for a reduction of the heavy taxes, rendered necessary by extensive public improvements in all parts of the kingdom during his father's reign, was met by such a coarse and even brutal refusal as to alienate at once ten tribes

---

[1] 1 Chron. 5-2 and 2 Sam. 7-16.

at the head of whom stood Ephriam, with the cry:—
"What portion have we in David? and what inheritance in the son of Jesse? every man to your tents, O Israel!" and now, David, see to thine own house." (1 Chron. 5-6).

The separation is complete and final until the days of the new dispensation, when Judah and Ephraim shall be reunited in a bond of brotherhood never to be broken, as said the Prophet Ezekiel:—

"I will make them one nation in the land upon the mountains of Israel: and one king shall be king to them all; and they shall be no more two nations, neither shall they be divided into two kingdoms any more at all; and David my servant shall be king over them and they all shall have one shepherd; and they shall also walk in my judgments and observe my statutes and do them." (Eze. 37-22, 24).

But though the kingdom is divided, let us not forget that Israel is yet through all the ages one and indivisible in the eyes of Him who sees all things from the beginning. This outward disruption is only for the better accomplishment of his purposes on the two lines of operations already indicated, by means of this twofold agency. He will surely fulfill the one object named at the beginning—the recovery of lost allegiance and love.

The same vital forces that animated the heart and head of Jacob when living, with all his tenacity of purpose and strength of endurance, are still in the body politic, directed better than they know, for the fulfill- of the divine promises. The shriveled and limping thigh of Jacob shall find its counterpart in the crippled and halting gait of Judah, until temple and ritual are laid aside for a purer worship received from the Son of David, the Prince of Peace, exalted to be a Priest forever after the order of Melchisedeck.

The other limb shall find in Israel a swift-footed though unwitting messenger of the divine purpose, strong for a wrestle with opposing forces until it shall be lost sight of and buried out of sight, only to come forth to become a "multitude of nations;" that they may "push the peoples together to the utmost bound of the everlasting hills."

The history of Judah from the secession of the ten tribes. is soon told. Notwithstanding the continued warnings of the prophets and the troubled course of her idolatrous sister, Israel, the hearts of the people, led away by the example of their princes and kings though still in the line of David, became so far corrupted by the introduction of heathen elements into the worship of the temple, that only about three hundred years sufficed to fill up the measure of their iniquity, when fire alone could wipe out the hideous emblems of idolatory in the temple dedicated by Solomon to the worship of the living and true God. Temple, palaces, groves and high places all fell under the devouring flame, and the great body of the people with their princes and rulers were carried into a seventy years captivity at Babylon as foretold by the prophets B. C. 606.

When the years of their captivity were ended God

raised up a deliverer in the person of Cyrus at the expense of the mighty Assyrian Empire, but so thoroughly alienated had the people become by reason of their long exile in the midst of an idolatrous people, that only about forty-two thousand, besides the servants, were found who had thought enough of Zion and her courts, the God given Law and the promises, to keep their genealogical tables or family records uncorrupted by strange marriages, and to desire to return to the home and soil of their fathers.

Henceforward we are to know these returned exiles as Jews or Hebrews, recognisable the world over as the true and lineal descendants of Abraham. Idolatry has been squelched out of them, and they hate it with perfect hatred. Those who staid behind either assimilated with the Assyrians among whom they dwelt, or they wandered into the surrounding countries for purposes of trade and commerce, but wherever they went they carried with them their peculiar Jewish traits of character, physiognomy, enterprise, and intellectual endowments. Travellers profess to recognise them in the far interior of Africa, in Abyssinia, in Malabar and Japan, as well as throughout Europe, by such physical and mental traits. Luke tells, in Acts 2–9, 10, 11, many of the countries from which they came up to Jerusalem to worship in his time.

But now the walls of Jerusalem rise once more around the beloved city and inhabitants once more tread her busy streets. The temple is rebuilt and the country settles down to peaceful habits for another trial of the divine favor. Two hundred years more of national life under a varied experience of freedom and dependency, prosperity and adversity, bring us to the time of Malachi, the last of the prophets through whom the divine Spirit will communicate with His people.

Four hundred years must now intervene before the Shekina, long since departed from the Temple, will manifest himself in the long promised heir of David's throne, the Messiah of God. This long period, while it resulted under the Macabees in throwing off the yoke of vassalage, left the kingdom to become the prey of contending factions and internecine strife, in which the line of David was lost in obscurity, only to be revived in Him who had been declared to be "as a root out of dry ground, without form or comeliness; despised and rejected of men, a man of sorrows and acquainted with grief." (Isa. 53-2, 3).

Resting against a background of such dark and portentous aspect as were these years of political and religious strife and entire absence of inspired prophet, it might naturally be thought an easy matter to detect and recognise, by the help of the family records and Daniel's definite prediction, the true heir to the throne. But, no. Their hearts had become hardened by a dead formalism and their eyes were holden that they should not see him until the "fullness of the Gentiles" should come in. The long promised Messiah has come to them but they see him not. The Living Presence is restored to the earthly House but "there is no beauty that they should desire him."[1] The Lord, whom ye seek, *has* "suddenly come to his temple, even the messenger of the covenant, whom ye delight in,[2] but "we hid as it were our faces from him ; he was despised, and we esteemed him not."[3]

Under the stinging rebukes of Christ for their hypocrisy, the rulers sought a balm for wounded pride and ambition by accusing him to Pilate—taking his blood upon themselves and their children—and HE IS CRUCIFIED ! The vail of the temple is rent from top to bottom, an evidence that the special mission of Judah is accomplished. But a few years more and the Temple and "City of the Great King" are destroyed, no more to be restored as the nucleus of a dead faith, the home of an extinct nationality.

"**Behold, your house is left unto you desolate. For the kingdom shall be taken from you and given to a nation bringing forth the fruits thereof.**" (**Matt. 23-35 to 38: 21-43: Jer. 23-39, 40: 12-17: 17-27: Isa. 65-14. 15**).

Not so, however, with Israel who had no hand in the crucifixion and partook not of the curse. Her mission lies along an entirely different route, and to her we return to follow her, as best we may, through all the devious ways of her most wonderful career. It was by no means to be expected that Israel with all her proclivities for idolatry should be a prosperous kingdom. Hence, we find her the continual prey of contending

---

[1] Isa. 53-2. [2] Mal. 3-1. [3] Isa. 53-3.

aspirants within, for the throne, and a bone of contention for enemies without, on either side of her. Having alienated themselves from their brethren of Judah by a system of worship based upon and but little removed from the temple service at Jeruslaem, the whole policy of the ruling powers of Israel was turned towards making the separation as wide as possible, that there might be no longing desire to return to the old forms and place of worship, with its divinely appointed ritual and priesthood. Hence their sensuous worship had always a tendency inclining more and more to the grosser forms of idolatry, and the introduction of the numerous gods of other surrounding nations.

Such a condition of things could not long continue if they are to retain those inherited qualifications by which they are to push the people to the ends of the earth, and be a blessing to the world by being its conquerors. To remain is death ; to go out is life. But what impulse shall be sufficient to induce them to leave home and fatherland, the home of Abraham and Isaac and Jacob ? God has answered it as he had said by all his servants, the prophets:—

"So Israel was carried away out of their own land to Assyria unto this day : and he placed them in Halah, and in Habor by the river of Gozan, and in the cities of the Medes." And the King of Assyria brought men from Babylon, and from Cuthah, and from Ava, and from Hamath, and from Sepharvaim, and placed them in the cities of Samaria instead of the children of Israel. (2 Kings 17-16, 23, 24).

Thus the kingdom of Israel continued after the secession only about two hundred and fifty-four years, when it is thoroughly wiped out by a complete interchange of populations as above stated, 740 to 713 B. C. [1]

To all human appearance this is the end of Israel, for we hear nothing further of them from Scripture, save an allusion in the "General Epistle of James" thus: "To the twelve tribes scattered abroad; greeting." But no indication is given as to their location and, seemingly, they are buried out of sight (at least the world has so considered) for more than twenty centuries. It may be well then, for a brief space, to look at the "waymarks" which the divine record tells beforehand shall be set up, and then we may proceed to enquire if profane history gives us any clue to their fulfillment.

At the very threshold of their captivity God declared by the mouth of Hosea :—

"O Israel, thou hast destroyed thyself; but in me is thine help. I will ransom them from the power of the grave: I will redeem them from death: O death, I will be thy plagues; O grave, I will be thy destruction : repentance shall be hid from mine eyes. Ephraim shall say.—What have I to do any more with idols! I have heard him and observed him : I am like a green fir tree ; from me is thine help. Who is wise, and he shall understand these things ? prudent, and he shall know them?" (Hosea 13-9, 14: 14-8, 9).

The only conclusion that can be drawn from these prophecies and others like them is, that God will yet bring Israel out of her grave and make her known to

---

[1] This event was contemporaneous with the founding of Rome; so long ago in the dim past did the dispersion commence.

the world as a monument of his abounding goodness and power.

The promises of superabounding blessings upon Ephraim and Manasseh, sons of Joseph, have never been fulfilled in anything that history has revealed to us in connection with the Jews. These have never become a "multitude of nations," though scattered everywhere. They have not increased, according to all accounts, above the number credited to them at the time of Christ, while it was declared of Joseph that *his* seed should multiply "*as the fishes do increase.*"[1] Hebrews have never in any *special* sense been a blessing to the world, nor have they been remarkably blessed themselves. They have kept aloof from the people and are hated of all nations for a special crime. Only since they came to this country have they enjoyed social and political freedom. In nothing do they fill the requirements of the prophetic record, save in those that immediately concerned themselves.

If the prophecies concerning Joseph and his sons Ephraim and Manasseh were not fulfilled in Palestine before the captivity, it is certain they are *yet to be* fulfilled. They have already been fulfilled in part since they left their land and are being fulfilled to-day. If the "times of the Gentiles"—the domination of the kings of the earth over Israel—are being fulfilled as all "signs of the times" indicate, then we must look for the realisation of these wonderful promises in some

---

[1] Mar. Ref. Gen. 48-16.

manner and among a people not yet discovered nor discoverable as Hebrews. Those who are seeking after the marvelous and the tragic in the developments of prophecy, will never see them wrought out into fact, for it is "the glory of God to conceal a thing." All the great moral epochs of God-in-Christ's government have been very quiet affairs and not introduced by the blast of a trumpet; but those who watch His secret and silent way of working, shall see things of wondrous beauty, even "The horsemen of Israel and the chariots thereof." "Who is wise, and he shall understand these things? prudent, and he shall know them?"

The word of God unfolds itself like life, ever opening and expanding into new forms, seen only by those who are led by the spirit rather than by the letter of the word. The promises made to the Patriarchs included the Jews of course, but those to the children of Joseph extend far beyond them, and while we do not deny that Jewish influence has been considerable in the world in some respects, especially in the field of finance and literature and state craft in modern times, yet these by no means fill the requirements of the case in respect of the line of Joseph. We feel warranted, therefore, in saying that the Jewish Church and national life filled up the full measure of their existence as such when the *last of the line of David*, the promised Messiah, was born, who lives forever a perpetual king.' There being no further use for the Temple and the family records, they were destroyed with the city.

But the national life of Joseph was promised to continue through *all time* (in one form or other, as will appear further on), and become the medium by which Judah herself should be gathered a *second* time, under a *new covenant* and a new *name*, into a *home* from which there should be *no removing* (Isa. 11-11 to 14 : Jer. 31-31 to 34 : 2 Sam. 7-10).

Meantime, great changes must take place in Israel before she can enter on her peculiar mission, for the tribes have become thoroughly demoralised by reason of idolatry. So conspicuous has Ephraim become as the leader of these idolatrous defections, that it is declared of him "Ephraim is joined to his idols; let him alone" (Hosea 4-17); so prominent indeed that his name stands as the representative of the whole house of Israel as God declares in his tender appeal by the same prophet : " O Ephraim, what shall I do unto thee. * * There is idolatry in Ephraim — Israel is defiled" (Chap. 6-4, 10).

The result is as predicted :—

"Ephraim, he hath mixed himself among the peo le" (Chap. 7-8). "Because Ephraim hath made many alters to sin, alters shall be unto him to sin (Chap. 8-11). "Israel is swallowed up : now shall they be among the Gentiles as a vessel wherein is no pleasure : for they are gone up to Assyria, a wild ass alone by himself" (Chap. 8-8, 9).

"He is like an unclean and broken urn cast into the sea as worse than useless. He forgot his Maker, yet built temples. In consequence of this attempt to do God service by flattering their own vanity, the very people who deemed themselves the peculiar inheritors of divine blessings, are now outcasts alike from their fatherland and their father's hopes. They shall forget all their traditions of Jehovah's covenant with their fathers, they are only to know themselves as utterly desolate and hopeless, incapable of recovery but through a manifestation of grace of which they have no record." Hosea continues the sad story of their defection thus :— "My God shall cast them away, and they shall be wanderers among the nations" (Chap. 9-17). Thus, also, the prediction of Moses is confirmed, as the result of their departure from the counsels of God. "The Lord shall scatter thee among *all people* from one end of the earth even unto the other" (Deut. 28-64). "And I will punish you yet *seven times* for your sins" (Lev. 26-24).

There were other peculiarities also which should result from this gross departure from God and accompany them in their wanderings until they should be fully prepared for their high destiny among and apart from the nations. Ephraim shall yet say, "What have I any more to do with idols?" But idolatry inbred as Ephraim's was is not to be eradicated by any easy process; nor would Israel be at all likely to return to the old paths so long since abandoned. The scriptures plainly declare that they should be cleansed only by great calamities and trials, adopting for a time a new religion whose refrain in song and temple service should be, "Lamentation, and mourning, and woe" (Eze. 2-10).

THE TWOFOLD AGENCY. 75

"And the songs of the temple shall be howlings in that day, saith the Lord God : there shall be many dead bodies in every place ; they shall cast them forth with SILENCE. And I will turn your feasts into mourning, and all your songs into lamentations ; and I will bring up SACKCLOTH upon all loins, and BALDNESS upon every head ; and I will make it as the mourning of an only son, and the end thereof as a bitter day" (Amos 8-3, 10).

"Therefore the Lord of hosts, the Lord, saith thus: Wailing shall be in all streets ; and they shall say in all the highways. Alas ! alas ! and they shall call the husbandman to mourning, and such as are skillful of lamentation to wailing. And in all vineyards shall be wailing: for I will pass through thee, saith the Lord" (Chap. 5-16, 17).

"And they shall wander from sea to sea, and from the north even to the east, they shall run to and fro to seek the word of the Lord, and shall not find it" (Chap. 8-12).

"But I will ransom them from the grave : I will redeem them from death" (Hos. 13-14).

We are then to look ultimately for a people not known as Israel, for how then could they be hid? we must look not for a people who are idolators, but for a people who have been recovered from it ; who have been delivered from their defilement by fiery afflictions in a very peculiar manner according to specified conditions, and whose minds are open to the reception of truth—for that is certainly God's *expressed purpose* in the trials—which shall so remodel all their previous conceptions of the divine government, as to make them willing and obedient subjects of His will, or inclined to it. In a word, we must look for the descendants of literal Israel among those who have already adopted or are ready to adopt the Christian religion ; in short, among Christian nations. We hope, therefore, to find many "waymarks" along the route traversed by Israel in his wanderings, which may help us to this conclusion.

It is then of the first importance to this discussion that we understand the precise localities to which Israel was carried, for it is on this point mainly that an intelligent understanding of their wanderings and subsequent career can be had. The divine record reads thus:

"In the days of Pekah, king of Israel, came Tiglath-pileser king of Assyria, and took Ijon, and Abel-beth-Maachah, and Janoah, and Kadesh, and Hazor, and Gilead, and Gallilee, all the land of Naphtali, and carried them captive to Assyria" (2 Kings 15-29). "And the king of Assyria hearkened unto him, and went up against Damascus, and took it, and carried the people of it unto KIR, and slew Rezin." 740 B. C. (2 Kings 16-9).

At nearly the same time—some have it three years between—this same king took the Reubenites, and the Gadites, and the half tribe of Manasseh and brought them unto Halah, and on the Chabor a river of Gozan[1] (1 Chron. 5-26). About twenty years later Shalmaneser besieged Samaria (Israel's capital), but died before it was taken, and Sargon finished the siege successfully and deported the captives to the number of 27,280 families (as the monuments tell us) into the same places as his predecessor had done, with this addition, "And into the cities of the Medes" (2 Kings 18-21). Esarhaddon completed the ruin of the people by deporting the balance and supplying their places by foreigners (Ezra 4-2).

---

[1] *Hara* is omitted from the text as not belonging to it.

That Kabor or Chabor was a river rather than Gozan (as the A. V. has it), and that the above rendering is the more correct one, seems more than probable from the fact that in 2 Kings 19-12 and in Isaiah 37-12, Gozan is represented as a country of which Shalmaneser boasted his fathers had destroyed or desolated. Moreover *Kir* is a river in the extreme north-eastern part of Armenia emptying into the Caspian Sea, while the Kabor is a river rising in the mountainous region of what is here called Gozan—now Kurdistan[1]—running through its western borders and emptying into the Tigris. Gozan was probably that part of Kurdistan now called Bhutan. for competent scholars say that the Aramean pronunciation of the letters of Gozan would convert the word into Buhtan or Bhutan.

The river Kabor—Habor or Chebor—is called by Strabo. Haborran. Ptolemy calls it Chaboras. and the Turks call it Al-chabur[2] It gives its name to a large district there. while the whole country is well watered and abounds in grass and is eminently fitted to a pastoral people like the Israelites. As long a journey as that from Palestine, when such vast numbers must be fed. would be impossible unless they took their flocks and herds with them. This they were permitted to do. as

---

[1] It is worth noting that this is the region where Dr. Grant claims to have found the remnants of the "Lost Tribes," some forty or fifty years ago, in the Nestorians.

[2] The famous "retreat of the ten thousand," described by Xenophon, was through this very region, and they crossed a river Chebar on their way from Batrai to the plains of Zakko or Sacho.

we learn from Amos 5-6. All of this country, as well as Media where we are *certain* some of the captives were placed, borders the western and south-western shore of the Caspian Sea.

How infinitely more probable it is that the captives were placed in this region, so eminently adapted to their needs and habits, rather than in the plains between the Tigris and the Euphrates as generally held. These plains were better adapted to an agricultural than to a pastoral people and besides were, probably, already occupied, while there is historical proof that Gozan had been devastated. It is not at all improbable that some may have been placed there, but the burden of proof is that the great body of the people were placed in the regions we have named.

There is another consideration which should have due weight with us, and it is this. If God reserve l "the best of the land" in Egypt and kept it comparatively free from occupation for the family of Jacob with their flocks, contiguous to the line of their retreat in after ages by the Red Sea, so that they would not be obliged to go through large bodies of the people in passing to that point. is it not just as probable that God would choose the most feasible point in locating his people, from which He could most easily scatter them into all quarters of the world as he had promised? The country bordering the western shore of the Caspian was in every respect adapted to all the requirements of the divine record, as a look at the map will show, which will be better seen as we proceed.

In that wonderful vision of Ezekiel (595 B. C.) when he was sent to them of the captivity by the river of Chebar to give his last testimony as a prophet to them, there was revealed to his astonished vision a sight which made his stout heart quail. Terrible visions of the fiery trials through which they would be called to pass to prepare them for their great mission of blessing to the world, were opened to him, and for the further purpose of fortifying his own soul for the delivery of God's last message to this rebellious house. "I remained there among them astonished seven days."

The prophet sees a "whirlwind coming out of the north, a great cloud, and a fire infolding itself."— flashing out or, as the margin has it, "catching itself":—

"And a brightness was about it, and out of the midst thereof came the likeness of four living creatures. As for the likeness of their faces, they four had the face of a man, and the face of a lion on the right side; and they four had the face of an ox on the left side; they four also had the face of an eagle. * * * Now as I beheld the living creatures, behold one wheel upon the earth beside the living creatures, for each of the four faces thereof; and their appearance and their work was as it were a wheel within a wheel. And over the head of the living creatures there was the likeness of a firmament like the color of the terrible crystal, stretched forth over their heads above" (Eze. 1st chap. which see).

That the living creatures represent *Israel*, through whom God has been through past ages and is working for the promised blessings, is fully evident from the fact that the various faces revealed in the vision have been the emblems of Israel from the time of their sojourn in the wilderness, when the four divisions of the camp were represented on their standards or banners by these same symbols.¹ There is reason to believe from Ezekiel's exclamation in chapter 10-20th, that these same symbols were in some way connected with the Cherubim of the Temple (see also chap. 9-3). Be this as it may. we are sure they are the emblems of the divine energy working through human instrumentalities for the good of the world, and that instrument is Israel.

It is well also to remember that these are the same symbolic faces of the "four living creatures" of the Apocalypse which stand around the throne and are *nearest* to it. transferred now to the Christian church, yet representing spiritual Israel, one and indivisible through all the ages, for the accomplishment of the divine purpose in the recovery of lost man. This is apparent in that they, with the four and twenty elders who represent the union of the *twelve tribes* with the *twelve apostles* (the union of the old with the new, and all who through them in all ages have received the adoption), are said to sing *together* the "new song" and to declare :

"**Thou hast redeemed us to God by thy blood out of every kindred, and tongue, and people, and nation, and hast made us unto our God kings and priests : and WE SHALL REIGN ON THE EARTH**" (Rev. 5-9, 10).

We, *Spiritual Israel*, a "remnant" of carnal or political Israel, but increased and multiplied a thousand

---

¹ So say the Rabbins.

times ten thousand times over by the power of Christ's matchless love "shall reign on the earth."

That the "whirlwind and the cloud and the infolding fire out of the north" are the symbols of some great influx of people driven by a resistless power from that quarter, who should in some way envelope Israel and by their very environment should become the agents of fiery trials by which they should become a changed, purified, hidden, and scattered people, is made plainly evident by the use made of similar symbols in other parts of scripture, as well as by the usage of classic writers.

"Therefore he hath poured upon him the fury of his anger, and the strength of the battle; He hath set him on FIRE round about and it burned him, yet he laid it not to heart. For behold, the Lord will come with FIRE, and his chariots like a WHIRLWIND, to render his anger with fury, and his rebuke like a flame of fire (Isa. 66-15; Jer. 49-36, 37). Yea, I will gather you and blow upon you in the fire of my wrath, and ye shall be melted in the midst. "I will bring the third part through the fire, and I will REFINE THEM" (Zec. 13-9). Behold, he shall come up as CLOUDS, and his chariots shall be as a WHIRLWIND: his horses are swifter than eagles (Jer. 4-14).

With such admonitions we are certainly warranted in concluding that Ezekiel's vision means nothing more nor less, so far as the cloud and the whirlwind are concerned, than an influx of an army of northern people which should infold Israel as in a cloud, and be the means of hiding them from the notice of the world.

The history of the Scythian tribes is involved in almost

impenetrable mystery, and the most conflicting accounts are given by different ancient authors as to their origin, place of abode and time of their appearance in Europe. This arises in great part, probably, from their being constantly mixed up with other nomad tribes from the same high plateaus and steppes of Southern Russia. Some say they came into Asia Minor through Media from the regions east of the Caspian Sea, from the land of the Chozar Tartars. Others say that in a war with the Kimmerians from the plateaus north of the Caucasian Mountains, which separate Europe from Asia, the Scythians drove the Kimmerians before them into the defiles of the mountains and were led by the eastern pass of the mountains bordering on the sea, into Asia.[1] This seems much the more probable theory since it is almost incredible that such a large body of warlike people could have appeared in the plains of Assyria, through Media, without attracting attention and meeting resistance.

The first definite notice of them that can be relied on is that they suddenly appeared in Asia at the time of the revolt of Cyaxares the Mede against the power of Assyria, on the occasion of the siege of Nineveh in connection with the Babylonians (B. C. 630). At this time there appeared, like a thunder-clap from the clouds in a clear day, a vast horde of northern barbarians called Scythians from the region of the Caucasus, who immediately attacked and defeated Cyaxares and the Babylonians, laid low the Assyrian power, and dominated Asia for

[1] Herodotus.

twenty-eight years.[1] They were then defeated and expelled (B. C. 598), retiring, probably, to the mountain regions around the Araxes and Kir from which they had so suddenly emerged. From this same region the Koords for generations have descended for robbery and plunder upon the defenceless villages of the plains.

In this region the ten tribes were located and, for now a hundred years at the time of the Scythian invasion, had been increasing in wealth and power and very rapidly in numbers. Is it not highly probable that the Scythians, coming into this region suddenly and finding a pastoral people ready for any marauding enterprise against their old time enemies and conquerors, with the added impulse of " manifest destiny," should join forces with them and make their descent upon the besieging army of Cyaxares, and then upon Nineveh itself. The tribes doubtless had long desired just such an opportunity, and when the occasion presented itself were not slow to accept the offer of coalition and augment the Scythian force by such vast numbers as to make resistance impossible, even in populous and warlike Assyria.

It is incredible to suppose that a Scythian *tribal* force could come through such a country as that occupied by our Tribes, a nation of fighting people and now become, doubtless, millions in number, on such an expedition as the conquest of Assyria, without receiving vast additions to their numbers, as well as providing themselves a base of supplies and perhaps a line of retreat in case of

---

[1] Herodotus.

defeat. But with such augmentation both the suddenness of the descent and its successful result are very easily accounted for.

It matters nothing that five or six years intervene between their defeat and expulsion from Assyria and Ezekiel's later vision. and that they are already enveloped in the cloud and the whirlwind from the north. The burden of his astounding vision was the fiery trials to which this environing cloud should lead them. So heavy indeed should these misfortunes be that the very songs of their sanctuaries should be, "Lamentation and mourning and woe." It is noticeable that the calamities were not revealed as being in the cloud but in the "roll" which was given to him, "written within and without." full to overflowing (Chap. 2–9, 11). The cloud was only the agency by which they should be led into the trials and be hidden to the world. In a word, they were to become a changed people.

Hitherto they seem to have led a quiet and peaceable life among the mountains and valleys of their allotted home, for we hear nothing whatever of them until this invasion of the Scythians. Not even then is the name of Israel mentioned as connected with them, except by inference from *after* circumstances. This is easily accounted for because the vision shows that they were enveloped by and hidden in the cloud, since the living creatures representing Israel, came out of the cloud. "And the living creatures"—with the wheels beside them—"*ran* and *returned* as the appearance of a flash of lightning" (ver. 14). "Their appearance was like burning coals of fire, and like the appearance of lamps ; it went up and down among the living creatures ; and the fire was bright and out of the fire went forth lightning" (ver. 13). This shows the intimate relations existing between the living creatures and the cloud, because they *ran out of* and *returned into* it. The *human* character of the living creatures is clearly shown by the coals of fire and the lamp which signify, in symbolic prophecy, purification, many evidences of which are found in the scriptures.

From the undeniable fact that soon after this time another people began to be mentioned with the Scythians under the name of Sacæ, as interchangeable cognomens, we conclude that the surrounding powers had begun to realise that these almost forgotten mountain captives of a hundred years, had more to do with this incursion of Scythians than at first sight appeared.[1]

It would be impossible for such an invasion as this to continue in power for twenty-eight years and extend its sway as far as to Syria and Palestine without giving the people and their previous rulers more correct information respecting its origin and the people or tribes composing it.

Still another result would follow if any of the tribes were located in Mesopotamia—between the rivers—and had recognised and become identified with their brethren of the mountain tribes because of their ascendancy over

---

[1] The Persians afterwards called the whole body of them Sac·e.

their oppressors, the Assyrians. They would certainly esteem it their opportunity as well as good policy to migrate in a body from the land of their captivity and, under the impulse of "manifest destiny," to join their brethren when the Assyrians regained the ascendency and expelled the Scythians and Sacæ from the country.

This would be a very natural result to be expected after such a domination when the Scythians and their mountain allies, the Sacæ, were expelled.

Be this as it may, it is certain the Tribes were somehow involved in the "cloud," and in it they lost their distinctive appellation of Israelites and came forth to the world as Scythians, whose chief element shall henceforth be Sacæ, Sacasuni (sons of Isaac) Saxons. Strabo calls Armenia, Sackasina. Pliny says the Sakai who settled in Armenia were named Sacassani, which is only another form of Saka-suna.[1] Ptolemy mentions a Scythian people sprung from the Sakai by the name of Saxons.[2] Diodorus says the Scythians came into Europe from Asia, about the river Araxes in Armenia. Turner thinks it probable the Saxons sprang from the Sacasenæ near Persia.[3]

It would seem then from the very best authority attainable, that here in this country of Armenia (part of which is now called Kurdistan), where the Ark was moored whence Noah and his sons went forth to people

---

[1] This word is said by some to mean in Hebrew, people who have changed their place of abode.
[2] Turner's "Anglo Saxons," page 12.
[3] Turner, note 5, page 182.

the earth anew. Israel found her living grave, in full accord with the prophetic record so that, being baptised anew "in the cloud and in the sea," the people might come forth from their graves unto a new resurrection and to a new and divinely appointed mission for the regeneration of the world. "Even so, Father, for so it seemed good in thy sight." To this baptism by the cloud, the flood, and the sword we will now turn our attention.

Hitherto the "Tribes" had lived in seclusion and quietness for more than one hundred years, but no sooner did they become involved with the Scythians than their troubles commenced. A taste of this predatory and martial life seems to have aroused the old fire within, and henceforth their career is to be one of conflict and "push" "unto the utmost bound of the everlasting hills."

Scarcely thirty years from their expulsion from the rule of Assyria we find Crœsus, the king of Lydia, with the Babylonians gaining a signal victory over the Sacæ, who are said by Athenæus to be a Scythian people. Twenty years later we find Cyrus, while extending unheard of bounties to the Jews of Babylonia on the occasion of their return from the seventy years captivity, bent on exterminating the Massa-Getæ[1] and Scythians

---

[1] This name Massa-Getæ (the Goths of Masha) is indissolubly mixed up with that of the Sacæ and Scythians, and after their dispersion we hear of them in the far East. May not the name Masha be the same as that mentioned in Genesis (10-23), and the very name of Getæ be derived from that of the inhabitants of Gath. The Getæ are mixed up with the Sacæ as the Gitites were

about the Araxes and Kir.[1] He penetrated their country with a large army and inflicted terrible sufferings upon them as appears from an inscription on the wall of a rock-temple in Kanari about twenty miles from Bombay. From this and others of the same kind it would appear that other and deeper afflictions by fire and flood had come upon them and changed their whole *religious* character at least and fulfilled to the letter the inspired record of their departure from God.

Jeremiah speaks of Ephraim in very tender terms, saying :

"I have surely heard Ephraim bemoaning himself thus:—'Thou hast chastised me and I was chastised as a bullock unaccustomed to the yoke: turn Thou me and I shall be turned; for Thou art the Lord my God.' Set thee up WAY-MARKS, make thee high HEAPS, set thine heart toward the highway, even the way by which Thou wentest; turn again, O virgin of Israel" (Jer. 31-18, 21).

Bear in mind this prophecy was spoken in Judea more than one hundred years after the Tribes were carried captive, and it is by these very "waymarks" and "heaps" that light is being thrown on the wanderings and sufferings of this hitherto hidden people. These inscriptions have been cut on pillars and temples, tumuli and rock-chambers, and on the scarped face of mountains from Thibet to lower India and Ceylon. Hitherto they have remained undeciphered and inex-

---

with the Israelites, and used the same language. There were Gitites (Getæ), men of Gath, in the body guard of David.

[1] Herodotus.

plicable on account of being written in an unknown language, with the alphabet of another language well known according to the locality in which the incriptions are found, some of them being in the Arian or Bactrian character, and some in early Pali, more than a thousand miles apart. All these inscriptions have the same general character, often being simple repetitions, and again differing materially in construction and manner of writing, while the sentiment is the same throughout the whole.[1] Only a few extracts can be given here to illustrate the fulfillment of the divine record respecting the calamities which were to overtake them.

Many of these inscriptions are now by fac-simile transfer, in the British Museum, and the sad refrain of every one is nearly in the words of the prophet. "Lamentation, mourning and woe." The following is the one recently found at Kanari already referred to but not in the above collection :

"The soft flowing of the wine-press from the white gushing fruit is as that which sets me at rest ; my drink, the refining of the fruit is the very grace of his mouth. Behold what thou possessest, yea, even the gladsomeness in it that is ministered to thee. Lo, the worship (or blood) of Saka is the fruit of my lip ; his garden (PARADISE) which CYRUS laid low was glowing RED ; and behold it is BLACKENED. His people being aroused would have their rights, for they were cast down at the parting of DAN, who being delivered was perfectly free. * * * Every one

---

[1] For further information we refer the reader to "Lost Tribes," by Dr. Geo. Moore, London, 1861. These inscriptions have been deciphered by Dr. Moore and found to be written in Hebrew.

grew mighty: your religion had saved even him from uncleanness. And his (Saka's) mouth, enkindling them, brought the Serim[1] together from the race of HARARI[2] My mouth also hastened the rupture, and as one obeying my hand thou didst sing praise. O unclean one, his religious decree is his bow. He who complains of inflicted equality turns aside. My gift is freedom to him who is fettered, the freedom of the polluted is penitence. As to DAN his unloosing was destruction, oppression and strife; he stoutly turned away, he departed twice. The predetermined thought is a hand prepared. The redeemed of KASHA wandered about like the (flock) overdriven. The prepared was the ready, yea, GOTHA, that watched for the presence of DAN, afforded concealment to the exile whose vexations became his triumphs; and SAKA also, being reinvigorated by the Calamity, purified the East, the vices of which he branded."[3]

Here are a few lines from an inscription found at "Joonur" on the wall of a rock-chamber near the summit of Naneh-Ghat Mountain, India, and translated by Dr. Moore:

"His perfection was as that of one purified,
BURNING COALS were the light of their fires (burnt offerings),
The guilt offering of those who were polluted.
He conceived a SEA (for purification).
Behold, my house (or temple) was a ruin,
My generation was polluted, we were unclean;

---

[1] "Serim—Seres (free or princes). A people called Seres have been the cause of much doubtful discussion." See "Latham's Ethnological Essays."

[2] People of the hill country of Ephraim are so called (2 Sam. 23-11, 33).

[3] Historical researches on the origin of the Buddha and Jaina religions by Jas. Bird, Esq.

The fire became a means of healing,
A root of exalted piety shot forth.
The equity (or equality) of Badh was set up.   *   *   *
The poor were enlightened,
Calamity, overruled by Saka, became a triumph and delight.
The decree of their mouth was BALDNESS.
The SILENCE of my bitterness was exaltation."

The following is the refrain of an inscription on a rock at Girnar, with a few lines following the *first two* out of more than five hundred :

" THE MOUTH OF RUIN HATH PLEADED THEIR CAUSE,
DESTRUCTION HATH BECOME THEIR ENLIGHTENMENT.
I will meditate, O God, on the woe that ruin hath wrought,
I will meditate, and the fire which smote shall be my grace,
The suffering thereof shall be my exaltation.
O sea, as in the day of thy trouble, thou breakest to pieces.
The perfection of Ruin, Calamity, and Truth, is my diadem,
   *   *   *   He hath made it the ornament of the head.
Here the choicest part of thy Calamity is its oppressiveness.
Why have I raised up a HEAP of ruin ?
Because the mounds thus afford a conception
Of the havoc the Calamity produced.
Behold it is even thy direction, the appointed guide.
Lo ! the sea is parched up whereby the Calamity came ;
As it is perfect (or ended), the sign is sufficient."

The inscription at Delhi is very nearly the same with the Girnar inscription but of a higher order, and appears to have been used as a hymn in the worship of the temple. In other inscriptions the name of Godama is said to be that of Saka or Sakya, and to have been given to him after death when, as Buddhists believe, he became like God.

In what way these calamities by fire and flood came, there are no means of knowing, but that in them and by them they were delivered from idolatry, seems certain from the inscriptions which throughout speak of them as the means of their purification, and that the heaps of ruin were but the mementoes of their afflictions.

The monuments of this new religion, which was introduced some time before the conquests of Alexander (B. C. 334), may be traced from Bactria, close on the borders of the Caspian Sea, through Mongolia and Thibet to China, through India to Ceylon, Burmah and Siam. In the providence of God the calamities may have followed close on to the disasters inflicted by Cyrus (B. C. 540) and were made the means at once of their purification and their dispersion as intimated in the Kanari inscription, for Saka or Sakya, soon after the reception of his "enlightenment" by "destruction," set about purifying the East.

It is by such inscriptions, waymarks and heaps as these, not a tithe of which can be given here, and all of which contain names and allusions pointing in a very marked degree to a Hebrew origin, that the way of the wanderers has been traced within a very few years in countries which have until recently been a *terra incognita* or unknown land to the world. By these we learn that Saka, or Sakya as in some inscriptions, whose name is intimately connected with the Sacæ, Scythians and

Getæ, or Goths, was the founder of a new religion in which negation of self, repentance and regeneration through submission to the divine decrees in suffering, were the essential elements. In his progress towards regeneration during a *week of weeks* he formulates his experience thus :-

> " All treasures must be emptied,
> All loftiness must fall.
> All earthly union must be broken,
> All that lives must die."

Further experiences in trial and suffering, voluntarily endured, ending in a still higher perception of Spiritual truth, are thus expressed :—

> " The strength of Mercy is firmer than a rock.
> Faith in unbounded Mercy is the rule,
> The path to holiness, the way to heaven."

The emblems of this new faith appear to have been "heaps" (mani) of rubbish, *sackcloth* and *baldness*, and this religion was none other than the Buddha whose festivals are mourning, and whose songs are lamentations, and those who are devoted to Buddha adopt sackcloth as their clothing and baldness is on all heads. The baldheaded devotees of Buddha are "sons of sackcloth," and the ordination of priests is to this day a refinement of austerity. According to their Book of Ritual they are required to wear a robe of filthy rags and subject themselves to every form of degradation.[1]

---
[1] Moore's "Lost Tribes," page 344.

In all this we see a complete fulfillment of the prophetic record, for Ezekiel says :

"That which cometh into your minds shall not be at all that ye say :—'We will be as the heathen, as the families of the countries, to serve wood and stone': and ye shall loathe yourselves in your own sight for all your evils that you have committed" (Eze. 20-32, 43).

"And the songs of the temple shall be howlings in that day, saith the Lord God ; there shall be many dead bodies in every place ; they shall cast them forth with SILENCE. And I will turn your feasts into mourning, and all your songs into lamentation ; and I will bring up SACKCLOTH upon all loins, and BALDNESS upon every head ; and I will make it as the mourning of an only son, and the end thereof as a bitter day" (Amos 8-3, 10:5-16).

"And they shall gird themselves with sackcloth, and horror shall cover them ; and shame shall be upon all faces, and baldness upon all their heads" (Eze. 7-18).

Now we know from various sources, especially from the primitive forms still retained in Thibet, that this was the religion of the Buddha as first introduced into the countries contiguous to the eastern and southern shores of the Caspian Sea. The Thibetans say that Sacke taught them their religion and that the people were called Sacki (Sackæ). The heaps of ruin and rubbish which they venerate and call *mani* are very suggestive of the words of Isaiah (65-11) : "But ye are they that forsake my holy mountain, that prepare a table for *Fortune*, that fill up mingled wine unto *Destiny*[1] (goddess of Fate) ; I will *destine* you to the sword and ye shall all bow down to the slaughter."

---
[1] Mar. Rev. Heb. *Meni*.

These heaps mark the graves of the Israelites, or rather now the "house of Isaac" (as Amos said they should be called) under their new names of Sackæ, Getæ or Goths, in all their wanderings. They were erected as an expression of a "covenant with Destruction."[1] But Isaiah, in speaking of Ephraim, says:

"Your covenant with death shall be disannulled, and your agreement with hell shall not stand: when the overflowing scourge shall pass through, then ye shall be trodden down by it" (28-18).

Very numerous are these coincidences between the ancient Buddhistic faith and the prophetic record of the wanderings of the house of Isaac. The most remarkable of these was the belief as taught by Saka, Sakya or Godama, that the ultimate Buddha—Bagava Metteyo, the Messiah—is yet to come, and this word *Metteyo* is said to be the very word used by the prophet Ezekiel (34-29). The legend of the Karens in Burmah is similar:

" When the Karen king arrives,
There will be but one Monarch.
There will be neither rich nor poor;
Everything will be happy;
The beasts will be happy;
Lions and leopards will lose their savageness."

But we are not entirely dependent on these rock records for our knowledge of the wanderings of the

---

[1] A heap of stones was raised over Achan and his family (Josh. 8-28); and this seems to have been a frequent usage with the early Hebrews. See Deut. 13-16; Gen. 31-52; 2 Sam. 18-17.

tribes into the far East, which must have occurred at some time between the wars of Cyrus against them (B. C. 540) and the conquests of Alexander in the Orient (334 B. C.) when we find them among his most formidable adversaries. Afterwards he found it to his advantage to enter into peaceful relations with them and employed large numbers in further expeditions. Ptolemy, in his geography of these parts (Afghanistan) locates the Aristophyli or "The Noble Tribes," near Cabul, a name at once suggestive of the Cabul of Palestine which Solomon gave to King Hiram, which signifies *sandy*. (1 Kings 9-13). Much of the country to which the name was transferred certainly warrants the application. He also places the "Tos Manassa" ("The far-banished Manasseh") in the land of the Gomeri[1] (the Gomer of the Bible). They are also called Isakzie and frequently by Herodotus the Sacæ.

The Hebrews in Mowr as well as those in Bokhara assured Rev. J. Wolff that there are many of the children of Israel of the tribes of Napthtali and Zebulun in the Hindu Cush, and that they lived by robbery and knew the exclamation, "Shama Yisrael!" (Hear, O Israel.[2]) The following passage from a letter written by an officer in India will throw some light on this subject. It is dated from *Headquarters*, Camp *Munikiala*, Jan. 20, 1852 :—

"Having just been through a part of Afghanistan Proper,

---
[1] Forster on Primeval Language.
[2] Wolff's Mission to Bokhara, vol. 2, page 165.

THE TWOFOLD AGENCY. 97

I cannot help writing to tell you how I was struck by the Jewishness of the people; and not only their appearance, but every possible circumstance tends to convince one that they are the descendants' of the Ten Tribes. They call themselves Bunnie Israel (Bunnie being exactly synonymous with 'Mac' in Scotland and 'Fitz' in England) and are proud of i ; whereas to *all* other Mahometans a more severe term of abuse cannot be applied than Yahoodee, or Jew. We may observe that these so-called Benee-Israel despise the Jews almost as much as any Mahometan people can. They pride themselves on being the sons of Israel in contradistinction from the people of Judah ; a strong presumptive evidence that they are really derived from the Israelites, especially as this distinction has been maintained from time immemorial amongst them. One of the tribes that at present are giving us a good deal of trouble is called " *Yousufzies*," or tribe of Joseph, "zie" meaning tribe ; and next to them are the Izakzie, or tribe of Isaac."

This certainly shows evidence corroborative of what we have shown by the inscriptions, some of which are located in the vicinity of these people, and also that they have adopted other names than those by which they were known in their old home in Palestine, but which the prophet declared should be their distinctive titles in the land of their wanderings (Amos 7-9, 16). "For in *Isaac* shall thy seed be called" (Rom. 9-7 : Heb. 11-18). We would like very much to quote in full a passage from the Apocryphal book of Esdras (2 book

13-39 to 46) which doubtless may be taken as *historical* evidence of their intention to go into a further country over the waters of the river (Euphrates), but will only quote a few lines. "For the Most High then showed signs for them, and held still the flood till they were passed over; for through that country there was a great way to go, namely, of a year and a half; and the same region is called Arsareth. Then they dwelt there until the latter time; and now when they shall begin to come, the Highest will stay the springs of the stream again, that they may come through; therefore sawest thou the multitudes with peace."[1]

This word Arsareth is held to be the equivalent of "Oriens, the Orient, the land of the far East, the country always called Oriental."[2]

The Casiphia to which Ezra sent for "ministers for the house of God" (8-17) is also recognised as the name of a country on the borders of the Caspian Sea.[3] But we think sufficient has been shown to prove that a very large portion of the tribes went into the far East and permeated the land from one end to the other with a new faith which, though a false one and now degenerated,

---

[1] Can it be that St. John alludes to this when he says: "The sixth Angel poured out his vial upon the great river Euphrates; and the waters thereof were dried up that the way of the kings from the sun-rising might be prepared" (Rev. 16-12).

[2] The country along the river Khorazan in Cabul is still called Hazara, believed to be the same with Bar-Zaura of the ancients, signifying the sons of Sarah.—*Dr. Moore.*

[3] Dr. Henderson's Russian Researches.

was a vast improvement over idolatry and prepared the way for Muhamadism which is iconoclastic to a degree. Let us now turn our attention to that branch that left Armenia to enter Europe for the regeneration of the world.

CHAPTER IV.

ISRAEL IN EUROPE, A MULTITUDE OF NATIONS;
THE TALL CEDAR PLANTED BY
GREAT WATERS.

"Ah, the land of the rustling of wings which is beyond the rivers of Cush;[1] that sendeth ambassadors by the sea, even in vessels of papyrus upon the waters, saying : ' Go, ye swift messengers to a nation dragged away and peeled, to a people terrible from their beginning onward ; a nation meted out and trodden down, whose land the *rivers have spoiled.*'" (Isa. 18-1, 2).

Having followed our Tribes into the far East by the monuments of a former age, but recently deciphered and found to be of Hebrew origin, written in the Hebrew language and telling in unmistakable terms the history of their terrible disasters which came upon them for their obstinacy and idolatry, we will leave them there

---

[1] Indo. Cush.

until the drying up of Euphrates shall prepare the way for their return in such manner and by such means as God in his infinite wisdom may provide.

We now return to the early home of the captives in Armenia, on the confines of Europe, to those who were delegated of God for a *western* migration, for the record says, "They shall wander from sea to sea, and from the North even to the East." This can have but one meaning, covering a hemisphere and stretching from ocean to ocean—from the Atlantic to the Pacific, because it is emphatically declared that their migrations and their "manifest destiny" for pushing things, should extend "to the utmost bound of the everlasting hills." Better accept the inevitable and go along with us as we follow the sons of Isaac and Joseph to the outer edge of the world's land surface, and then by faith Israel shall take a "new departure" to a new home from which she shall never be moved.

Doubtless the Scythians who had received such information from the Tribes on their entrance into Asia of the rich plunder to be obtained by a descent upon the Assyrians, were now able to reciprocate the favor and tell the Tribes of the rich spoil to be had from the southern nations of Europe, lying along the Mediterranean. Since they had become objects of hatred to the Medo-Persian kings, and had met so many evidences of the Divine judgments in their own mountain home, after their environment by the northern cloud, we may fairly suppose they were desirous to get away from a place of such sad reminiscences, and betake themselves to a predatory and pushing life which promised such rich spoils. We may fairly suppose also that such a vast country as Europe must have been represented to them, though but little known save that it was but thinly inhabited by nomad tribes and offered immense fields for their flocks and herds, would offer a strong inducement to the Tribes that were left to follow the northern trail past the Caucasian Mountains and into Europe.

But suppositions are not arguments by any means and we desire if possible to connect the Scythians, who are now generally admitted to have peopled Northern Europe, with the Scythians and Sackæ who were found, not long after Cyrus' conflict with them on the Araxes and Kir, to have migrated to the far East and to have been at first the most formidable adversaries of Alexander two hundred years later, and afterwards his most trusted allies. By the inscriptions, the Buddhist faith and the divine record, we have a reasonable basis for connecting these of the far East with the Hebrews of the house of Isaac and Joseph. But what reason have we for supposing that any of the Tribes were left in their mountain homes. In the absence of monuments how are we to connect the Scythians and Sackæ of the East with those who entered Europe.

Let us remember that God's way of proving the, prophetic records is to look at *results* rather than at causes; at the *end* of the race, rather than at the beginning for the time and circumstances of the starting. On this hypothesis, if we are able to find a people in the latter days filling all the conditions of the prophecies, by whatever name they may be called, we have found the true Israel and should be satisfied. But as human minds will not be satisfied in full with that kind of evidence, we must hunt up something additional.

In what is known as the "Behistun" inscription found inscribed on a rock in Persia not much later than the time of Cyrus, three classes of Sacæ are mentioned, namely: "The Sacæ named next to India, the Sacæ who use arrows, and the Sacæ who are said to be beyond the river." We have already considered those located on the borders of India and here we find two other divisions; one distinguished as bowmen, and the other as that "beyond the river," but what river is not named. Could it be that any considerable number still remained between the rivers Tigris and Euphrates where popular belief has located the whole body? Or could it have been the Araxes where Cyrus encountered them, and to which the popular attention might have been turned on that account?.

Be this as it may, we are disposed to believe that the third division at least—the one famous in the use of the *bow*, with which arrows are of necessity connected—was the division which entered Europe, since all accounts agree that the Saxon element of the Scythian invasion was also famous in the use of the bow. Even as late as the conquest of England by the Saxons they were famous as bowmen. But since Dr. Moore thinks that the word translated from the inscription—"beyond"—has the meaning of "gone beyond"—and this would fully agree with the record of Esdras—we feel quite persuaded to believe that the second division joined their brethren of the third division and entered Europe with them, rather than have attempted to join their brethren in the far East, which would have been a difficult undertaking through hostile Media. We hear of no great body of these people anywhere in Western Asia after this great exodus a little later than the time of Cyrus, though doubtless some of them did remain and continue to this day in those regions.

We have still to connect these Scythians with the Sacæ of the East and with the house of Isaac, for we have only got so far as to separate them into three great divisions, and that they did not all "go East" as many have supposed. In that case not one-tenth of the conditions of prophecy would have been complied with. In most of the early accounts of the Scythian invasion of Europe we find the Saxons and Goths mentioned as forming a large component part with other minor divisions, but altogether a vast horde who were a constant menace to Southern Europe. They were known to the Latins as Sacæ and to the Greeks as Sakai.

Here again the Behistun inscription comes to our aid, for the name is there rendered from the Scythic version Saakkà, but which Dr. Moore renders into its Hebrew equivalents and finds the very word Isaac without the initial which properly forms no part of the name—a name so peculiarly Hebrew that it can hardly have any other derivation than that given to it in Holy Writ. The people dwelling by the Chebar are called in the Assyrian monuments Sucki or Saake, as translated by Rawlinson. From either word, if derived from any Hebrew word common also to the Chaldee, it would mean according to the same authority, a people emptied from one place into another. We have the same wo in use to-day in our word to *sack* a city. The second would simply mean sons of Isaac as the prophet Amos speaks of them. So that in whatever form we find the word we seem forced to the one conclusion that it is indissolubly connected with the Hebrews and the Patriarch Isaac. We shall presently see that all accounts agree that the Scythians came from Asia. If the Scythians came from there so did the Saxons, and the Sacæ, Sakai, Saxons are of Hebrew origin.

The earliest occupation of Europe of which we have any account was by the Kimmerian and Keltic races, the first of which was said to have led the Scythians into Asia. But the second influx of peoples were the Scythian and Gothic tribes. From these, all the modern nations of Europe are descended and known to us as Anglo-Saxons, Lowland Scotch, Normans, Danes, Swedes, Germans, Dutch, Belgians, and Lombards.[1] Herodotus gives the time of their first appearance in Europe as between the seventh and eighth centuries before Christ. This is evidently altogether too early

---

[1] Turners's Anglo-Saxons.

ISRAEL IN EUROPE. 105

since very little was known of the wild tribes in those far off regions, and they might easily be confounded with the Kimmerians. Ptolemy is the first to mention the *Saxons* in Europe, and he says that previous to his time (140 A. D.) they were a considerable people on the north side of the Elbe. Diodorus says the Scythians commenced their career about the Araxes, just where we have shown the marauding bands of Scythians from the Caucasus to have met our Tribes and with them to have made their descent upon Assyria and to have ruled it for twenty-eight years. This, the monuments prove conclusively, took place B. C. 641 to 633. They were certainly there as late as the time of Cyrus one hundred years later, so that the statement of Herodotus can hardly be credited.[1]

Having by fair deductions and historical evidences brought the history of our Tribes—or a very considerable part of them—from their graves in Asia into the borders of Europe, it is comparatively an easy task to trace them the rest of the way, for they remain true to the prophetic record :—

"With them he shall push the people together to the ends of the earth ; and they are the ten thousands of Ephraim, and they are the thousands of Manasseh."

The earliest notice we have of these invaders in re-

---

[1] Herodotus lived only 450 B. C. and was largely dependent, according to his own account, on hearsay and is often incorrect, especially in matters before his time. His account would make it synchronous with the founding of Rome.

spect to *location* is of a people called Saxoi on the western shores of the Euxine or Black Sea, said to have been left there as a colony when the great body of them was passing on to the more central parts of Europe.[1]

We learn, moreover, that just before Alexander undertook his conquest of Asia he crossed the Danube, which empties into the sea on the West, to attack the Getæ who had been making inroads upon the outlying settlements of his kingdom. This was B. C. 335.[2] Now, as we know the Getæ and Sacæ or Saxoi—or Sakai as the Greeks called them—pertain emphatically to our Tribes and to no others, we have here fair proof that they had got as far as the western shore of the Black Sea, near the Danube, as early and as late as Alexander's time. This is probably the earliest and only *authentic* record of their first appearance in Europe.

It will be noticed that the time between Cyrus and Alexander will give ample time for all the mighty changes which came to them by reason of flood, fire and the sword, and enable them to move at their leisure with families, flocks and herds. It is not to be supposed that such warlike tribes could move over such vast spaces of territory without meeting everywhere other warlike tribes to contest for a time their progress, so that their movements would necessarily be slow. "Manifest Destiny" is also an impelling power not to be lost sight of, respecting which no precise calculations can well be made. The time for the punishment of the

---

[1] Turner's Anglo-Saxons, page 83.   [2] Cyc. Brit.

nations, grown corrupt and effete by reason of their idolatrous practices, had not yet come. But because the Merciful Father will not strike until ample opportunity has been given for repentance, these hordes of marauders who have not inaptly been termed "The Scourge of God," were held in restraint until the gospel had been "preached in all the world for a witness unto all people."

But time speeds on and the "cup of indignation" has come to the full, and Rome with its gathered treasures from all quarters of the globe, offers a rich harvest of spoils to these hungry freebooters for extensive and long continued depredations. Between 408 and 410 A. D. Rome was besieged three times by them and only delivered by immense ransom or by pillage. In 490 A. D. one of their number (Odoacer) ruled Italy, at which time the fate of Rome had for a long while hung upon the sword of these formidable strangers who began to trouble the Empire as early as the third century after Christ.[1]

Gibbon gives a minute and comprehensive account of these ravages under Alaric and those following him, and the almost incredible amount of plunder of every description which they carried away. Yet amidst all the barbarities incident to such times, there are recorded many traits of character showing them to be altogether superior in many respects to the corrupt nobility whom they displaced. Alaric himself gave special orders that

---

[1] Gibbon's "Decline and Fall of the Roman Empire."

unarmed citizens should not be molested, and that *Christian churches should be inviolate.* War, indeed, drove the people from the fields; but famine, pestilence and the forty thousand slaves of Rome were the chief causes of the terrible destruction of the people.

As a general thing they did not assimilate with the conquered people but drove them before them and supplied their places with better and more robust material with which in after years to continue the life of the nations just ready to drop out of line. Charles Kingsley says: "These wild tribes (the Gothic) were bringing with them into the magic circle of the Western Church's influence the very materials which she required for the building up of a future Christendom. The new invaders divided Europe among themselves." This same influence was exerted wherever they came, which served to give new life to the old effete civilisations of southern Europe. They introduced new customs, laws, and language, which so intertwined with the existing order of things as to impart to them a new tone and vigor; indeed, they gave a new lease of life to that which was ready to die out from sheer exhaustion. Such was the case in a very marked degree throughout Italy and Greece, and the influence was but little lessened in the remoter portions of the Empire.

But not alone on the borders of the southern States of Europe are these Saxon and Gothic nations penetrating with their almost resistless arms. They are stretching across to the northern shores of Europe on the Baltic and North seas, and westward along the channel. Everywhere they are pushing the people before them to find escape or an asylum in large or small bodies wherever they can, but preserving in the main their own individual and tribal characteristics of race, language and customs. We learn that they were so proud of their descent and stalwart physique that marriages with other nations were rare.[1] Especially was this the case with the Sacæ or Saxons, and to such an extent was this carried that it is asserted of those who afterwards settled New England, that a race of purer blood could hardly be found the world over.

Having renounced the worship of idols—as we have shown—before leaving Armenia, it is not surprising that we find the Tribes, six or seven hundred years later, with a sort of conglomerate faith and worship hard to be understood, about which ancient historians have very little that can be relied on, so conflicting are their accounts. Doubtless they are indulging in very many rites and usages more or less heathenish. Yet if they had not renounced idolatry, how then can we account for the immunity granted to Christian churches which not only afforded in themselves rich fields for plunder but were made the receptacles of treasures by many when this fact became known?[2] Moreover, it is pretty well established that the Saxons paid divine honors to

---

[1] Turner's Anglo-Saxons, page 143. Tacitus also testifies that monogamy was the universal rule and polygamy almost unknown.

[2] Gibbon's Decline and Fall.

Godam[1] which is, doubtless, an abbreviation of Godama, a name very early applied as we have seen to Saka or Sakya the founder of Buddhism and meaning God-like. From this source we have our name of God and Wednesday—Wodensday or God's-day—Woden being first known as Goadem, then Godem and finally Woden. Odin of the Scandinavians, celebrated in song as the soul-giver is, probably, another form of the same word. Doubtless many other forms, modified by time and changing dialects, are to be found among these Saxon, Gothic and Scythian tribes, which have been charged to them by ancient writers as veritable heathen gods.

It cannot be denied that these so-called Scythic nations—especially that portion entitled *Saxon*—were far above the heathen nations in general in all physical, moral and intellectual endowments. Their agility, the swiftness of their movements, great endurance and bravery, are especially noted. In this, one is reminded of Saul and Jonathan (2 Sam. 1-23) who "were swifter than eagles, they were stronger than lions;" also, of the Gadites who "separated themselves unto David," "men of war fit for the battle, that could handle shield and buckler, whose faces were like the faces of lions, and were as swift as the roes upon the mountains" (1 Chro. 12–8); also, of the quotation at the head of this chapter: "To a people terrible from their beginning onward." The whole history of these "multitude of nations" in

---

[1] Mengel's History of Germany, and Latham's Ethnology of the British Isles.

the far East and of those who went into Europe, tells the same story that the prophets declared ages ago, and points as with a pen of iron to a future destiny at once irresistible and immeasurable.

Among the more conspicuous of these pushing conquerers were the Engels from Engel-land bordering on the Jutland peninsula between the Baltic and North seas. Whether invited over by the public council of the king and chiefs of Britain to resist the inroads of the Irish and Picts, or seeking for further conquests on their own account, matters not. Certain it is that about the year 449 or 453 A. D., some three hundred men[1] headed by Horsa and Hengist, all pure Saxons, crossed the Channel and entered Britanny—to stay. But a few years elapse and we find them assuming the government of that portion of the kingdom in which they were located—the county of Kent—and inviting more of their people over from the main land for future operations.

True to their nature and "manifest destiny" we find them pushing the native Britons more and more to the boundaries of the island, being constantly reinforced [2] by their brethren from Jutland and Saxony until but a remnant of the original Kimmerian and Keltic settlers of Britain were left, principally in Cornwall and Wales. "The ancient inhabitants and the progeny of the Roman settlers disappeared as the new conquerors ad-

---

[1] Turner's Anglo-Saxons, page 181.
[2] Turner's Anglo-Saxons, page 75.

vanced—or accepted their yoke—and Saxon laws, Saxon language, Saxon manners, government, and institutions, overspread the land."

There are many interesting circumstances connected with the influx of the Anglo-Saxons, which go to show some connection with a people of Hebrew origin. We give below a portion of a poem as the prayer of five hundred men who came over in five ships, which is suspected to be Hebrew in consequence of Taliesen the bard (600 A. D.) having declared that his lore had been delivered to him in Hebrew [1] or Hebraic. A translation by Dr. Moore is offered : [2]

> " And I have made a covenant—a Heap,
> A home of wood is a home, my guide,
> I have made a covenant, O ship,
> SAK is my guide, my guide, he is my Friend."

There are said to be more than five hundred words of Persian origin in the English language, derived, probably, by the Sacæ or Saxons in their early intercourse with Persia and thus brought into England. There are also very many words with Hebrew roots—good authorities say one thousand—which can only be accounted for on the supposition of a Hebrew origin and a connection with the Sons of Isaac.

. The cut on the page opposite the preface shows the essential features of the English Coat of Arms and the

---

[1] Rev. E. Davies' Mythology of the British Druids.
[2] Lost Tribes, 173.

star banner, somewhat modified indeed in the lapse of time since they were cut in the vast rock chamber of Ajanta or engraved on the gates of the tope at Sanchi or Sachi. The trident is peculiar to British coins. The star banner is little known and quite in disuse; doubtless, that the stars might become the peculiar legacy to the "man child," "the stone of Israel" across the water, since "*westward the star of empire* takes its way."

The Saxons always boasted of their As-Khan, that is Asian prince. An old MS. in the Vatican says they came from Esco or Yisico (Isaac ?), (2) Arminius (Armenia ?), and (3) Ingo or India.[1] Capt. Wilford has shown from the Puranas that the British Isles were called Saccam.[2] The "White Island in the West" (England) was called in India, Sacana, from the Sacæ who conquered it. The Karens of Burmah told the first missionaries that messengers would come from the "White Island" to teach them the true way. These are only "straws," but they serve to "show which way the wind blows."

Though many benefits were conferred by the Roman conquest and occupation of Britain, the influx of the Saxons offered a vastly superior foundation for a more enduring civilisation in that, while they were by nature and occupation freebooters and rovers, they brought with them—strange as it may appear—superior domes-

---

[1] Dr. Moore's "Lost Tribes," page 354.
[2] Asiatic Res. II., page 54.

tic and moral character and the rudiments of new political, judicial and intellectual life.[1]

While they adopted many of the usages of the conquered, they greatly improved them by the addition of their own, and continued as heretofore to keep themselves a unique and predominating race, both in language and social life. To them we owe not only the name but the very idea of true home life, so foreign to the civilisations of Greece and Rome. But with all these qualifications there was yet needed a softening influence, a toning down of the terrific harshness of the Saxon tongue, and of exterior manners born of their wild, predatory life. Leaving our Anglo-Saxons to "'push' things," let us turn our attention very briefly to this mollifying agency.

The time never seems to have been when wars and conflicts were not in progress between the numerous States of the Teutonic or Gothic races and the older civilisations of the south of Europe, as already noticed; while the roving expeditions by sea from the northern countries, afforded a constant menace to the coast inhabitants and cities, from the North Sea to the Mediterranean and made the very name of Northmen a terror. Early in the 9th century they entered Gaul or France, but not content with simply entering, their roving disposition led them to keep on pushing and plundering until they came out on the other side, when many of them settled down in Sicily and Lombardy. In the

---

[1] Turner's Anglo-Saxons.

early centuries they were freebooters ; in the eleventh and twelfth they were the best of Crusaders and, in fact, aided very materially in stemming the tide of Turkish invasion which threatened to overspread Europe.

Early in the ninth century these Northmen in large numbers settled down in Normandy, a province in the north of France bordering on the English Channel, who were destined to exert a very powerful influence for all time on their Saxon brethren across the Channel, from whom they differed in one important particular. While partaking of the same restless, roving, spirit, and fondness for martial enterprise, they were not averse to assimilating with the conquered people instead of pushing them on before to seek a home elsewhere.

They were great imitators of all they saw and they greatly improved what they adopted. They did not leave behind them anything peculiarly and distinctively Norman, nor build up a Norman state after the example of their Anglo-Saxon brethren of England, but they accepted even the language of the province in which they settled, and greatly enriched it by the addition of their own, making it a polished and comprehensive medium of literary and poetic thought. They introduced customs and habits of life which gradually moulded the people to a new and better order of things, awakened a love for church establishments on a solid and enduring basis, and by apt architectural designs wrought their sanctuaries into a "thing of beauty and a joy forever." They moulded law into precise forms and a substantial science, for it has been truly said, "If they were born soldiers, they were also born lawyers."

With this enrichment in language, social bearing, love for church endowments and architecture, and his natural born legal acumen, all improved by his connection with the polite Gaul and his Gallo-Latin tongue, the freebooter Northman of two centuries ago is transformed into the Norman of the eleventh century, and ready to enter on his God-appointed mission to enrich his brother Saxon across the Channel. In the year 1066 William "the Conqueror" laid claim to the English throne on a purely legal basis and maintained it, right or wrong, by a *posse comitatus* of 60,000 soldiers, adventurers and retainers, and, on entering England proceeds at once, like an old-time Democratic administration, to apply the shibboleth, "To the victors belong the spoils," though Edward the Confessor had in a measure prepared the way by filling his own court and offices with Norman favorites.

Norman nobles and retainers are again put into all places of power and emolument in Church and State. The whole social, political, and ecclesiastical, goverment of William is in great measure changed into Norman hands (made necessary by internal troubles) and he proceeds to work out "manifest destiny" in behalf of those who had hitherto known no permanent conqueror. There was no special humiliation in this, for were they not brethren of the same original stock, and working under the divine hand for the accomplishment of the same ultimate object? Two centuries sufficed for the schooling in manners, language, literature, jurisprudence, architecture, and love of endowments, which characterise our brethren of to-day across the waters. They are not *over* polite yet, what must they have been before this schooling?

But now Israel (for we shall have her resume her maiden name now) has pushed the people to "the utmost bounds of the everlasting hills." She has given birth to a "multitude of nations" and kings without number. She has possessed the "gate of her enemies," carrying new life and promise of better things to come wherever she has sojourned. She has, by her children, been sifted among the nations, yet has gathered to herself the "precious things of heaven, of the *dew* (fogs?), and of the *deep* that croucheth beneath, and of the chief things of the ancient mountains." She lends but does not borrow and, enriched by the fiery trials through which she has passed, she has become the best conservator of all that is true, noble, valiant and free. She has become indeed "an holy nation" in the sense of being set apart and consecrated to the accomplishment of the Divine purpose, that purpose being the political mastery of the old world and the destruction of Imperialism and the Papacy. "The highest branch of the high cedar" has indeed been "planted in a good soil by great waters, that it might bring forth branches and that it might bear fruit, that it might be a goodly vine" (Eze. 17–8, 22).

But is this the end of Israel? Are the promises all fulfilled save those pertaining to the punishment and destruction of those old-time enemies of the church—Imperialism and the Papacy? By no means. In the first chapter on "Signs of the Times" we have shown how political Israel has already indicated her purpose to complete the circuit of the old world and occupy again at no distant day the initial point of her journeyings—the objective point of the divine purpose, so far as the old world is concerned. Is that all? Not by any means. Her career is in one sense but *just begun*. DAVID'S THRONE MUST BE ESTABLISHED.

But David has been "a man of blood," and cannot be allowed to build the temple of God. The commission is therefore committed to his son Solomon, whose reign and kingdom have in all ages been taken as the type of Christ's kingdom on earth. David may gather the materials in rich abundance, but Solomon alone is fitted to build the temple of the living God, who accepts it at his hands by the presence of the Heavenly Shekina. Even so in this ultimate temple of the ages, "built by workmanship divine," of heaven-born material, no bloody hands may control the work. Israel may provide the baser material, and may purchase at a goodly price the land whereon the temple shall be built, but she shall have no hand in its construction. Yet out of her shall come the gold of human character, tried in the fire until it reflects the image of the Heavenly Architect and Builder, and fitted to be the chief adornment of this living Christian temple, each human block of which may have within his consecrated and sanctified heart the *living presence* of the Heavenly Shekina ; while the larger, aggregate, temple of the Theocracy shall be so governed and controlled, that in all the untold ages of the future it shall not cease to fill the earth with blessing. "For the law shall go forth from Mount Zion, and the word of the Lord from Jerusalem." To the erection of this temple we will give our attention in the next chapter.

CHAPTER V.

SPIRITUAL ISRAEL PLACED IN THE NEW WORLD; THE TENDER TWIG PLANTED UPON AN HIGH MOUNTAIN.

"At that time shall a present be brought unto the Lord of Hosts *of a people* dragged away and peeled, and *from a people* terrible from their beginning onward ; a nation meted out and trodden down whose land the rivers have spoiled, *to the place* of the name of the Lord of Hosts, the Mount Zion."

"All ye inhabitants of the world, and ye dwellers on the earth, when an ensign is lifted up on the mountains,—SEE YE: and when the trumpet is blown, *hear ye*" (Isa. 18–7, 3: also Zach. 9–16, 17).

"For, behold, I create new heavens and a new earth: and the former shall not be remembered, nor come into mind " (Isa. 65–17).

"For as the new heavens and the new earth which I will make shall remain before me, so shall your seed and your name remain:

and it shall come to pass, that from one new moon to another, and from one Sabbath to another, shall all flesh come to worship before me, saith the Lord" (Isa. 66-22, 23: see also 51-16: 43-18 to 21).

"And I saw a new heavens and a new earth; for the first heaven and the first earth were passed away; and there was no more sea" (Rev. 21-1).

We have come now to a very critical point in Israel's history, and we desire to make future developments so plain that no one who desires to know the truth can stumble or make a mistake. One of the most difficult things in connection with this subject is to realise that one is passing through the actual developments of prophecy, so prone are we to look for the marvellous. "As for this fellow we *know* whence *he* is: but when Christ cometh no man knoweth whence he is," said the astute Pharisees. Those who passed through the stupendous events of the French Revolution of 1793-4 could not realise their greatness, but left it to those who should come after them to measure their significance. It is of the utmost importance to us to grasp if possible the import of the mighty, yet quiet, events through which, as a people, we have been and are now passing.

Hitherto we have followed Israel's career by historical and monumental evidence, yet only suggestively lest we trespass our bounds. We have given authorities for various statements, which can be consulted for a deeper study of the subject if desired. We have seen how completely the facts of the case have fitted the prophetic record. But the most wonderful part of all is yet to come, and to this we ask your careful and serious attention, because it will be found so completely at variance with all your preconceived ideas and opinions. But if the conditions of the record are filled, you cannot honestly refuse your approval and acceptance of the truths thus opened to you, and to God and your own conscience you are answerable for your conclusions.

To make the case plainer we shall first name the conditions of scripture necessary to be complied with and then proceed to state the historical facts. The conditions referred to are these: the "remnant" shall be delivered,

(a) "At *that time*,"—"in *that day*,"—"In the latter days ye shall consider it" (Jer. 30-24),—in the "Consummation of the age" (Matt. 13-39).

(b) "A *present* to the Lord of Hosts."—a free will offering; "Ye shall not go out with haste, nor go by flight" (Isa. 52-12).

(c) "*Of a people* dragged away and peeled" hitherto and now afflicted:—"They shall come with weeping and with supplications will I gather them" (Jer. 31-9).

(d) They must come out for religious convictions:— "Depart ye, depart ye, touch no unclean thing: be ye clean that bear the vessels of the Lord" (Isa. 52-11).

(e) They come out because of trials put upon them by their brethren:—"As for my flock they eat that which ye have trodden with your feet, and they drink that which ye have fouled with your feet" (Eze. 34-19).

(*f*) A *small* portion of people from a *nation* :—"The stone of Israel" (Gen. 49-24); "A *stone* cut out of the *mountain* without hands" (Dan. 2-45) : "a remnant" (Jer. 31-7; 23-3).

(*g*) They shall act at once as a fold and a "shepherd" (Gen. 49-24) :—"He that scattered Israel will gather him, and keep him as a shepherd doth his flock" (Jer. 31-10; Isa. 11-10).

(*h*) The "present" must be "*from a people* terrible from their beginning onward, whose land the rivers have spoiled," as Israel's was in Armenia.

(*i*) The "remnant" must come from a *North* country:— "Behold, I will bring them from the *North* country, and gather them from the *coasts* of the earth" (Jer. 31-8 : 23-8).

(*j*) It must be a *tender twig* from "the *highest* branch of the *high cedar*" : "In the *mountain* of the height of Israel will I plant it" (Eze. 17-23).

Here are ten peculiar conditions pertaining to Israel and to no other person, people or nation, which must be observed (and many more of the same character are left for the reader to hunt up) in connection with further developments in the progress of Israel. She has got to the "utmost bounds," into a *North* country, in "the uttermost parts of the earth" from where the prophet wrote, her land is all "coasts" but—a wide ocean confronts her and she can go no further. *Yes she can.* Faith can leap the waters "*dry shod.*" The "remnant" shall be "baptised in the cloud and in the sea ;—but we will not anticipate. Hunt the world over and history through, and you cannot find any event whatever that will fill all these conditions without straining, twisting and whittling, to make it fit. save the one event we are about to relate. Nor is it at all likely that such an event with all these requirements and a hundred others which will be named in their proper place. will ever again occur in this world. and he must be dead to all conviction who refuses to see the hand of our God in all this most remarkable career of Israel.

There is hardly a necessity to enter into any detailed account of the condition of the English Established Church previous to the year 1620, with its dead formalism and rites borrowed from the anti-Christian forms of Rome. to find reason for the spirit of non-conformity which grew out of a godly desire for a purer and simpler form of worship. The history of it is well-known by large numbers and open to all. Suffice it to say that the spirit of non-conformity was abroad in the land and taking a deep hold upon the hearts of many godly people, notably in the little town of Scrooby in the north of England. on the borders of Nottinghamshire, Yorkshire. and Lincoln. where was gathered a little congregation who held their meetings every Sabbath in one place or another for about a year. when they resolved to go over to

Holland for greater freedom in the exercise of religious worship. There had always been non-conformists in the English Church from its very foundation, but in 1559 during the reign of Queen Elisabeth, the act of uniformity was passed, imposing severe penalties for conducting public service in any other manner than that prescribed in the Book of Common Prayer; so that it became necessary for those who could not in conscience conform to what seemed to many pious people only popish superstitions, to worship by themselves and in secret.

These at Scrooby were among the more pronounced of non-conformists, who were ready to leave all the endearments of home for purely religious causes, so deep were their convictions of the sinfulness of remaining longer in fellowship with a church so corrupt in form and practice as the English Established Church had become. In mockery they were termed "Puritans," for the name "Non-conformist" was not publicly recognised until the act of 1656.

"Depart ye, depart ye, go ye out from thence, touch no unclean thing; go ye out of the midst of her: BE YE CLEAN, that bear the vessels of the Lord" (Isa. 52-11).

The troubles they experienced in effecting this change on account of the rigor of ecclesiastical laws and the tyranny of a church and priesthood but little removed from the formulas of the Roman, were indeed pitiable to behold. Says one account,[1] "They were robbed of

---

[1] Palfrey's New England.

their worldly goods, betrayed through treachery and
sent to prison, families were separated by reason of a
storm which drove the vessel to sea, on which part of
their company had embarked with all the goods left to
them; and thus, deprived of their homes which they
had sold and having none other to which they could immediately go, they were indeed in a pitiable plight most
affecting to behold."

"For thus saith the Lord: behold, I will bring them from
the north country, and gather them from the uttermost part
of the earth, a great company shall they return hither; they
shall come with weeping, and with supplications will I lead
them; and they shall walk by rivers of waters in a straight
way wherein they shall not stumble: for I am a father to
Israel and Ephraim is my first born" (Jer. 38-8, 9).

After many mishaps and much hardship they arrived
at last in Amsterdam in 1607-8. Here they remained
a distinct community, though they found there the
London congregation which had emigrated some twelve
or fifteen years before, and the Gainsboro congregation,
their former neighbors in Nottinghamshire. Not finding their residence there pleasant on account of dissensions in the two above named societies, they determined
to remove to Leyden, some forty miles distant. All
these troubles were however but the premonitory signs
—the quickenings—of a birth from the womb of the
symbolic "mountain" to be accomplished later on in
quietness and peace at Delft Haven:—

"For ye shall not go out with haste; nor go by flight for the
Lord will go before you, and the God of Israel shall be your
rearward" (Isa. 52-12).

Twelve long years of tedious residence in Leyden were fully sufficient to make them devoutly tired of the indolent security of their "little sanctuary," and in 1620 a small company, having determined to embark for the New World, gathered with their friends to hold their last religious service together, "pouring out prayers to the Lord with great fervency mixed with abundance of tears." When they were just ready to leave, the brethren who were to remain behind gathered them at the pastor's house, "where we refreshed ourselves, *after tears*, with singing of psalms, making joyful melody in our heart as well as with our voice." After this they accompanied the "*Pilgrims*" to Delft-Haven, fourteen miles distant, where they were to embark; when, with tears, prayers and much sorrow at parting, "we lifted up our hands to each other and our hearts for each other to the Lord our God, we departed," some ninety persons in all, on board the *Speedwell* for Southampton, July 22, 1620.

There they were joined by the *Mayflower* and on the 5th of August they were ready to sail with one hundred and twenty persons on the two vessels, the first of sixty tons, and the last of one hundred and eighty tons burden.[1] After getting to sea the *Speedwell* proved leaky and

---

[1] It is worthy of note as at least a remarkable coincidence that this "remnant" coming out as "the shepherd, the stone of Israel," should consist of just one hundred and twenty, or twelve each for the ten seceding tribes of Israel. This connects it at once with the twelve disciples chosen from the one tribe of Judah for the

both vessels put back, when some concluded to remain behind, so that when the *Mayflower* at last sailed, Sept. 6, there were one hundred and two passengers on board, men, women, and children. They were at last out on the bosom of the broad ocean, but whither were they bound? Where else can they go but to "*the place* of the Lord of Hosts. the Mount Zion" of the ages to come, as saith the prophet Nathan:—

"Moreover I will appoint A PLACE for my people Israel, and will plant them. that they may dwell in a PLACE OF THEIR OWN. AND MOVE NO MORE: neither shall the children of wickedness afflict them any more as before time" (2 Sam. 7-10).

"For, behold, I create new heavens and a new earth: and the former shall not be remembered nor come into mind" (Isa. 65-17). "For as the new heavens and the new earth which I will make shall remain before me, so shall your name and your seed remain: and it shall come to pass that from one new moon to another, and from one Sabbath to another, shall all flesh come to worship before me, saith the Lord of Hosts" (Isa. 66-22, 23: 51-16: 43-18 to 21).

Where else can they go but to the *New World*, prepared of God in ages past for his people and his kingdom when in his good providence it should please him to bring them thither? We will now leave our pilgrims on shipboard on the bosom of the broad ocean while we

---

Prince of the house of David. It matters not that eighteen remained when they were obliged to put back and abandon one vessel, no more than the defection of Judas destroyed the unity of the body of the disciples. It only serves to make the cases more coincident and remarkable, since both losses were made good afterwards.

consider this subject of the New World for which they are heading.

I am fully aware that I am treading on what may be termed by some timid souls "dangerous ground." But truth is never dangerous ground to stand upon; and if old, delusive, fossil, rocks, even though they be component parts of ideal new worlds such as have been cherished from time immemorial, have become honeycombed by the disintegrating elements of time, research and common sense, it is high time that some sharp blows from the "hammer that breaketh the rock in pieces" should cause them to crumble and go down.

Let us look calmly and without prejudice at these passages we have quoted, without asking what is the orthodox or received view respecting them, or what authorities sustain the old notions that have so long prevailed, but let us ask what is the truth and what is a plain, common sense interpretation of these strange passages. If the truth is reached on this basis, be true to God and to yourself by acting on your convictions. The quotations from Isaiah are certainly plain enough it would seem, without symbolism or circumlocution of any kind. A plain statement is made that God will create new heavens and a new earth with its festivals and new moons —by which the beginning of the festivals was determined —and Sabbaths, all pertaining to present life and religious enjoyment, which one would hardly suppose necessary if we are to be "caught up and changed in the twinkling of an eye" and the world given to devouring flame.

But then says one. John declares there is to be a
"new heavens and a new earth wherein dwelleth righteousness." If there is to be indeed a new earth—a new
creation—it can only be, according to the plain word of
scripture, "when the elements shall be dissolved with
fervent heat, the earth also and the works that are therein
shall be burned up." But that cannot be (as we shall
conclusively show in the final chapter) until the need of
Sabbaths, festivals and new moons, and all the cumbersome machinery of "church work" are no longer needed
and we shall have entered into an eternal Sabbath of
rest.

Better give up, dear reader, looking for the marvellous
and tragic and look about you and behold the "new
earth" on which you tread, and the "new heavens,"
more wonderful than any the world has ever seen, your
very environment.

The reign of righteousness is in great measure at your
own disposal: first, in your own heart after the pattern
of Him who hath called you into the glorious liberty of
the sons of God: and, again, in the domain of your own
social circle ever widening into the circle of the world at
large.

Again, the record says, "As the new heavens and the
new earth shall remain before me, so shall your *seed*
and your *name remain.*" Pray where is the necessity of
seed and names *remaining* if the earth is purified by fire
and our whole organism changed to suit the new order
of things? Absurd! There is not the shadow of a claim

on which to build such a theory. Why not then acknowledge at once that there is no light to be gained from the old, accepted expositions of these passages, and admit that your conception of "the new heavens and the new earth" must in some way be defective and needs remodeling.

It is of no use to fall back on the Apocalypse and say, as so many have done, that the later revelation explains the earlier, and that John says expressly there is to be a new heavens and a new earth, *for* the first heaven and the first earth were passed away, and "*there was no more sea.*" This reminds me of a good Christian, a hard-working mechanic who prided himself somewhat on his intellectual attainments and general reading and who, in making some remarks in the weekly prayer meeting, said that he found it difficult to express himself in Engglish, he would therefore give it to them in Latin,—and he did. So, my brother, you would take Revelations, confessedly a book of symbols from the fourth chapter throughout, which you do not understand, to explain simple, straightforward, Isaiah who, as a general thing, explains himself as we shall presently see. In Isa. 34–4 are these words :—

> "And all the host of heaven shall be dissolved, and the heavens shall be rolled together as a scroll; and all their host shall fall down, as the leaf falleth off from the vine, and as a falling fig from the fig tree; for my **SWORD** shall be bathed in heaven; behold, it shall come down upon **IDUMEA**, and upon the people of my curse, to judgment."

Does any one for a moment suppose that this strong language was literally fulfilled ? or did it mean, simply, that judgments should come upon the people and their rulers and that their princes and their great men should be driven from their seats of power by war, and their political heavens "dissolved." To this there can be but one answer. Political revolutions based upon the arbitrament of the sword, are meant and nothing more. Take this from Isa. 13–10, 11, 14, spoken of Babylon:—

"For the stars of heaven and the constellations thereof shall not give their light; the sun shall be darkened in his going forth, and the moon shall not cause her light to shine; and I will punish the world for their evil, and the wicked for their iniquity; and I will cause the arrogancy of the proud to cease, and I will lay low the haughtiness of the terrible; therefore I will shake the heavens, and the **EARTH SHALL REMOVE OUT OF HER PLACE**, in the wrath of the Lord of Hosts, and in the day of his fierce anger."

Here, again, no one for a moment supposes that there was a literal fulfillment of any of these grand natural phenomena, but that Babylon should be humbled and her name as a nation, yea, the very kingdom itself should be removed out of her place ; all which was long ago fulfilled. Yet the heavens still remain, albeit a new *political heavens* are above us and our dull eyes fail to see their surpassing beauty, and old earth moves on in her accustomed course as she is likely to do for untold ages to come. So also are we to understand the following passages, especially the last named, all of which we will leave the reader to look up and carefully ponder (Isa. 24–19, 20, 23: Joel 2–10: Rev. 6–13, 14).

In reading the Apocalypse of John the general reader needs to bear in mind that it is an Oriental book, written for Orientals and, consequently, in a language abounding in metaphor and symbols or picture language, in which we may say, in a general way, all historical events were recorded on the monuments and termed to-day hieroglyphics. These symbols were well understood by educated Orientals and every symbol had a definite and well established meaning, not understood by us at this day whose language is precise and definite and without symbolism, or even metaphor to any great extent. Yet if I say that man is an ass, or is brazen faced, or that boy is a calf, any one at once understands that I mean nothing of the kind as a matter of fact, but that the persons addressed have the qualities supposed to belong to the animals or object named. The animals themselves may be used as the symbols; the statement in connection with them is a metaphor which in plain terms may be stated thus—to speak *otherwise* than one really means.

Now the Apocalypse is just such a book as described in few words, above. It is made up entirely of metaphors and symbols which, continued or woven into a complete story, make an allegory. The book is made up, moreover, of material furnished in large part by the older prophets and a continuation—with amplification and minuteness of detail—of the previous visions of Daniel in particular, and of Isaiah, Zecheriah, and other prophets in general. Thus the figures and symbols employed have the same value throughout, being inspired by the same Divine Spirit. This will be made clearer and more apparent as we proceed. But the trouble has been that general readers, and exegetes as well, have dropped the symbolism where there *appeared* a statement of facts, and have wholly ignored the value of symbols explained in great measure by the older prophets. Thus the whole of the last two chapters of Revelations have been taken as a veritable description of heaven or the purified earth, because of the highly tragic statements of the previous (20th) chapter. Let us see.

John says he "saw a new heaven." What! new planets, new stars, new sun, new moon ? Must all this beautiful planetary system and the constellations be destroyed or moved out of their place because this little earth of ours is to undergo a change? or must this earth be moved into other regions of space and made to take its place in some other galaxy of planets to move on for countless ages in its new found path among the stars ? That is what is involved if we take his statement of what he saw as literal, in its entirety. How much more reasonable to believe that this new heaven has the same meaning here that similar phrases have throughout the scriptures where they are used as symbols of great and mighty changes in the *political world*—an entirely new political firmament, as compared with that of the Old World. It may here be observed that symbolic prophecy takes no cognizance anywhere of the destruction of matter, only of moral and political changes. It is also a rule of correct interpretation that the character of a symbol once obtained as used, is *good for the whole Bible*. It is never materially changed and may be relied on throughout, otherwise there would be confusion and we could know nothing certain. But "order is Heaven's first law" and confusion is found nowhere—except in modern interpretations of symbolic prophecy. These slight changes in symbols had better be named that we may not be misunderstood :—The one horn of Daniel's beast, which represents the ecclesiastical power that should grow up out of the civil or imperial power of Rome, becomes two horns in the Apocalypse to fit the double character of the Papacy, civil and ecclesiastic. The fourth beast "great and terrible" becomes the great red dragon of Revelation, but still a beast. The four living creatures of Ezekiel's vision—representing Israel, as shown in the previous chapter—are reproduced in the "four living creatures in the *midst* of the throne and *round about* the throne" of the Apocalypse. The "wheels" are absent because these symbols of the on-goings of the Almighty are no longer necessary in the new dispensation, since Christ is there represented as the moving power and is himself present by "a Lamb as it had been slain." So it is throughout; the changes do not destroy the value of the symbol, for the horns still represent civil or ecclesiastical powers and the "four living creatures" always represent Israel. With this digression we pass on.

Having obtained the character and value of the "new heavens," let us determine about that "*sea*" that was to "be no more." The sea was generally regarded by the Ancients as the home of monsters of a rapacious and destructive character: hence, a beast rising out of the sea would indicate in symbolic language a cruel and rapacious political power growing out of a corrupt and debased social and political condition of the people, which should exercise all the instincts of a wild animal. Such was the Roman imperial power which persecuted the people of God with such terrible severity at ten different times. This power is represented in Daniel 7-7 by the "fourth beast, dreadful and terrible," which "devoured and brake in pieces" the other three beasts or national powers, and by the great red dragon of Rev. 12-3, and the "beast" of chap. 13-1 representing the *civil* power of *Papal* Rome. All are repacious beasts out of the *sea* and stand as symbols of Rome in her political power, whether under Imperialism or the Papacy.

The Abyss, as in the Revised Version, is a different original word from that used for sea, but has the same general characteristic as a symbol, and means simply bottomless. There is nothing to necessitate its being used with "pit," as in the Common Version, save in chap. 9-1 where *phreas* is used for pit. In all other cases it may just as well be attached to sea and doubtless belongs there to indicate that when the dragon is cast back into the sea from whence he came, it will take him a thousand years to rise to the surface again. No wonder it was called *bottomless;* but to have mentioned the *sea* would have made the meaning too plain, and "it is the glory of God to *hide a thing.*"

That this interpretation is not strained is apparent from chap. 11-7 where the "beast," which we know in all cases to have arisen from the *sea,* is there represented as rising out of the abyss—*abussos*—" bottomless." Now if the sea is a symbol for vast masses of corrupt people,—smaller bodies being always symbolised by rivers, streams, and fountains of waters,—is it not evident that when the people become sufficiently intelligent to deny the "divine right of kings" and are able to rule themselves by elected representatives, that there is "*no more sea*" from which "beasts" and dragons can rise? Of course it is, and that is the meaning, nothing more nor less. Having discovered the value of two factors in the problem, it ought not to be a difficult matter to find the third—the " new earth."

No symbol stands for the earth because there was no one in use for a subject that could not by any means have entered into the wildest imaginations of men unless by divine impulse. John adopted. therefore, the plain language of the older prophets and trusted to the symbolisms of the balance of the verse to hide his meaning, in which he succeeded, we think. most admirably, for eighteen centuries have passed and the Christian world is still puzzled over the whole subject. We can, perhaps, get a more intelligent view of this subject if we will only place ourselves, in imagination, where John was in the lonely isle of Patmos, and see with his eyes what he saw "in the Spirit," he says :—

"I saw a new h aven and a new earth: and he first heaven and the first earth were passed away; and there was no more sea."

There was revealed to his enraptured vision something exceeding the wildest flights of his imagination in a normal condition:—for, be it observed, he saw it in an advanced condition, since he seems to have seen this after the dynasties of the old world had been cast into the abyss, and after the thousand years were ended and those old-time oppressors of the race had dared to attempt a revival, in some form, of their lost power. If it was at this stage of the world that he got his first view. in the very height of Christ's beneficent reign, what must have been his joy at seeing this "new world" with its boundless wealth of hill and dale, valley and field ; with its almost limitless expanse of waters in lakes. rivers and streams, emptying into harbors. bays. gulfs, and ocean on either hand. What signs of busy life in multiform phases in shop, mill and farm, or flying as on wings of wind over prairie and up the mountain side. What lovely and beautiful homes in city. town. and village, all betokening a happy and prosperous people. Seeing all this in his mind's eye, and the old world lost to view, could he say ought else than "I saw a new earth, and the first earth was passed away" ?

But John saw more than this :—He saw what was foreign to the highest conception of old-world imperialism with its thrones bathed in blood and sunk in corruptions of the worst form. He saw a happy and multitudinous people electing their own rulers "from amongst themselves," as the prophets had declared they should "*in that day.*" Millions of happy people he saw going to their appointed places to elect these rulers, and as quietly and happily returning to their usual avocations without strife or revolution, so different from all that the old world had ever seen. Could he say aught else than "I saw a new heaven"? He says nothing more of all this, for his eyes followed his heart with rapt attention to the glorious condition of the Church for which he was then suffering banishment; he saw the holy city, new Jerusalem, and was satisfied.

Awhile back we left our Pilgrims heading for an almost unknown country, like their fathers of the olden time:

"They went out not knowing whither they went, and confessed that they were strangers and PILGRIMS on the earth." For they who say such things declare plainly that they seek a country. * * * But now they desire a better country, that is a heavenly; wherefore God is not ashamed to be called their God; for he hath prepared for them a city."[1]

Even one of divine make and workmanship, "a new heaven and a new earth," uncorrupted by the curses of the old world. To this New World we introduce our Pilgrims at Plymouth Rock Nov. 11, 1620, to commence the foundations of an empire which shall, by its God-

---

[1] Heb. 11-14, 16.

appointed institutions, cause ancient, imperial dynasties, foreshadowed in Nebuchadnezar's golden image, to crumble and fall to the ground. "The stone cut out of the mountain without hands" shall yet become itself a "great mountain and fill the whole earth." Although our "pilgrims" at Southampton were but one hundred and two—a "remnant," a "little one,"—yet in twenty years nearly forty thousand had arrived of those who sought for "freedom to worship God." "A great company," to be enlarged by an innumerable number out of all kindred and languages and people. Here we leave them, to seek in the next chapter, if possible, a God-appointed name for our New World.

CHAPTER VI.

THE GOD-APPOINTED NAME—AMERICA.

"For thus saith the Lord God: Behold, I, even I, will both search my sheep, and seek them out: I will feed them in a good pasture, and upon the *high mountains* of Israel shall their fold be : there shall they lie in a good fold, and in a fat pasture shall they feed upon the mountains of Israel" (Eze. 34-11, 14).

"Thus saith the Lord God: I will also take of the highest branch of the high cedar and will set it ; I will crop off from the top of his young twigs a tender one, and will plant it upon an *high mountain and eminent*" (Eze. 17-22).

"For in mine *holy mountain*, in the mountain of the height of Israel, saith the Lord God, there shall all the house of Israel, all of them in the land, serve me; there will I accept them, when I bring you out from the people, and gather you out of the countries wherein ye have been scattered" (Eze. 50-40, 41).

"Every one that keepeth the Sabbath from polluting it, and taketh hold of my covenant; even them will I bring to my *holy mountain* and make them joyful in my house of prayer" * * * "He that putteth his trust in me shall posess the land, and shall inherit my holy mountain" (Isa. 56-6,7: 57-13: 40-9: 65-9; Micah 4-1; Zech. 8-3; Zeph. 3-10, 11).

The very frequent and peculiar emphasis laid upon the phrases "My high mountain," "My holy mountain," "In the height of the mountain of Israel," &c., in passages where there would seem to be no symbolism intended, had for a long time excited my curiosity to know what could be meant by these phrases. That they had no reference to the mountains of Judea, seems evident from the palpable absurdity of the statement in such case. Although all Palestine is an exceeding hilly country, no real *mountains* are there if we except the Lebanon range in the extreme north, of which Mt. Hermon, the highest peak, is only 6,000 feet high. If in the license of poetic imagery the hills about Jerusalem were denominated mountains, they were never by any license termed, as a matter of fact, *high* mountains, and inasmuch as Israel had wholly left the country when these words were spoken, they seem more strange still.

If we take the word *holy* mountain in its scriptural sense of consecrated and set apart for a specified religious purpose, we can see still further the inappropriateness of the phrase, since the land had already been set apart for such a purpose and failed entirely of accomplishing the results that should have been expected. But how much more appropriate they seem when spoken with reference to a new kingdom which the God of heaven should set up in the latter days in a land whose very name means "high mountain" which, as a kingdom of people, should so enlarge itself as to fill the whole earth—realm or continent where it should be located—in the same sense as the scriptures use the phrase "the whole world" of the old Roman Empire. Without violence it can also take a broader meaning and refer to the time when the principles and institutions of this God-given land shall so permeate Old World social and political life as to bring them into harmony with our own, and thus in the larger sense it shall fill the whole earth.

From these considerations there can be but one conclusion, that there was some hidden meaning not yet revealed which would appear in due time as the explanation of these very peculiar and emphatic phrases, so simple and plain in their straightforwardness. It is with great pleasure therefore that we present a copy of an article on the origin of the name AMERICA which we stumbled upon some ten years ago, which led us to see the significance, force and beauty of these phrases as originally intended. Surely, God takes strange methods to hide his secrets till such time as he sees fit to reveal them, not always to the "wise and prudent" but to "babes." It affords one more link also in the mighty chain of evidences that this Continent has been reserved through a period of nearly six thousand years, unknown to the civilisations of the Old World, and set apart to a holy purpose for the accomplishment of the Divine plan.

ORIGIN OF THE NAME AMERICA.

The controversy as to the priority of discovery and the honor of bestowing a name on the New World has been so long undecided—almost three centuries—that any light thrown upon this intricate problem may help its true solution, if the truth be discoverable at this late day ; and with this hope I offer the following contribution.

Americ, Amerrique, or *Amerique,* is the name in Nicaragua for the high land or mountain range that lies between Juigalpa and Libertad, in the province of Chontales, and reaches on the one side into the country of the Carcas Indians, and on the other into that of the Ramas Indians. The Rios Mico, Antigua, and Carca, that form the Rio Blewfields ; the Rio Grande Matagalpa, and the Rios Rama and Indio, that flow directly into the Atlantic ; as well as the Rios Comoapa, Mayales, Acoyapa, Ajocuapa, Oyale, and Terpenaguatapa, flowing into the Lake of Nicaragua, all have their sources in the Americ range.[1]

---

[1] See public documents of the Nicaraguan government; and The Naturalist in Nicaragua, by Thos. Belt, 8vo, London, 1873.

The names of places, in the Indian dialects of Central America, often terminate in *ique* or *ic*, which seems to mean "great," "elevated," "prominent," and is always applied to dividing ridges, or to elevated, mountainous countries, but not to volcanic regions; for instance, Nique and Aglasinique in the Isthmus of Darien (*Estados Unidos de Colombia*); Tucarique and Amerrique in Nicaragua; Amatique, Manabique, Chaparistique, Lepaterique, Llotique, and Ajuterique in Honduras; Atenique (*Estados Unidos de Mexico*); Tactic and Polochic in Guatemala; Tepic, Acatic, and Mesquitic in the State of Jalisco, Mexico. The list of Indian local or other names, with the termination of *ique* or *ic*, as Cacique or Cacic, great Chief, might be easily lengthened.

It is now well known, through the learned researches of philologists for the last twenty years, that no denominations are more securely established than the names of localities—mountains, valleys, lakes and rivers. Even the most absolute conquest, unless it totally exterminate the aboriginal race inhabiting a country, does not destroy entirely the names of localities, or *lieux-dits*, as the French so well express it. These names may be slightly modified, by various spelling, but the primitive sound remains. And even where the aboriginal race entirely disappears, the names of places are often preserved, at least as synonyms; of which there are many examples in Canada, in New England, in the state of New York, and elsewhere throughout the Union.

The question to be decided is, whether the word Americ or Amerrique, designating a part of the *terra firma* discovered by Cristoforo Colombo, on his fourth and last voyage to the New World, was known to the great navigator, and consequently could have been repeated by him or by the companions of his voyage. There is no certainty of this; for the word is not found in the very brief account he has left us. But as the origin of the word Americ has been until now an enigma, in spite of the different interpretations of it that have been given, and as Vespuchy had nothing to do with this name, entirely unknown to him—the inventor of the word Americe or America being a printer and bookseller in a small town hidden in the Vosges Mountains—it is well, perhaps, to review the facts, and to show where lies the greatest probability for a true solution of this word America which denominates alone a hemisphere.

In the Lettera Rarissima of Cristoforo Colombo giving an abridged description of his fourth voyage, 1502-3, he says that after having passed the Cape Gracias a Dios, on the Mosquito Coast, he reached the Rio Grande Matagalpa, which he called the Disaster River, and after remaining anchored there for several days, he stopped some time for repairing his ships and giving rest to the crews, between the small island of La Huerta (the Garden Quiribiri) and the Continent, opposite the village of Cariaï or Cariay. Cariaï is so like Carcaï, or the dwelling places of the Carcas Indians, who still live in that neighborhood, that it is possible the variation is caused by an error in reading the manuscript letter of Colombo, the c having been mistaken for an i.

The great object of the desires and researches of Colombo and his company was the finding of gold mines; and of these the inhabitants of Cariaï or Carcaï had much to relate: they led Colombo to another village called Carambaru, whose inhabitants wore golden mirrors round their necks. These Indians named several places where mines of gold existed, the last named being Veraqua, twenty-five leagues distant on the coast.

Colombo and his company were struck by the number of sorcerers (medicine men) among the Cariaï or Carcaï; and the sailors afterwards thought they had been bewitched by them, as they suffered from the many tempests and mishaps of all sorts they were obliged to endure for the rest of the voyage.

What was the geographical position of Cariaï (Carcaï), Carambaru, and Veragua? Veragua is known to be in the great Bay of Chiriqui (Costa Rica): Colombo says in his narration, "It is the custom in the territory of Veragua to bury the chief men with all the gold they possess"; and in these last years gold has been found in the tombs of the aborigines of the country. Carambaru was at least twenty-five leagues distant from Veragua (Chiriqui), which brings up a little to the north of the Rio San Juan and Greytown. Cariaï (Carcaï) must have been a little farther north, in the neighborhood of the mouth of the Rio Blewfields (of which the Rio Carca is one of the affluents), where are several islands, and this accords with the narration of Colombo. The Carcas Indians inhabit all this region, and work to-day in the gold mines of Santo Domingo and Libertad, on the Rio Mico, another affluent of the Blewfields, at the foot of the Americ (or Amerrique) range. Carambaru was probably near the Rio Rama, and in the country of the Ramas Indians. Now the Ramas and Carcas Indians have always resisted all attempts at civilisation; most of them, especially the Ramas, are wholly savage, and allow no one to penetrate into their country; they have remained the same as they were when Colombo visited them in 1502.

It is well known with what tenacity the Indians attach themselves to all their surroundings; and the Americ or Amerrique range forms the highest chain of mountains in the country of the Carcas and Ramas Indians, the average being three thousand feet; making a dividing line between the waters flowing directly into the Atlantic, and those that empty into the Lake of Nicaragua. According to travelers who have visited certain places in the neighborhood of Libertad, Juigalpa, and Acoyapa, this mountain range is very conspicuous; it is seen from afar, with its precipitous rocks, great white cliffs, and huge, isolated, rocky pinnacles. This ridge divides the country into two parts, distinguished by totally different climates. To the east continual rains have caused impenetrable forests, and to the west of this dividing line the country is arid and unproductive for want of rain.

The Americ range prevents the passage of all the moisture from the Atlantic. The direction is from north-northwest to south-southeast, and the last spur of the range is on the Atlantic coast a little to the north of Greytown; the ramifications being in the country of unapproachable and savage Ramas Indians.

There is the strongest evidence that this word, denoting the range and the rocks of Amerrique, Amerique, or Americ, is an indigenous word, the terminal *ique* or *ic* being common for the names of locality, in the language of the Lenca Indians of Central America, a part of Mexico; and that this name has been perpetuated without alteration since the discovery of the new world, by the complete isolation of the Indians who live in this part of the continent, who call their mountains by the same word to-day as they did in 1502, when Colombo visited them, Amerrique, Amerique, or Americ. These mountains are auriferous; at their foot lie the gold mines of Libertad and Santo Domingo, and further, the gold of the alluvium or the *placers* is entirely exhausted, which can only be explained through a previous washing by the Indians themselves; at present the gold is to be found only in the veins of quartz rock.

Colombo says the Indians named several localities rich in gold, but he does not give the names in his very curtailed account, contenting himself with citing the name of the province of Ciamba; but it is highly probable that this name Americ or Amerrique was often pronounced by the Indians in answer to the pressing demands of the Europeans of the expedition. The eagerness for gold was such among the first navigators that it formed their chief preoccupation everywhere; and it is almost certain that to their continual questions as to where the gold was found that the Indians wore as ornaments, the reply would be, from Americ, this word signifying the most elevated and conspicuous part of the interior, the upper country, the distinguishing feature of the province of Ciamba.

It does not follow that Colombo was ignorant of the word Americ because he has omitted it in the Lettera Rarissima, which was addressed by him to his Catholic Majesty, the powerful King of Spain. It is evident, from his mention of several places where gold was to be found, as the Indians had told him without giving their names, that he did not tell all he knew; and it must be remembered that the Lettera Rarissima was written under the most painful circumstances. He was a prisoner in the island of Jamaica, loaded with chains, old, infirm, and overwhelmed by suffering and injustice, and not in a position to make a very full report of his expedition. His account of his fourth voyage is the least clear and precise of all his writings, showing in its confused and melancholy style the sad condition to which he was reduced, and although the name Americ is not seen therein, the region may have been considered by Colombo and his companions as an unexplored El Dorado, occupying the interior of the country in the province of Ciamba, along the coasts of which they had navigated.

We may suppose that Colombo and his companions on their return to Europe, when relating their adventures, would boast of the rich gold mines they had discovered through the Indians of Nicaragua, and say they lay in the direction of Americ. This would make popular the word Americ, as the common designation of that part of the Indies in which the richest mines of gold in the New World were situated.

The word Americ, a synonym for this golden country, would become known in the sea-ports of the West Indies and then in those of Europe, and would gradually penetrate into the interior of the Continent, so that a printer and bookseller in Saint Die, at the foot of the Vosges, would have heard the word Americ without understanding its true meaning as an indigenous Indian word, but would become acquainted with it in conversations about these famous discoveries, as designating a country in the New Indies very rich in mines of gold.

Hylacomylus[1] of Saint Die, ignorant of any printed account of these voyages but those of Albericus Vespucius—published in Latin in 1505, and in German in 1506—thought he saw in the Christian name Albericus the origin of this, for him, altered and corrupted word,

---

[1] This teacher, bookseller, and printer of Saint Die (Vosges) is so little known that even his name is not exactly known; it is thought to have been Martin Waldseemuller or Wallzemuller, and that the Latin name of Hylacomylus was adopted by him in accordance with the custom of the time.

Americ or Amerique, and renewing the fable of the monkey and the dolphin, who took the Piræus for a man, called this country by the only name among those of the navigators that had reached him, and which resembled the word Americ or Amerique.

In order to accomplish this it was necessary to change considerably the Christian name of Vespucius, and from Albericus, Alberico, Amerigo,[1] and Morigo—which are the different ways of spelling the first name of Vespuzio, or Vespuchy, or Vespucci—he made Americus! Thus, according to my view, it is owing to a grave mistake of Hylacomylus that the aboriginal name of the New World, Americ or Amerique, has been Europeanized and connected with the son of Anastasio Vespuzio.

Had this mistake occurred in Spain, Portugal, or the West Indies, evidently it would have been corrected; for Vespuzio and many of the companions of Colombo were still living. But in the little town of Saint Die, the name of which was, probably, never known to Cristoforo Colombo or Alberico Vespuzio, distant from any sea-port, this little pamphlet of the book-

---

[1] It is important to remark that Hylacomylus knew only the names Albericus and Alberico, which renders the creation by him of the name America still more improbable, if he had not heard the indigenous name Americ. The first name of Vespuzio was only spelt Amerigo and Morigo in Spanish documents that remained unpublished until many years after the death of Hylacomylus.

seller Hylacomylus[1] was restricted to a small circle; and, in truth, it is around this limited area that the error was propagated and prolonged by the publication of a new edition of the pamphlet of Hylacomylus at Strasburg in 1509, and by the appearance at Basle, in 1522, of the first map upon which was seen *America Provincia*.

This map, with the name America upon it, reached Spain long after the death of Cristoforo Colombo, which took place in 1506; and the companions of his expedition, almost all unlearned men, were, also, either dead or gone back to the Indies, and no one was there who could correct the mistake, even supposing that the map gave the origin of the word.

The name Americ had been heard, not as that of a man, but of a country, of an undetermined portion of the *terra firma* of the New World, and it was accepted without difficulty, no attention being paid to the mistake of the printer and bookseller of Saint Die whose pamphlet was, probably, unknown in Spain.

There can be little doubt that the word Americ was not only known, but popularised to a certain extent, in the sea-ports of Spain, Portugal, and the Indies, or it would not have been thus at once accepted by universal consent, without discussion. This is all the more probable from the fact that Hylacomylus, beside the marked alteration of the first name, Alberico, disregarded the

---

[1] Entitled, Cosmographiæ Introductio cum quibusdam Geometriæ ac Astronomiæ principis; ad eam Rem necessariis insuper quatuor Americii Vespucii Navagationes; p. 52 in quarto, 1507.

rule which has always been followed in naming countries, by giving the first name instead of the family name of his hero; he should have called the New World Vespuzia or Vespuchia.

The Christian name of an ordinary man is never used to designate a country, but only that of an emperor king, queen, or prince; thus we say Straits of Magellan, Vancouver's Island, Tasmania, Van Dieman's Land, etc., while we have, on the other hand, Louisiana, Carolina, Georgia, Maryland, Filipinas, Victoria, etc. There is no exception to this rule in the case of Cristoforo Colombo, for no one has thought of giving the name of Cristoforia to a country, and that of Cristoforo to a town; while at several epochs many names of Colombia, Columbia, Columbus, and Colon, have been given. Furthermore, in giving to Vespuzio the honor of naming the New World, Hylacomylus, using the Christian name contrary to all precedent, should have named it Albericia, or Amerigia or Amerigonia or Morigia, and not America.

The only way to explain this name, reached with such difficulty, is that Hylacomylus had previously heard pronounced the name of Americ or Amerique. Amerigo Vespuchy (as the name is written by Cristoforo Colombo in his letter dated Seville, 5 Feb., 1505), died in 1512, long before the publication at Basle of the map in *Mela cum commentatio Vadiani*, without knowing "the dangerous glory that was preparing for him at Saint Die," as Humboldt expresses it; he believed until the end of his life that the New World was the coast of

Asia, and died as he had lived, *piloto mayor de Indias*.

This belief in the Indies and the nearness to the River Ganges of their discoveries, prevented Colombo, his contemporaries, and his successors, from giving the countries they found a collective name. The idea originated with men in the interior of the continent of Europe, unacquainted practically, with the navigation of those times, so feverish with the excitement of voyages ; and who, repeating the sayings of the sailors, without knowing very well what they were about, applied a name already known to those who had returned from the Indies, but which was without any geographical position, to an entire group of newly discovered lands, hardly then recognised as a whole.

The mistake of the theoretical geographers of Saint Die, Strasburg, and Basle. could hardly have been corrected, unless by Colombo, who was no longer in this world : and then the discoveries of Cortez, Pizarro. and others, came to change the direction of ideas as to the countries fabulously rich in gold.

Although Nicaragua was conquered in 1522 by Gil Gonzales de Avida, a part of it remained wholly unknown, especially the region extending from the Atlantic to Lake Nicaragua, in which lies the Amerrique range : and the ignorance of this part of America has continued so long, that the Californian emigration, even. has passed by it across the Isthmus of Nicaragua without any knowledge of or interest in its existence. It may be said that the region of country lying between the Caribbean Sea and the dividing line for the waters that flow into Lake Nicaragua is to this day entirely unknown; the Carcas and Ramas Indians, especially the latter, oppose any entrance into their country, rejecting even the Indians who search for caoutchouc, and who intrepidly pursue their work in countries as yet closed.

The theory I have presented has some great advantages. In the first place, it takes nothing from the glory of Colombo, the name of the continent discovered by him being an indigenous name which, from designating a small and limited country, has been extended to include the whole New World, through the mistake of a teacher, printer, and bookseller in a little town hidden among the Vosges Mountains.

The accusations of plagiarism from which Alberico Vespuzio has suffered are abolished, and there is no longer any reason to reproach him with having imposed, or having suffered to be imposed, his Christian name on a whole continent; inasmuch as this name was never Americ or Amerique, but Alberico or Amerigo. The name Amerique, although aboriginal, makes no confusion between a part and the whole, because the locality where it exists as *lieu-dit* is too small, obscure and insignificant to give rise to any false or double meanings of the term. Finally, this name appears to be admirably chosen, extending as the Americ range does from the center to the extremities of the continent, radiating as it were, giving one hand to the North and one to the South, looking to the Antilles and to the Pacific, and being even the central point of the immense chain of mountains which extends from the Tierra del Fuego to the borders of the Mackenzie River, and forms the backbone of the western hemisphere; in truth, the longest range of mountains upon our globe.

It is well chosen, also, as it probably was heard by the great Admiral Colombo on his fourth voyage; the illustrious discoverer of the New World being the first European who heard and pronounced the word Americ or Amerrique, although we have no material certainty of this. Had the name belonged to a part of either extremity of the Continent, it would hardly have been so readily accepted; but it grasped and took the new world round the centre, vaguely, merely signifying a region very rich in gold mines; and it was employed and accepted without a thought of the pilot Alberico Vespuzio; it was a long time after that discussions arose among learned geographers, and that the gross mistake of Hylacomylus was imposed upon the world as truth. In a word, the word *Americ* is American.

JULES MARCOU,

Atlantic Monthly, March, 1875.

CHAPTER VII.

MATERIAL ENDOWMENTS OF THE LAND.

"Moreover, I will appoint a place for my people Israel, and I will plant them, that they may dwell in a place of *their own*, and *move no more;* neither shall the children of wickedness afflict them any more as beforetime" (2 Sam. 7–10).

"And he shall set up an ensign for the nations, and shall assemble the outcasts of Israel, and gather together the dispersed of Judah from the four corners of the earth: but they shall fly upon the shoulders[1] of the Philistines *toward the west*" (Isa. 11–12, 14).

"Hear, Lord, the voice of Judah, and bring him in unto his people : let his hands be sufficient for him" (Deut. 33-7).

"Thine eyes shall see the king in his beauty: they shall behold the land that is very far off" (Isa. 33-17).

Here are some very singular statements especially in the first verse. It seems strange that the prophet Nathan, in speaking to David of the establishment of his throne *forever*, should speak of a "home of their own" for his people and of *moving no more*, when they were at that very time well settled in the very land promised to their fathers, in which they expected to remain forever. They were now under David consolidated into a united and well established kingdom with not the slightest sign of the future rupture but three centuries distant, which should scatter them into all corners of the earth.

---

[1] Or "ships," as the LXX. render it.

But there was every prospect under the promise just then given for the eternal continuance of his house and kingdom, of long continued prosperity and happiness—and so David himself expected, as witness his seventy-second Psalm. Where then was the occasion of speaking in the future tense of appointing a "place for Israel," "a place of their own" from which they should "move no more" and should be no more afflicted? Only one answer can be given.

God saw clearly what would be the inevitable result of their idolatrous propensities manifested so early as at Sinai; and that only when by terrible afflictions and trials they should be thoroughly cured of idolatry, would they be fitted for their future far-off land which they could fully call "*their own*," and from which they would never move.

"Behold, the former things are come to pass, and NEW THINGS do I declare: before they spring forth I tell you of them" (Isa. 42-9). "Behold, I will do a new thing; now it shall spring forth: shall ye not know it? I will even make a way in the wilderness, and rivers in the desert" (Isa. 43-19).

"The children of wickedness shall not afflict them any more," for "they that afflicted thee shall be far removed from thee" by reason of a wide ocean on either hand that separates spiritual Israel from her old time enemies, which also fulfills in a remarkable degree the prophecy of Balaam (Num. 23-9).

> " For from the top of the rock I see him,
> And from the hills I behold him:
> Lo, it is a people that dwell alone,
> And shall not be reckoned among the nations."

Here also in this "place of their own" where we have landed the "pilgrims" of Spiritual Israel, God has "set up an ensign" and given us the "Eagle" as an emblem of kingly power, with a royal priesthood, and to it a call is made by Isaiah : "All ye inhabitants of the world, and ye dwellers on the earth, when an ensign is lifted up on the mountains, *see ye;* and when the trumpet is blown, *hear ye*" (18–3 : see also Zech. 9–16, 17).

Yet the Christian Church has neither seen the ensign nor heard the trumpet sound calling the dispersed of Israel and Judah, and the downtrodden of every land to this "Land of the free, and the home of the brave."

But Judah is listening to the sound and obeying the call, if we may judge by the "signs of the times." On a Fourth of July celebration some years ago in San Francisco, the following sentences were uttered by two of the leading Rabbins as reported in the *Alta California :* "Of all other people, the Jews have reason to be thankful for America. To them God has created it a *New World.*" * * * "We can only compare this Republic to the old commonwealth of Israel delivered from Egypt." * * * To the American Jew the history of America is the history of his redemption from a second Egypt, and his finding a *second land of promise* where he can resume the songs of Zion." Multitudes of passages of the same tenor, uttered from time to time, could be given, all tending to show that Judah at least is beginning to realise the marvelous manner in which God is bringing to a close her long, long years of bondage and trouble, and this answers to the third peculiarity of our heading, "Hear, Lord, the voice of Judah, and bring him in unto his people." God grant the time may soon come when

"**They shall look on Him whom they have pierced, and shall mourn for him as one mourneth for an only son**" (**Zech. 12-10**).

It would seem also that even their oppressors are urging them on with all speed by persecution, oppressive taxation, and other disabilities, before their own day of wrath comes. "The unprecedented success which has accompanied the efforts of the Russian Immigrant Aid Association for the last few months, has induced its managers to conclude a contract with a leading steamship company to transport five thousand Jews to this country as fast as their facilities will allow; the expressed intention being to drain Russia completely of its Jewish element and to transplant it to these shores. The project is greatly simplified by the favor with which the Imperial Government contemplates the movement."[1]

Simultaneous with this decision comes the news that the Alliance Israelite Universelle, of Paris, has entered into a similar contract with another steamship line for the transportation of other thousands from that country."[2]

---

[1] Russia contains all told about 3,000,000 Jews, nearly half the whole estimated number of them in the world, and it is expected that all will be in this country within the next five years. I have no means of knowing the number in France.

[2] *New York Truth*.

"Who are these that fly as a cloud and as doves to their windows? Surely the isles shall wait for me and the ships of TARSHISH first, to bring thy sons from far, their silver and their gold with them, for the name of the Lord thy God, and for the Holy One of Israel, because He hath glorified thee" (Isa. 60-8, 9).

This whole chapter is most wonderful in its minute details of marvelous material blessings that are to be the portion of spiritual Israel in this "place of their own." We cannot accept the commonly received idea that all this refers to Christ's kingdom, for we are in the full enjoyment of these material gifts and Christ's temporal kingdom is not yet set up and will not be until God, working through and by means of the people, *shall give it to him*, since it must be, to be acceptable to Christ, a purely voluntary offering. Neither can it refer, as held by some, to the return of the Jews to Palestine, for the reason that Judah has lost all chance of being gathered again as a nation, by reason of Christ's denunciation as recorded in Matt. 23-38 : 21-43; read also Amos 9-8 ; Isa. 65-15 ; Jer. 7-14, 16 : 19-11 : 23-39, 40. Nor for the further reason that Palestine can in nowise answer the conditions of the record in *any particular*, save by a mighty miracle and an entire reconstruction above and below ground, which is not at all likely to occur while the "New World" is already made to our hand, and the process of *returning* already begun long ago. Wake up, my brother, and behold what mighty things the Lord hath wrought in the earth! (Job 9-10 ; Dan. 4-3).

Nor for the additional reason that if the promise is not already fulfilled, there are insurmountable difficulties in the way of any future fulfillment, for who that has studied human history believes that Latin Spain, born in paganism and nurtured by the "Mother of Harlots," will ever rise again to commercial supremacy so as to be the *first* to carry the "dispersed among the Gentiles" to trodden down Jerusalem? Who will tell us what "*isles* shall wait" for them? Reverse the scene to the Western Continent, and how complete the picture in the first voyages of Columbus.

Marvelous indeed seems this vision of the prophet in connection with the historic story that Roman Catholic Spain—the sworn enemy of both spiritual and carnal Israel in all ages, and who showed her hatred of Judah by expelling the Jews from all her territory in 1492, the very year of the discovery of America by Columbus—should be the first to discover Israel's and Judah's future home, but would not be permitted to establish herself in it, nor enjoy the fruit of her discovery:—

"They that swallowed thee up shall be **FAR AWAY**; but the sons[1] of them that afflicted thee shall come bending unto thee" (Isa. 6-14).

Not only does the record state that old time enemies should be far removed, but that Israel's future home should be vast in extent, and far in excess of anything

---

[1] In Mexico?

any single country of the Old World could show, even a "*New World*" created or kept expressly for her. How insignificant is Palestine beside it, even in its palmiest days. Why, the whole country of David's kingdom could be put inside the San Joaquin valley of California, with thousands of square miles for playroom on the borders. Hear what David says of the "new home" as described in the seventy-second Psalm, which has always been held to describe Christ's kingdom—as it will be ere long:—

> "He shall have dominion also from sea to sea,
> And from the river to the ends of the earth.
> They that dwell in the wilderness[1] shall bow before him,
> And his enemies shall lick the dust.
> The kings of Tarshish and of the isles shall bring presents,
> The kings of Sheba and Seba shall offer gifts."

"It is not generally known, even in cultivated circles, that the amount of arable soil in America is greater than in Europe, Asia and Africa put together, and can therefore sustain more lives. I speak from a scientific basis, and I will show you what that basis is: Our continent is narrow and therefore the winds of the ocean water it well. The mountain chains on the east side of the American continent are low; on the east side of the Old World they are high. From this it results that the trade winds, laden with the wetness of the sea, are attracted to our land. The breadth of the Old World and its high eastern ranges, cause the rainless interiors of

---

[1] Aborigines?

Asia and Africa. Again, America is the land of fertile plains; the Old World of scorched plains. Our plains run north and south, and so attract and receive the rains. America is higher under the equator, the Old World is wide, hence with us a small surface is exposed to the scorching sun. The result is that the productive soil in the Old World is 10,000,000 square miles, and in the New 11,000,000. Thus bursts upon us in all the light of scientific truth the fact that America can sustain a greater population than the Old World, and if she can it is unquestionable that some day she will."[1]

This was just what the prophets declared should be the case :—

"The wilderness and the solitary place shall be glad; and the desert shall rejoice and blossom as the rose: for in the wilderness shall waters break out, and streams in the desert" (Isa. 35-1).

"And I will make them and the places round about my hill a blessing; and I will cause the shower to come down in its season; there shall be showers of blessing" (Eze. 34-25).

The prophet must certainly have had this vast extent of territory in mind, and seen its comparative freedom from opposing forces, when he stated in substance that there was enough to give all who should come, " as well the *stranger* as the children born in the land," a home and a chance to live. Hear what Isaiah says (54-2, 3 : 49-20, 21) :—

"Enlarge the place of thy tent, and let them stretch forth the curtains of thy habitations: spare not, lengthen thy cords and strengthen thy stakes: for thou shalt break forth on the

---

[1] *Coal Trade Journal.*

right hand and on the left; and thy seed shall inherit the Gentiles, and make the desolate cities to be inhabited." "The children of thy bereavement shall yet say in thine ears, 'The place is too strait for me: give place that I may dwell.' Then shalt thou say in thine heart, 'Who hath begotten me these. seeing I have been bereaved of my children, and am solitary, AN EXILE, and wandering to and fro? and who hath brought up these? Behold, I was left alone; these, where were they?'"

But now if we look at Eze. 34-25 we shall see a peculiarity worth mentioning, which should distinguish this God-given land and that is, it should be free from ravenous wild beasts. When we consider that twenty-five thousand human lives are lost annually in India by serpents and wild beasts—and Asia and Russia are greatly troubled by ferocious animals—we may well be surprised and thankful that so large a territory as ours is so free from such pests to civilisation.

"And I will make with them—Israel—a covenant of peace. and will cause the evil beasts to cease out of the land; and they shall dwell safely in the wilderness, and sleep in the woods" (Eze. 34-24).

"And they shall no more be a prey to the heathen, neither shall the beast of the land devour them; but they shall dwell safely, and none shall make them afraid" (Ver. 28: also Isa. 35-9).

This is somewhat surprising inasmuch as the record declares that the land should abound in forests, the peculiar home of wild beasts and serpents. All sorts of wood of every kind and those peculiar to Old World climes and soils, should be found here in abundance, even those considered of the highest value and exceeding scarce :—

"I will open rivers on the bare heights and fountains in the midst of the valleys. I will plant in the wilderness the cedar, the acacia tree and the myrtle and the oil tree; I will set in the desert the fir tree, the pine and the box tree together: that they may see, and know, and consider, and understand together, that the hand of the Lord hath done this, and the Holy One of Israel hath CREATED IT" (Isa. 41-18, 19, 20).

"The glory of Lebanon shall come unto thee, the fir tree, the pine tree, and the box together, to beautify the place of my sanctuary; and I will make the place of my feet glorious" (Isa. 60-13).

But there are two peculiarities seemingly at variance, and one of them is always taken as a sure evidence that Palestine is meant, and that nothing but the return of the Jews to that country will satisfy the record; and so we must needs speak of them. We do not by any means state that Palestine will not be occupied again by Israel and Judah and the "old wastes" builded, for I think it very probable that it will be. But I do deny that the scriptures show any good ground for supposing that a Jewish state and polity will ever be established in Palestine or anywhere else, for reasons already given. But so far as virgin soil in connection with a land full of wasted cities and depopulated places is concerned, it would seem that God anticipated even this and provided for it in some way, so that not one jot or tittle should be wanting in the New World. Only think of it—old deserted cities and broken down fortifications in the *New World!* Yet such is the fact. While we are accustomed to speak of our fair land as "virgin soil" in the largest and truest sense of the word, we have left to us the record of a former civilisation in the "mound cities of the West"—silent cities of the dead whose history is but slightly known, and whose inhabitants are but recently being traced, but whose monuments will continue for ages to challenge the wonder of men. In choosing the sites for their cities and fortifications, this mysterious race of the mounds were moved by the same motives that control peoples of to-day in fixing the abodes of men and choosing strategic points.[1] .The centers of population are to-day near by the places of the "mound builders" who flourished ages ago, and we are filling out the scripture record to the letter:

"The wilderness and the solitary place shall be glad for them: and the desert shall rejoice and blossom as the rose" (Isa. 35-1).

"And I will multiply men upon you, all the house of Israel even all of it; and the cities shall be inhabited and the wastes shall be builded" (Eze. 36-10, 33).

"In that day will I raise up the tabernacle of David that is fallen, and close up the breaches thereof: and I will raise up his ruins, and I will build it as in days of old" (Amos 9-11).

This last verse has primary reference to the house of David as a regnant line which will certainly be established again on a surer and more enduring foundation than ever, when Christ takes the offered kingdom not far hence. But we pass on to other material endowments far surpassing all these, which challenge and override all past conceptions in old world history. We will not stop to dwell upon the promise of "broad rivers and

---

[1] Smithsonian Contributions to Knowledge, vol. 1.

streams" which should be a peculiar heritage of the new home and singularly wanting in the old—except to give a single quotation in its place and to say that these happy springs of life and sources of joy certainly speak of material blessings of the largest kind, and invite a happy people to "sow beside all waters" for ages to come—but will pass on to show what God has provided for us in this new home of the "remnant," "the stone of Israel:" "The chief things of the ancient mountains, and for the precious things of the lasting hills. and for the precious things of the earth and the fullness thereof, and for the good will of him that dwelt in the bush, and for the precious things of the fruits of the sun, and for the precious things of the growth of the moons " (Deut. 33-14, 15, 16).

"And I will make the place of my feet glorious: for brass I will bring gold, and for iron I will bring silver, and for wood brass, and for stones iron " (Isa. 60-17).

"But there the glorious Lord will be with us in majesty, a place of broad rivers and streams; wherein shall go no galley with oars, neither shall gallant ship pass thereby " (Isa. 33-21).

It does not need to be said that our boundless wealth of minerals and precious metals makes us the treasure house of the world, all the coinage of which was not equal to the production of California for twenty-five years. From 1870 to 1880 we produced over seven hundred millions of dollars worth of precious metals. and last year the valuation is estimated at seventy-five millions of dollars, and we have hardly touched the mines as yet. Two hundred thousand square miles of coal fields already discovered, with new deposits added every year, tell what ample provision has been made for the teeming millions of future generations. England, France, Russia, all the German States, and Spain, together, cannot boast of a twelfth as much.

All this does not begin to tell the story, vast as it is. We are fast becoming the granary of the world in productions, as well as its treasure house in precious metals. According to official statistics our products amounted in 1885 to the enormous sum of three and one half thousand millions of dollars. The mind almost staggers at such enormous wealth as the product of one year, and little of our soil is yet touched by the plow. Here are a few of the leading products : One thousand seven hundred million bushels of corn=$580,000,000; four hundred and fifty million bushels of wheat=$355,000,000; six and a half million bales of cotton=$250,000,000. Other smaller products bring up the full sum.

The growth of our national wealth is beyond all precedent in the world's history. Other nations in the past have grown suddenly rich and mighty, but it has always been at the expense of some other nation destroyed, whose accumulated wealth of centuries suddenly passed into other hands to be in turn an object of cupidity and plunder. Not so the wealth of this God-given land— this *Jerusalem* of peace and quiet habitations. We have earned it ourselves and robbed nobody.

In 1880 our national wealth, according to the general census of that year, amounted to forty-four thousand millions of dollars. All this is the growth of a century, and the most of it is the outcome of the last twenty years. for in 1860 we only estimated our wealth at sixteen thousand millions of dollars. In ten years from 1860 we increased our wealth by eight thousand millions of dollars, and in the next ten years we increased it by twenty thousand millions. ·· This enormous national wealth exceeds the wealth of Great Britain by two hundred and seventy-six millions of dollars," and that of Russia by at least ten thousand millions of dollars. Who can fully comprehend the fact that two thirds of this enormous national wealth was gained by peaceful industry in twenty years preceding the last census of 1880.

Does it not seem a marvelously strange story that half a world with such wondrous resources could remain for more than five thousand years utterly unknown to the advanced civilisation of the other half? How can we account for this except on the hypothesis that God created it and kept it in store for his spiritual Israel until it should become necessary to transplant ·· the tender twig of the topmost branch of the high cedar·· from the corrupting influences of old world life? in a word, that he might introduce his chosen ones—the " finest of the wheat"—to a new heavens and a new earth which for four hundred years we have been pleased to term. in tacit acknowledgement of the verification of scripture. '' The New World." How slow and dull we are to perceive God's wondrous dealings with us. Hitherto expositors have found nothing in scripture relating to these mighty events of the ages save an obscure passage in the Apocalypse (chap. 12-6, 14) relating to the woman fleeing into the wilderness,[1] an event that occurred about the time of the Apostles, or shortly after, in relation to the Jewish Church.

"**And he shall give the rain of thy seed, that thou shalt sow the ground withal; and bread of the increase of the ground, and it shall be fat and plenteous; in THAT DAY shall thy cattle feed in large pastures. The oxen likewise and the young asses that till the ground shall eat salted provender, which hath been winnowed with the shovel and with the fan**" (Isa. 30-23, 24).

"And I will bring them out from the peoples, and gather them from the countries, and will bring them into their own land ('a place of their own'); and I will feed them upon the mountains of Israel, by the water courses, and in all the inhabited places of the country. I will feed them with good pasture, and upon the mountains of the height of Israel shall their fold be: there shall they lie down in a good fold, and on fat pasture shall they feed upon the mountains of Israel" (Eze. 34–13, 14).

We think we have quoted sufficiently to show the vast superiority of this "home of their own" above anything offered by Palestine, even in its palmiest days, in extent of domain and vastness of resources, to convince any candid mind that this land and this alone is the future

---

[1] Rev. Ethan Smith's "Key to the Revelation."

home of spiritual Israel, and the kingdom of the future for the Son of David.

We think by this time our Pilgrims have increased in numbers and in wealth enough to desire to cut away from leading strings and set up for themselves, and so we will pass over intervening time and come to the year 1776 when the God of Israel proposes to enter a little more prominently into the government of the people, and for a time take charge of it, and to that we will now turn in the next chapter.

CHAPTER VIII.

THE GOD OF HEAVEN SHALL SET UP A KINGDOM.

" And I heard a voice in Heaven, saying :—' Now is come salvation, and strength and the *kingdom of our God*, and the power of his Christ; for the accuser of our brethren is cast down, which accused them before our God day and night" (Rev. 12-10).

" And in the days of these kings shall the God of heaven set up a kingdom which shall never be destroyed : and the dominion shall not be left to other people, but it shall break in pieces and consume all these kingdoms, and it shall stand forever" (Dan. 2-44).

" Who hath heard such a thing? Who hath seen such things? Shall a land be born in one day? Shall a nation be brought forth at once? For as soon as Zion travailed, she brought forth her children. *Before* she travailed, she brought forth; *before* her pain came she was delivered of a man child" (Isa. 66-8, 7).

One hundred and fifty years of Colonial growth " in good soil by great waters " have indeed made our "tender twig" a "goodly vine," but they have also brought it to the time when stays and props are no longer needed, and to the time when—to change the figure—the furnace fires of oppression and wrong shall consume as tow, the cords which have bound Israel to the mother country, and to a still better time when by a strange and peculiar birth, he shall enter into a new life for his mission of regeneration among the nations.

"Kings have been his fathers and Queens his nursing mothers,"[1] but having attained his majority he no longer needs their fostering care and desires to set up for himself. There is prepared for him however a new and strange political birth, "stranger than fiction," stranger than any birth the world ever saw before, whose *after-pangs* shall shake the world and dispel the darkness, oppression and gloom which have hung for so many ages like a funereal pall over the earth :—a birth which shall be the ushering in of the morn of a better day—the dawning of the new dispensation—only to be exceeded by the full morning glory of that day when " the Sun of Righteousness shall arise with healing in his wings " at " the consummation of the age."

---

[1] Isa. 49-23.

"Arise, shine; for thy light is come, and the glory of the Lord is risen upon thee. For, behold, darkness shall cover the earth, and gross darkness the peoples; but the Lord shall arise upon thee, and his glory shall be seen upon thee. The little one shall become a thousand, and the small one a **STRONG NATION**: I the Lord will hasten it in its time" (Isa. 60-1, 22).

"**Open ye the gates, that the righteous nation which keepeth the truth may enter in**" (Isa. 26-2).

" In that day, saith the Lord, will I assemble her that halteth, and I will gather her that was driven far off, and her that I have afflicted; and I will make her that halted a *remnant*, and her that was cast off a *strong nation;* and the Lord shall reign over them in Mount Zion from henceforth even forever. Now why dost thou cry out aloud? is there no king in thee? is thy counsellor perished, that pangs have taken hold of thee as of a woman in travail? be in pain and labor to bring forth, O daughter of Zion " (Micah 4-6, 7, 9).

Were it not for the dullness of our apprehension these passages, with a few others added, would make out a continuous history of the inception and birth of the new kingdom. But " in *this mountain*"—or by means of it—" will the Lord destroy the vail that is spread over all nations," and show the wonderful fulfillment of all that is written concerning his people Israel, and hence we must explain.

Chronologically this strange birth of a nation in " one day " ought to—and really does, according to the calendar by which the time for each is reckoned—take place in 1794 on the occasion of the ending of the "mystery of iniquity"[1] and the proclamation of the angels at the sound of the seventh trumpet, saying, "THE kingdom of this world is become the kingdom of our Lord and of his Christ"[2] In a succeeding chapter we hope to show beyond the peradventure of a doubt that the Papacy received its death blow at that date. At present we must confine ourselves to the setting up of the kingdom of the God of heaven and show by the very peculiar circumstances attending the birth of that kingdom, that this event is the only true and common sense solution of that most perplexing prophecy of Isaiah (66-7, 8) respecting a nation to be born in one day.

It was eminently proper that the ending of the mystery of iniquity and the birth of the new kingdom—two of the most stupendous events of all the ages, inasmuch as it is the pivotal point of Bible history—should not only be simultaneous, but should be marked by extraordinary circumstances. Yet how could they be marked by any marvelous events without calling undue attention to the events themselves, and so reveal what it was the evident intention of God to conceal, as in the case of the extraordinary and apparently conflicting circumstances connected with the advent and exit of the Son of Man. These events of the "kingdom" and the "mystery" are quite as extraordinary, as conflicting, as pronounced, as difficult and yet as easy of solution as were those, if only our minds are open to the truth and we are not as per-

---

[1] Rev. 10-7.
[2] Rev. 11-15, also 12-10 at the head of this chapter.

sistently blind as were the Pharisees who settled the whole question of Christ's claims with that most convincing (?) argument, " Look and see, for out of Gallilee ariseth no prophet."

Assuming, for the time being, what I shall hereafter prove—that 1794 marked the ending of the "mystery of iniquity "—how does it happen, as we have declared, that the birth of the kingdom in 1776 was synchronous with that event and the death blow (not actual death) given to the Papacy in 1793–4. Herein lies the truth of that saying of " The Preacher," " It is the glory of God to conceal a thing, but the honor of kings is to search out a matter (Prov. 25-2: Isa. 45-15: Deut. 29-29). We will therefore settle this matter if possible as a " condition precedent " to further progress.

In the eleventh chapter of Revelations which marks the ending of the second division of the book and a partial winding up of the affairs of the Papacy, it is declared by two different statements that the duration of that "mystery of iniquity " should be 1260 years. In chapter 13-5, it is again declared that " power was given unto him to make war forty and two months= 1260 years. Daniel says, also, of the same power that the saints should " be given into his hand until a time, times and the dividing of time "=1260 years (chap. 7-25).

But since in scripture language a thing *begun* is well nigh *done*, we are taught that when the *death blow* is given to the Papacy her days are short and she is as *good as dead*, though she may live some time after—as it is plainly declared she should—until the "vials of wrath" should be poured out upon her closing days. So in the same way the angels speak of "the kingdom" as established for all the world when "the mystery" is ended and the kingdom of the God of Heaven is set up, although it has only just entered on its infant days. This is a peculiarity of scripture language and we must accept it for all it is worth.

We come now to a very peculiar distinguishing feature of the "little horn"—the Papacy—as described by Daniel. "For he shall think to change times and laws" (7–25). In perfect accordance with this prophecy we find Pope Gregory XIII. in 1582 abolishing the Julian Calendar which had been in use for more than sixteen hundred years, to the gain, indeed, of ten days over actual solar time. Russia alone of all nations holds to the old Julian Calendar and her gain in time is twelve days to the present. This calendar Gregory XIII.[1] changed to meet correct solar time, and this is the accepted calendar of to-day. By this time the twelve hundred and sixty years end as we have assumed, in 1794.

But if we are reckoning the same number of years by the same calendar for the continuance of the treading of "the holy city" under foot, we shall be mistaken in our

---

[1] It is of no earthly consequence what was the reason of this change, right or wrong. God saw fit to have him do it that it might be fulfilled which was spoken by the prophets.

calculations, for we are dealing with God's people and kingdom and must not reckon by the time of the "man of sin," however correct it may be as solar time, but we must reckon by sacred time, which was lunar time and reckoned in round numbers at thirty days to the month or 360 days to the year—at a loss of five days. We are led to this surmise of the use of sacred time by noticing that the time during which the Church is to be in gloom and trodden by "the Gentiles"—occupied by unholy people—is named as " forty-two months," as distinguished from the twelve hundred and sixty days during which the "two witnesses"—the Old and New Testaments—were to "prophecy in sackcloth." Reckoning then by sacred rather than by papal time we have the date 1794, when the " mystery of God" was finished, reduced by eighteen years, which bring us back to 1776. Considering the confusion usually attending the computation of sacred time and chronological data, this is very remarkable. If we could find out the precise time of Daniel's writing we should find, very probably. that his twenty-three hundred days ended at the same time as above noted. Other remarkable circumstances which we embody in an appendix, confirm us in our conviction that 1776 marks the close of the 1,260 years of gloom for Israel.[1]

But why this setting back of the date of the birth of the "man-child" from 1794 to 1776 if the time of the ending of the "mystery of God" and the setting up of "the kingdom" are synchronous events, as would appear

---

[1] See appendix A.

from Rev. 11-15 and 10-7 ? We have already given one reason, but the real scriptural reason is that the birth of the man-child might correspond to the prophetic record of Isaiah, as follows :—

"**A voice of noise from THE CITY, a voice from the TEMPLE, a voice of the Lord that rendereth RECOMPENSE TO HIS ENEMIES: BEFORE she travailed, she brought forth ; BEFORE her pains came, she was delivered of a man-child."**

The time has come that the cup of indignation should be drunk to its dregs by the "mother of harlots and abomination of the earth." This was accomplished in the chief city of the chief kingdom of the "man of sin" "which is spiritually called Sodom and Egypt, where also our Lord was crucified." "Therefore shall her plagues come in one day, death, and mourning and famine." "In the cup which she hath filled fill to her double." Therefore "the Lord rendereth recompense to his enemies"; but the birth of the "man child"—the God-appointed kingdom—must be accomplished *in peace* as was the birth of the Son of David eighteen centuries before.

But this event being of world wide significance for the ages to come, it is in the highest degree fitting that the mighty events of the French Revolution, which affected the Papacy as no other event ever did—events which filled to the letter the terrible woes pronounced against her for her crimes, second only to her final doom—should do double duty and serve as *after pangs* for the birth of the "man child" eighteen years before, for whom the whole course of political nature was reversed that it might be a standing memorial to the world of his divine paternity.

Lest some may be doubtful of this application of these tremendous revolutionary scenes, it was ordained that Zion should have her own immediate after pangs. Hence we have the very singular political phenomenon of a nation born in one day, July 4th, 1776,[1] and fulfilling to the letter the divine record by fighting for seven long years to establish her right to live. Surely such a birth was never witnessed before, since the universal custom for all revolutionary action has heretofore been for a people *first* to establish their right to live—*and then live.* Can anything be clearer than this? The prophecy in no wise refers to nations being born in a day, as this passage is so often misquoted and misapplied, reference being made to such cases as the Sandwich Islands and Japan. The conditions are clear cut and concise, and any interpretation that does not fill the requirements of the prophecy, however ingenious, is a failure. Our solution meets all these and is therefore the only true one.

Now it becomes necessary to look a little more closely at this youngest of the nations and see if we can divine

---

[1] It is a remarkable coincidence and one worthy of record, that this date is also the anniversary of the destruction of the Temple at Jerusalem, and was so commemorated by pious Israelites in this country, July 4th, 1776, as we learn from Jewish sources.

her character, future position and influence, from the scripture record. The first characteristic, then, of this fifth kingdom—this "stone of Israel" "cut out of the mountain without hands"—is that it is of Divine origin:—

"And in the days of these kings shall the God of Heaven set up a kingdom which shall never be destroyed : but it shall break in pieces and consume all these kingdoms, and it shall stand forever."

The context of the prophecy shows that "these kings" or kingdoms are symbolised by the ten toes of the image, pertaining to the fourth kingdom, which should continue in their general integrity until the latter day when the stone kingdom should smite the image, because the image was smitten on its *feet* (ver. 34) and not on its legs, or breast, or head. Also for the further reason that Daniel says in another vision (chap. 7), which is a duplicate in another form of this one, that this fourth kingdom in a dual form (which John makes over into a triple form) should continue for twelve hundred and sixty years. So that the conclusion is inevitable that this fifth divine kingdom of the "stone" is set up at or near the close of the career of the ten kingdoms which formed the Imperial power of Rome and the Papacy.

The second characteristic of this fifth kingdom is that it is a political and not in any paramount sense, at least at present, a spiritual kingdom, for it being proven that parts are political necessitates the whole must be political. This character is given to it by the interpretation itself which says that it would break in pieces all the kingdoms existing before it. Now as the Roman or fourth kingdom brake in pieces all the kingdoms before it by the most bloody and devastating wars, it follows that the breaking of the fourth kingdom by the stone would be by violence and war as before. There is no getting rid of this conclusion without violating a plain rule of interpretation by assigning a different sense to an author's words than he himself has given. Hence we conclude that the breaking power must be a martial and political kingdom, for no earthly kingdom was ever yet *broken* up by spiritual forces. least of all by a Christian, spiritual. kingdom. the weapons of whose warfare are not carnal but spiritual. mighty though they be to the pulling down of strong holds.

Again. the political character of this stone kingdom is still further shown in the very fact of its being cut out of the *mountain*. which we intimated when we narrated the historical fact of the sailing of the Pilgrims from England to lay the foundations of a new empire on the shores of the New World. The commonly received exposition of this "stone cut out without hands" is that it refers specifically to Christ's kingdom because he is called the "chief corner stone." a "stone of stumbling," and "rock of offense," etc. In symbolic prophecy a mountain always means an eminent nation, a powerful kingdom. Babylon, a city of the plain, is called by Jeremiah, "a destroying mountain." It is always so held by expositors.

Now in the natural world no one would think of attributing to a rock cut out of a mountain, a character very much different from the mountain out of which it was cut. It might be richer rock as in the case of marble, or quartz from a vein in the mountain, but it is still rock or stone in its general characteristics. Why then change the essential character of a part of the same symbol, contrary to all sound rule of interpretation as given above? If the mountain is a nation or kingdom, a portion of that kingdom cut out will partake of the same character and have of necessity a political organisation, for no kingdom ever yet existed without one and never will, not even excepting Christ's millennial kingdom.

We are reminded furthermore by a friend at our side, if the church of Christ was intended to be represented by any symbol in connection with this vision it would certainly not have been by a *"stone* cut out of the mountain" but rather by something much more precious, as was afterwards done in the Apocalypse in connection with the latter-day glory of the Church. There gold is taken for no higher use than for walls, houses and pavement of the streets.

To represent Nebuchadnezar's kingdom in the image by a head of gold, the Grecian kingdom by silver, and even the cruel Roman kingdom by iron, would seem to be exalting them to a very high point of honor if the kingdom of our Christ can find no better symbol to represent it than that of a stone. No, no! His kingdom is represented by something more precious than all these together—as we learn from chap. 7–13—even by "a Son of Man" who is declared by the Spirit to be the very temple of God, the object of Christ's love and the especial abode of the purifying Spirit.

But this fifth kingdom has still another characteristic in that it is represented as antagonistic to all other kingdoms represented by the image, inasmuch as they were broken to pieces by it with great violence, and these represent Imperialism in one form or other the world over. Hence it follows again as another inevitable necessity that the stone kingdom must be republican, since all governments *must* be either republics or monarchies. There may be aristocratic, democratic, representative, and confederate republics : but they all agree that there is no right of government except by the expressed consent of the governed. There may be absolute, limited, constitutional, and hereditary monarchies; but they all agree in the doctrine that the right of governing does not rest in the consent of the governed. These two can never exist harmoniously in juxtaposition, because their principles are essentially and originally antagonistic. This is shown by the words, "They became as the chaff of the summer threshing floor ; and the wind carried them away" (ver. 35).

It is also an undeniable fact that all the various forms of monarchy grew out of estrangement from God in heathenism or idolatry. Hence it is fair to presume that God himself is antagonistic to every form of government but a theocratic democracy in which God himself shall be recognised as the source of all right to govern, and his law the basis of all legislation on moral questions for the good of the people. This was the character of the early Israelitish kingdom of "ancient days," and such we may fairly conclude from the record, should be the character of the fifth kingdom—the stone of Israel of which we are speaking:—

"And their nobles shall be of themselves, and their governors shall proceed from the midst of them. And ye shall be my people, and I will be your God" (Jer. 30-21, 22).

"And I will restore thy judges as at the first, and thy coun sellors as at the beginning: AFTERWARD thou shall be called the 'The city of righteousness, the faithful city'" (Isa. 1-26).

"And they that serve the city shall serve it out of all the tribes of Israel" (Eze. 48-19).

We have now to consider, further, the influence of this fifth kingdom in its relations with the other four kingdoms represented in the image. Of this "stone" it was said:—

"Then was the iron, the clay, the brass, the silver and the gold, broken to pieces together, and became like the chaff of the summer threshing floors: and the wind carried them away, that no place was found for them; and the stone that smote the image became a great mountain and filled the whole earth" (Dan. 2-35).

The explanation says that the kingdom represented by the stone not only brake in pieces but "shall consume all these kingdoms." This explicit and imperative language here employed has led many expositors to argue with great skill that this fifth or stone kingdom should itself do all this work of destruction, and that too by one sudden, irresistible and overwhelming blow. Dr. Adam Clark, for whose expositions we have generally great respect, says, " The falling of the stone upon the feet of the image was like the stroke of a stone discharged violently from a Roman catapult : there was but one stroke of the stone upon the feet of the image ; it was plainly a swift stroke and therefore a sudden one ; there was no protracted effort on its part to break up the monarchy ; there was no repetition of the blow by the stone, for the image fell the moment its feet felt the force of the single disrupting blow."

Yet this exposition is given in face of the fact that the fifth or stone kingdom could in no wise be set up until the seventh angel should sound at the end of the "time, times and the dividing of time." when only the kingdom represented by the toes remained of the four mighty monarchies symbolised by the image. Each of these kingdoms was in its turn destroyed by the succeeding one ; the Assyrian or head of gold, by the Medo-Persian ; this, by the Macedonian ; and this, by the iron kingdom of Rome ; while this last was divided—not destroyed—into the kingdom of the feet and ten toes of the image. But the vision shows a *complete* image, *suddenly* struck by the stone, and as suddenly collapsing into fragments, ground to chaff and blown away.

The only way out of the difficulty has been, hitherto, to suppose there will be a reunion of the broken empire represented by the feet of iron and clay (and if of a part, then why not of the whole image?) for the special purpose of being *suddenly* destroyed by the stone kingdom. Shades of the prophets! what an interpretation! build a man of straw for the special purpose of knocking him down.

In this age of enlightenment when the very air is surcharged with a spirit of liberty; when iconoclastic nihilism is stalking over the world on the very edge of the abyss; when the whole creation groaneth together, waiting for the adoption: to wit, "the manifestation of the sons of God," can any man for a moment suppose that these powers will ever again be what they have been, the persecuting, hell-deserving minions of the mother of harlots and abominations of the earth? But if we suppose that which is much more reasonable, that the image represents the secular, imperial, idea of government concentrated and embodied in these kingdoms from Daniel's time to the present, as opposed to the divine, republican, idea of government represented by the "stone" and working in all ages through Israel, we have an easy solution of the difficulty, and one that will harmonise perfectly with all scripture, as well as with historical facts.

In this view it matters little *where* these kingdoms are located at any particular time, or by what names they are called, provided they represent imperialism; though I have no doubt the number ten will be preserved throughout to continue the integrity of the image.¹ The *when* must, of course, be in the last days of their full glory, coinciding with the " time, times and the dividing of time "=1260 years, which we have assumed for the time to end in 1794. At the same time we intimated that these kingdoms were *not* to be destroyed at one fell stroke for the reason "their lives were prolonged for a season and a time" (Dan. 7-12), the same as the co-existent Papacy. This corroborates the supposition that principles are represented, not things.

Moreover, we must remember continually that scripture prophecy makes very little use or account of time and always assumes that a *predicted* result, once entered upon its fulfillment, is spoken of as already accomplished. In fact, the prophets often went even further than this and counted that as already finished for which the *causes* only were already at work. Isaiah says:—

"**Thy holy cities ARE a wilderness. Zion is a wilderness. Jerusalem IS a desolation: our holy and beautiful house.**

---

¹ As a matter of fact, however, only *eight* kingdoms are needed to fill the requirements of the vision, because Daniel declares (chap. 7-8, 20, 24) that *three* of the kingdoms would be plucked up by the roots—which was done by Pepin and Charlemagne—to constitute the temporal estates of the Church for which Rome would naturally be the equivalent as the eighth power, as follows:—France, Spain, Portugal, Sardinia, Austria, Hungary and Russia—and Rome as the eighth. Turkey, which occupies the capital of the ancient Roman empire of the East, is left out, for she will soon be absorbed by the other powers and cease to be.

where our fathers praised thee, IS burned with fire ; and all our pleasant things are laid waste" (Isa. 64-10, 11).

"Therefore my people are gone into captivity, because they have no knowledge : and their honorable men are famished, and their multitude dried up with thirst" (Isa. 5-13, 25).

These words were spoken of Judah nearly two hundred years before the prediction was realised, so certain was the prophet of its accomplishment from causes then already at work. Even the last words, if spoken of seceded Israel, were some years before they began to be carried away.

Nor does it matter, on the other hand, in what particular form or by how many repetitions the blow is struck, provided *Israel* gives it and proper results are obtained. As a historical fact it will be found that the fifth kingdom, being in its inception and ultimate power a spiritual one, can give no *blow* at all, on account of her isolated position and her peculiar political policy; for it is distinctly stated of the latter-day kingdom of Israel, "They that oppressed thee shall be far removed from thee," and that must needs be outside of Europe and Asia, for Israel has been oppressed in almost every land under the sun. Yet none the less will her influence be found to be world wide, to the utter discomfiture of old-time monarchies. But of Zion's *elder brother*, the "mountain" across the water—who, being "a man of war,"[1] could not be allowed to build this latter-day temple—God has said:—

---

[1] 1 Chron. 28-3: 22-8.

"**THOU art my battle axe and weapons of war: for with thee will I break in pieces the nations, and with thee will I destroy kingdoms: and with thee will I break in pieces the horse and his rider : and with thee will I break in pieces the chariot and his rider**"[1] etc. (Jer. 51-20, 21).

Contrast this with the kind of warfare that is to be waged by Zion, and we may get a very good conception of the nature of the kingdom, and the true relation it bears to the nations of the world represented by the image:—love and mercy to peoples, death to iniquitous rulers and wrong doing; martial wars in Europe against wrong government, moral warfare on this side against wrong doers.

"**And I saw heaven opened, and behold, a white horse: and he that sat upon him was called FAITHFUL and TRUE, and in righteousness he doth judge and make war. And he was clothed in a vesture dipped in blood: and his name is called THE WORD OF GOD. And out of his MOUTH goeth a sharp sword, that with it he should SMITE the NATIONS:**

---

[1] It is a singular fact well worth noting as a precursor of things yet to come, that while France, the "chief daughter" of the papacy, was made to inflict the severest blows upon the papal church at home through the length and breadth of the empire, and Napoleon was the appointed "scourge of God" in the same line at Rome, the seat of the beast, and upon all the kingdoms that formed the cohorts of Roman imperialism—it was political Israel, after all, that was appointed of God to inflict the final, crushing blow upon Napoleon himself when he assumed the Imperial purple and lorded it over the people in the very spirit of the Powers which he sought to overthrow. Can any one fail to see in all this the hand of the mighty God of Jacob working through his beloved Israel for the world's good ?

and he shall rule them with a rod of iron: and he treadeth the wine-press of the fierceness and wrath of Almighty God" (Rev. 19-11, 13, 15).

We therefore conclude that the kingdom of the God of heaven, the "stone of Israel," the stone kingdom of the mountain, must be, to fill all the requirements of scripture, a political kingdom with all the habiliments of place and power and also a Republic which shall become in the not distant future a theocratic republic, the influence of which shall so permeate old-world society as to cause thrones to tottle and the abyssmal theory of government with its unholy alliance of church and state to become "as the chaff of the summer threshing floor." Having established our republican kingdom under the special care of the "God of Heaven," we will pass on to see what the divine record says of her moral and political characteristics.

CHAPTER IX.

MORAL AND POLITICAL CHARACTERISTICS OF

THE KINGDOM.

"Thus saith the Lord God: This shall be the border whereby ye shall inherit the land according to the twelve tribes of Israel : Joseph shall have two portions " (EZEKIEL, 47-13).

"And over against the border of the priests the *Levites* shall have five and twenty thousand in length, and ten thousand in breadth : and they shall not sell it, neither exchange, nor alienate the first fruits of the land ; for it is holy unto the Lord. * * * And they that serve the city shall serve it out of all the tribes of Israel " (EZEKIEL, 48-13, 14, 19).

"And it shall come to pass that ye shall divide the land by lot for an inheritance unto you, and to the *strangers* that sojourn among you, which shall beget children among you : and they shall be unto you as home-born among the children of Israel. And it shall come to pass that in what tribe the stranger sojourneth, there shall ye give him his inheritance, saith the Lord God " (EZEKIEL, 47-22, 23).

This vision of Ezekiel has greatly puzzled expositors. and, failing to find any satisfactory solution, they have wisely left its interpretation to future generations, and the sequel of fulfillment. Connected as it must be with all other prophecies relating to latter-day Israel, we feel constrained to offer a solution, so far as it bears directly on our subject.

In the original division of Canaan among the tribes,

Levi was left without a portion because he was set apart for the service of the Temple. But since it was promised that latter-day Israel should become a "kingdom of priests" at the setting up of the kingdom of the "God of Heaven" in the latter day, it follows that Levi is no longer recognised as the only legitimate depository of the priestly robes and insignia, but that in the re-adjustment which the vision is evidently intended to illustrate, Levi should be reinstated in his inheritance.

But this arrangement breaks up the mystic number, which can no longer stand in its symbolic relation to completeness, fullness, and entirety, because it is distinctly stated that "Joseph shall have *two portions.*" In other words, Ephraim and Manasseh should still retain their portions, notwithstanding the re-instatement of Levi; thus making *thirteen* divisions to the land, which corresponds exactly to the original thirteen States of this latter-day kingdom of Israel.

But there is still another peculiarity which must not be overlooked, viz., a portion besides all this is set aside "for the priests, the sons of Zadok which have kept my charge; which went not astray when the children of Israel went astray, as the Levites went astray." (EZE. 48-11.) "And they shall not sell it, nor exchange it, nor shall the first fruits of the land be alienated: for it is holy,"—consecrated to a sacred purpose—"unto the Lord" (verse 14). Now if there is no established priesthood, since all are priests in the new regime, who can these "priests, the sons of Zadok," be but those who "serve the city out of all the tribes of Israel," and the place of their service "*the sanctuary in the midst thereof,*" set apart and consecrated to a special purpose for the benefit of all the tribes or states ? This denotes the character of the priesthood in the latter-day kingdom in respect of the spiritual and political branches of it. Levi being relegated to the ranks of the people, spiritual advisers are recognised in whomsoever God calls, while those who serve the city—the nation—shall be by fair adjustment out of all the tribes or states.

The coincident historical fact is found in this piece of legislation peculiar to this country. Shortly after the organization of the political or civil branch of the government, the rulers "chosen out of all the tribes of Israel," set apart a certain "portion" or district—containing about sixty square miles—for the special and perpetual use of the nation, as the permanent seat of government, free and independent of the rest of the land, and proceeded to build the national capitol—called in the text, "the sanctuary"—in the midst of it. These certainly are very remarkable coincidences unless we accept them, as far as they go, as a complete fulfillment of the divine record. We leave the specific measurements to the curious in symbolic art. We have no use for them, and so will proceed to consider other peculiarities of Israel's dowry.

A UNITED PEOPLE UNDER ONE HEAD.

"Thus saith the Lord, I will take the children of Israel from among the heathen whither they be gone, and will

gather them on every side, and bring them into their own land: and I will make them one nation upon the mountains of Israel: and one king shall be king to them all; and they shall be no more two nations, neither shall they be divided into two kingdoms any more at all" (Eze. 37-22, 23).

"Then shall the children of Judah and the children of Israel be gathered together and appoint themselves one head, and they shall come up out of the land; for great shall be the day of Jezreel" (Hosea 1-11)

These and similar passages are usually held to refer to the return from the seventy years captivity at Babylon or, by a sweeping generalisation, to the spiritual kingdom of Christ, neither of which seems to us to be the true sense here intended, for the reason that this great gathering is to be the *second* one in respect of Judah and the *first* one of Israel, unless the handful of Israel who returned with Judah from the captivity might give the right to reckon that gathering as the first one of *all* the tribes. If the coming together to 'appoint themselves' one head' refers to the time not far distant when the people shall choose Christ for their king, we have no objections to the view. But inasmuch as that event is in nearly all cases connected with the house of David, or the allusion to it is so plain as not to be mistaken, we are inclined to think it refers to the grand quaternial gathering of the people for the choice of a Chief magistrate.

A CHRISTIAN PEOPLE UNDER A NEW COVENANT.

"And it shall come to pass in that day that the Lord will set his hand the *second* time to recover the remnant of his people, which shall be left, from Assyria, and from Egypt, and from Pathros, and from Cush,[1] and from Elam, and from Shinar, and from the islands of the sea. And he shall set up an ensign for the nations, and shall assemble the outcasts of Israel, and gather together the dispersed of Judah from the four corners of the earth " (Isa. 11-11, 12).

"Behold, the days come, saith the Lord, that I will make a new covenant with the house of Israel and with the house of Judah. * * After those days, saith the Lord, I will put my law in their inward parts, and write it in their hearts; and I will be their God and they shall be my people" (Jer. 31-31, 33).
"And thou shalt be called by a new name which the mouth of the Lord shall name" (Isa. 62-2; Hosea 2-16,17).

These passages are often pointed to as evidence that the Jews are to be gathered again to Palestine with a new lease of national life and a new temple with its festivals, new moons, and oblations. But Israel must be gathered as well, and where will you put them all so as to answer all the conditions imposed by the record? What about the new covenant and the *new name* since you are expecting them to go back as Jews? If on the other hand they refer only to the *spiritual* reign of Christ, then there is no need of any gathering at all, for one place is as good as another for Christ's reign in the heart. But if they refer, as we believe they do, to the gathering of both Israel and Judah into this God-given land, under a new covenant and with a new name for

---

[1] Indo Cush.

people, country, government and religion, how appropriate the whole account seems.

THE PEOPLE SHALL ALL HAVE ONE LANGUAGE.

"**Thou shalt not see a fierce people, a people of deeper speech than thou canst perceive; of a strange tongue that thou canst not understand.**" (Isa. 33-19).

"**For then will I turn to the people a pure language, that they may all call upon the name of the Lord to serve him with one consent**" (Zeph. 3-9).

The gift of tongues was given to the Apostles for the multitudes who came up to the Feast of Pentecost at Jerusalem, that each and all might hear in their own language the wonderful things of God. But whoever should join himself to the latter-day people and kingdom, would adopt the new language of God's Israel and become interwoven with the customs and institutions of the land of his adoption. It needs no prophets tongue to declare that the English language is, ere long, to be the medium of communication among all nations. The testimony of our wisest and best men for a generation back, as well as the foreshadowing incidents of old-world life, point to this certain result in the not very distant future. From thirty millions in 1800, the English speaking populations of the world are now fully one hundred millions, and now that Japan is seeking to adopt our alphabet and advocating the adoption of our language, we shall soon find the ratio of increase rapidly advancing.

THE PEOPLE SHALL BE MARRIED TO THE LAND.

"**Thou shalt no more be termed 'Forsaken': neither shall thy land be any more termed 'Desolate': but thou shalt be called Hephzi-bah, and thy land 'Beulah': for the Lord delighteth in thee and thy land shall be married: for as a young man marrieth a virgin, so shall thy sons marry thee": and as a bridegroom rejoiceth over the bride, so shall thy God rejoice over thee**" (Isa. 62-4, 5).

Here is a statement which can in no wise find a fulfillment save in an entirely new country and on virgin soil. It could not certainly be verified in Palestine, since that country is already owned and largely occupied by a people having no particular regard for Jew or Gentile, and their rights would have to be respected. The very diminutive area of Palestine precludes the possibility of supporting such a vast population as "the whole house of Israel even all of it," as well as the seven millions of Jews of the house of Judah. Such an idea could only obtain under the prevalent belief that the Jews represent all of the Hebrew people, which we have already shown to be very far from the truth.

The law of pre-emption is peculiarly an American institution which obtains nowhere else in the world to any extent that we are aware of. Wittingly or unwittingly we have followed, strictly, the commands of God as already given from Ezekiel 47-22, 23. Certainly it was never an institution of ancient Israel, save that the land was originally divided by lot among the children only and not to strangers, and ever after that was inherited, with no choice in the matter. But in the broad expanse of the New World, embracing almost every known variety of climate, soil, and commercial advantage, what a field for choice! What splendid brides, and what a dowry! (Hosea 2-14 to 19).

IT SHALL BE A LAND OF HOMES.

"And they shall build houses and inhabit them; and they shall plant vineyards and eat the fruit thereof. They shall not build and another inhabit; they shall not plant and another eat; for as the days of a tree are the days of my people, and mine elect shall long enjoy the work of their hands" (Isa. 65-21, 22; also 62-8, 9).

In this respect the new land of promise is not unlike the old, although both are very different in this respect from all countries not controlled by Israel. Our Heavenly Father would have every man happy in his own home. There are no homes and no conception of home under any system of religion originating with men. In the matter of possession there is no country in the world where homestead property is so easily acquired or where so large a proportion of the people do in fact own their homes as in this country.

The strength of this American Republic rests very largely, under God, in this universal desire to own a home; and this desire is serving to mould the people, native and foreign, into one homogeneous whole, and makes them intensely interested in whatever tends to the good of the people, and antagonistic to everything pointing to misrule and anarchy. They may be led away for a time by specious reasoning and unscrupulous leaders, but there will come division of sentiment and counsels when dangers threaten the homes of the people. Therefore, if capitalists wish to preserve their own interests and their own homes, let them encourage the possession of homes by the artisans, laborers and employees under their control, and these alien leaders of nihilistic proclivities who never own a home, will shortly be left out in the cold to go to work or starve.

Out of a population in 1880 of fifty millions, nearly four millions were farmers who are able to "sit under their own vine and fig-tree with none to molest or to make them afraid," and one-quarter of our entire national wealth, or ten billions one hundred and ninety-seven millions of dollars are invested in farm property. In England, on the contrary, only two hundred and fifty thousand are farmers, of whom only sixty-two thousand four hundred can boast of the possession of fifty acres and upwards, and that too in a population of thirty-five millions.

In the country towns and villages and even in the smaller cities of America, most of the people own their own homes, and as soon as aliens enter this magic circle they become seized with the idea of owning a home. This is as it should be and helps much in the stability of government and social order.

WISDOM AND KNOWLEDGE SHALL PREVAIL.

"Wisdom and knowledge shall be the stability of thy times and strength of salvation: the fear of the Lord is his treasure" (Isa. 33-6).

"Many shall run to and fro, and knowledge shall be increased" (Dan. 12-4).

"And all thy children shall be taught of the Lord, and great shall be the peace of thy children " (Isa. 54-13).

"For the land shall be filled with the knowledge of the glory of the Lord as the waters cover the sea" (Isa. 11-9; Hab. 2-14).

Many other passages occur which hold the same thought if not expressed in the same words, all tending to show in a very marked degree, as in contrast with all past times, the increase of knowledge and general information among all classes, especially in religious instruction. It is not at all unreasonable to suppose, from the minuteness of details in many places, that the prophets had actual visions of large bodies of children and youth under instruction in day and Sabbath schools.

While it is true that the Pilgrims brought with them the *seeds* of our present free-school system and a free church—the outgrowth of the Reformation—it is nevertheless equally true that only in the sturdy soil of New England did they first find their proper developement, until they have become the peculiar heritage of spiritual Israel in all lands. Especially have our schools, both secular and religious, become by common consent the stability of our times and strength of salvation, or as some are pleased to term them, "the bulwarks of Liberty."

IN "THAT DAY" THE BLIND SHALL SEE AND THE DEAF HEAR.

"Is it not yet a very little while, and Lebanon shall be turned into a fruitful field, and the fruitful field[1] shall be

---

[1] Heb. Carmel, a fruitful field.

counted for a forest? And in that day shall the deaf hear the words of the book,[1] and the eyes of the blind shall see out of obscurity and darkness" (Isa. 29-17, 18).

Although this, like many another prophecy, might have been uttered respecting some local events, yet the phrase "*that day*" widens its import and brings it down to these days to find its full significance. Lowth says it was "a proverbial saying, expressing any great revolution, and when respecting two subjects, an entire reciprocal change." Taken in connection with the next verse we may see its full import. The eighteenth verse is generally supposed to have been fulfilled by Christ's advent and ministrations, according to the prophet's record that he should be "for a light to the Gentiles, to open the blind eyes," etc. This was true in fact, but it was only an earnest of better things to come. That was limited in extent, and the fulfillment of to-day is universal in its application. The evident meaning of the verse is that the blind should be able even in their "obscurity and darkness," to read the book (a book, any writing), and through this to perceive the things of the kingdom; and that the deaf by equally clear methods, should be able to hear and understand "in that day", the gospel of good will to all men. Shall we call it simply a coincidence that the first institution for the blind was established in 1783, in the "yet a very little while" when the Carmel of the Papal states "shall be esteemed as a forest" like Lebanon; and the Lebanon,

---

[1] A book or writing.—Marg. R.V.

or forest of America, be turned into a fruitful field coincident with the birth of the nation? Call it what we will, and interpret the passage as we may, of one thing we may rest assured; it was delivered to the prophet as one of the peculiar legacies of the latter-day kingdom of Israel.

HAPPY CHILDREN AND YOUTH SHALL ABOUND.

"**Thus saith the Lord of Hosts:— There shall yet old men and old women dwell in the streets of Jerusalem, every man with his staff in his hand for multitude of days. And the streets of the city shall be full of boys and girls playing in the streets thereof**" (Zech. 8-4, 5).

"**Thy wife shall be as a fruitful vine, in the innermost parts of thine house:
Thy children like olive plants, round about thy table.
Yea, thou shalt see thy children's children.
Peace be upon Israel**" (Ps. 128-3, 6).

This subject may appear of little importance to many, but we need to be careful lest we call that "common and unclean" which God has sanctified to the use of earnest seekers of the truth. If He has not thought it beneath his notice to introduce it as one of the 'wedding presents' of Zion's typical son, why should we turn away from it as insignificant and beneath our notice. It certainly distinguishes us from the usage of the old world from time immemorial, where titled aristocracy has so long held sway, and the common people have had very few rights which the privileged few felt bound to respect. In no place was this more conspicuous than in the streets and thoroughfares of city and town. Those who rode controlled the streets and highways, and pedestrians had no rights which the drivers of lordly carriages were expected to regard. If one was run over, it was the pedestrian who was fined for being in the way; consequently great insecurity was felt in traversing the streets. Add to this their narrow, crowded, and generally filthy condition, and one can readily see why children were seldom seen in the streets at play, save perhaps in the 'market place' in company with their parents. Still less frequently were the two sexes seen together beyond the days of mere childhood, and as they grew in years, the separation was made complete.

In the new home the usage should be directly the reverse of all this, so much so as to constitute a peculiar feature which only finds its complete fulfillment in happy, free, America. Here the sovereign people hold the "right of way" and pedestrians are accorded privileges above all others, causing a deep feeling of security well becoming the "habitations of peace." Add to all this our broad highways and sideways and we arrive at the result mentioned by the prophet, and are continually reminded of his happy thought by the troops of laughing boys and girls to be met any day on their way to and from school. "Great shall be the peace of thy children."

THE ONE RELIGIOUS FESTIVAL OF THE PEOPLE SHALL BE THANKSGIVING.

"And it shall come to pass that every one that is left of all the nations which came against Jerusalem shall even go up

from year to year to worship the king, the Lord of Hosts, and
to keep the Feast of Tabernacles" (Zech. 14-16).

This, like many another passage from the prophets, is to be taken in its spirit rather than in its letter; for the idea in the mind of the prophet is, evidently, that as Jerusalem with her temple service was the place to which "the tribes went up, the tribes of the Lord unto the testimonies of Israel" year by year, so latter day Israel in her "cities of peace" should assemble to celebrate in song and worship, God's goodness for the bounties of the year. A curse is pronounced upon those who refuse thus to offer an oblation to the Lord.

The "Feast of Tabernacles" was the annual Thanksgiving of ancient Israel, occurring in October after the ingathering of harvest. As with our Puritan fathers in a local and restricted sense but now with us become national, it was made the occasion for reunion of families and for general and hearty, social and religious, rejoicing for the bounties of the year. It was to Israel a reminder also of their journeying in the wilderness in their exodus from Egypt, yet it was foretold of latter-day Israel that they *should no more rejoice* in the Lord who "brought them out of the land of Egypt," but in the Lord "who brought up and who led the seed of the house of Israel out of the *north country*, and from *all* countries whither I had driven them; and they shall dwell in their own land" (Jer. 23–8).

The prophet calls attention especially to this feast as the only one of the three great annual festivals of the nation that would be left to God's people in their new home, and *denounces those who keep it not.*

Passover is no more of any significance to us because Christ is our Paschal Lamb, and the commemoration of his death is our continual Passover. No more is Pentecost of any worth to us, for "Christ is become the end of the *law* for righteousness to every one that believeth." We are "dead to the law through faith" and have no need to commemorate the thunders of Sinai.

Not so shall it be with the "Feast of Harvest," for God's continual and prodigious bounties to Israel call for songs of loudest praise. It may be well to bear in mind that ours is the only nation on the earth that celebrates such a day after the manner of ancient Israel, and the day is not far distant when Judah also will celebrate with us this annual Thanksgiving, if events connected with recent festivals are indications.

THE CHINESE SHOULD BE A DISTINGUISHING FEATURE.

"Behold, these shall come from far: and, lo, these from the north and from the west; and these from the land of Sinim. Sing, O heavens; and be joyful O earth; and break forth into singing O mountains: for the Lord hath comforted his people, and will have mercy upon his afflicted" (Isa. 49-12, 13).

Most commentators agree that China is intended by the "land of Sinim." Is it not very singular, to say the least, that among all the peoples and languages from every corner of the world who should of their own free choice become participants of the great material blessings of the latter-day kingdom, China alone should be singled out as worthy of special mention by name? When, however, we find in strange contrast with these free-will emigrants from the "Flowery Land," that the Ethiopians are mentioned as coming, *not* of their own free will but in *chains*, to signify their condition of servitude, it would seem that God had taken every pains to indicate to us by every possible hint, where to look for the land of his special creation as the place of Israel's permanent home, as distinguished from every other land under the sun; but here is the contrast:—

"Thus saith the Lord, The labor of Egypt and the merchandise of Ethiopia and of the Sabeans, men of stature, shall come over unto thee, and they shall be thine; they shall go after thee; in CHAINS they shall come over: and they shall fall down unto thee, they shall make supplication unto thee, saying, 'Surely God is in thee: and there is none else, there is no God'" (Isa. 45-14).

No comment is necessary on passages so plain as this, and so we hasten on to state of the new kingdom:—

IT SHALL CONTROL THE COMMERCE OF THE WORLD.

"Then shalt thou see and be lightened, [1] and thine heart shall tremble and be enlarged; because the abundance of the sea shall be turned unto thee, the wealth of the nations shall come unto thee. Thou shalt also suck the milk of the nations, and shalt suck the breast of kings: and thou shalt know that I the Lord am thy Saviour, and thy Redeemer, the Mighty One of Jacob" (Isa. 60-5, 16).

"Ye shall eat the wealth of the nations, and to their glory shall ye succeed" (Ibid. 61-6).

The whole of the sixtieth chapter is a panegyric upon the wonderful commercial wealth and strength of the

---

Ps. 34-5.

new kingdom which could in nowise be spoken of Palestine, for that land was never fitted for any but a pastoral and agricultural people, and for this reason was especially chosen as the home of God's ancient people. But how truly may it be spoken of this country with its boundless wealth of inland waters and seaboard, opening out on either hand to Europe and the Orient, and giving every facility for exchange of its limitless resources of material wealth. Our exchanges reach to every quarter of the globe, and we are even now in successful competition with those who have heretofore had no rivals in the choicest results of human skill. Our exports for 1885 reached the large sum of seven hundred and twenty millions of dollars and are constantly increasing.

Kings, queens, and titled nobility, are not unmindful of their interests in providing against the unsettled future of the old world, though they may not comprehend the full extent of the coming storm of wrath and indignation so near at hand. Some of the best real estate in New York city is held by foreign princes. Several of the most expensive buildings in Broadway, Broad and Wall streets, are owned by the ex-Empress Eugenie who derives an annual income of sixty thousand dollars from them. The Duke of Nassau, one of the erstwhile German princes, brought over in 1868 $1,500,000, which he invested in Allen street, which yield him twelve per cent. on the capital invested; the property stands in the name of German lawyers. The Grand Duke of Mecklenburg-Schwerin, Frederick Francis II..

is the owner of lots and houses in Elm street; and even Queen Victoria owns considerable real estate in Broadway, which stands in the name of an Englishman. The king of Sweden owns half a million dollars worth of real estate in New York, and the Grand Duke Alexis owns a hotel in Broadway. King Bomba, as far back as 1852, bought six houses in Greenwich street, held by Italians for his son Francis II. Doubtless many more have invested since these statistics were gathered some years ago. What is invested in other cities of the land, in agricultural lands and vast cattle ranges, must be very large indeed from what we have heard, but having no precise data we cannot say definitely. We think their investments are pretty safe, for the promise is:—

NO FOREIGN ENEMY SHALL ATTACK US.

"But there the Lord will be with us in majesty, a place of broad rivers and streams; wherein shall go no galley with oars, neither shall gallant ship pass thereby. For the Lord is our judge, the Lord is our lawgiver, the Lord is our king; he will save us. Thy tacklings are loosed; they could not strengthen the foot of their mast, they could not spread the sail: then was the prey of a great spoil divided; the lame took the prey" (Isa. 33-21 to 23).

"Thy gates also shall be open continually; they shall not be shut day nor night: that men may bring unto thee the wealth of the nations, and their kings led with them" (Isa. 60-11).

Here is a very graphic description—which could in nowise apply to Palestine—of the difficulties to be encountered in any attempt of an enemy's ships to enter our "rivers and streams." Even cripples might capture them, so sure is the prophet of God's protection. In this we have an assurance for the peace and security of our land from all foreign invasion for the generations yet to come. But if we are comparatively free from any fear now, what will be our security when Christ takes charge of the kingdom in the not distant future. Then, we feel assured, the enormous annual expenditure for navy and war departments will be put to better account for the good of men.

The only enemies we have to fear are those within our own borders, "they of our own household" who, by their iniquities and defiance of God's law, are bringing judgments on the land. They whose trust is fixed in the God of Jacob need have no fear, for yet a little while and the land shall be cleansed of its foul blots. and we shall enter on a reign of perpetual peace under the "Prince of the house of David."

PERPETUAL PEACE AND PROSPERITY ARE ASSURED.

"But now will I not be to the remnant of this people as in former days, saith the Lord of Hosts: for the seed shall be prosperous, the vine shall give her fruit; and the ground shall give her increase, and the heavens shall give their dew, and I shall cause the REMNANT of this people to possess all these things" (Zech. 8-11, 12).

"And I will make thee an eternal excellency, a joy of many generations.**They shall INHERIT THE LAND FOREVER; the branch of my planting. And they shall dwell therein, even they, and their children and their children's children FOREVER; and MY SERVANT DAVID SHALL BE THEIR PRINCE FOREVER" (Isa. 60-15,21: Eze. 37-25: Hosea 3-5).

Here then we leave this young giant of a hundred years until such time as he shall see fit to apparel himself anew for an audience with the King of kings, and is ready to enter into covenant relations with the Son of the Highest.

A well-defined and clear-cut outline of the kingdom has been presented as *now existing* under God's appointment, to which we challenge the attention of every Christian reader who is "waiting for the consolation of Israel." We have shown by fair interpretation of scripture, beyond successful controversy, that the kingdom which the God of heaven was to set up is not in the dim and uncertain future, but is even now, already, entered upon its glorious career, only to be eclipsed beyond all conception by the reign of the Son of David, who is made a King throughout all generations.

It may seem strange to many that if this nation was the special creation of the God of Heaven, why was not His name recognised in the organic law at the very inception of the Government! This omission has been from the first a matter of great regret with many good and wise men. But to our mind it is the very best evidence of Providential arrangement that such recognition should be deferred until the nation, in the fulness of her moral and political powers, should be able intelligently to make deliberate choice of God, and his Son Jesus Christ, as her own rightful rulers in all national life, and stand forth on "open confession" to the world as a Christian nation.

No person is held to be a Christian until he decides of his own choice to give himself to Christ, no matter how religiously he may have been taught and trained. For various reasons the nation was not in condition to intelligently make such a choice one hundred years ago, neither is she now able; but we are happy to say she is under "deep conviction," and a few years hence she will assuredly give with a will what she "forgot" or did not think worth while to do in infancy, or to have done for her by her sponsors in convention without her deliberate consent. This idea corresponds fully with the thoughts we have all along expressed, that spiritual Israel is yet to do this very act in accordance with the prophetic vision of Daniel 7-13, and then, and not until then, she will be a Christian nation.

Let us go back now to the point from which we started, 1776—or by Roman-papal time 1794—and take up the momentous events connected with the death-blow to the Papacy and Imperialism, which will be considered in the next chapter.

CHAPTER X.

DEATH BLOW TO PAPACY AND IMPERIALISM.

"But in the days of the voice of the seventh angel, when he shall begin to sound, the mystery of God is finished, according to the good tidings which he declared to his servants the prophets" (Rev. 10-7).

"And the seventh angel sounded; and there followed great voices in heaven, and they said, 'The kingdom of the world is become the kingdom of our Lord and of his Christ;' and he shall reign forever and ever: "And the nations were wroth, and thy wrath came, and the time of the dead to be judged, and the time to give their reward to thy servants the prophets, and to the saints, and to them that fear thy name, the small and the great; and *to destroy them that destroy the earth*" (Chap: 11-15, 18 see also Dan. 7-26).

"He that leadeth into captivity shall go into captivity; he that killeth with the sword must be killed with the sword. Here is the patience and faith of the saints" (Chap. 13-10).

"And the ten horns which thou sawest upon the beast,[1] these shall hate the whore, and shall make her desolate and naked, and shall eat her flesh and burn her with fire" (Chap. 17-16).

There is, perhaps, no point in Revelations that has received more attention, and over which there has been more controversy than in connection with the beginning and ending of the 1260 years of the "man of sin." On this point hangs all the mystery of the ages, until itself

---

[1] The ten kingdoms of Imperio-Papal Rome.

has become a mystery which no man seems able to fathom. But the "Lion of the tribe of Judah" prevailed to open the seven-sealed book, and he is able by the Spirit to tell us of the "times and the seasons" of this mystery of iniquity. Hitherto this matter seems to have been hid for good and wise purposes from the wise and prudent, as it is written. "For the wisdom of the wise men shall perish, and the understanding of the prudent men shall be hid" (Isa. 29-14).

Now it is generally conceded and nearly every one understands that these kingdoms—symbolised by the feet and toes of the image in the vision of the king— are the ten kingdoms of Imperial Rome which gave her "power" and "her seat" to the Papacy, and continues to do so in one form or another until the time of the end at the close of the "time, times, and the dividing of time"=1260 years (Dan. 7-25 : Rev. 12-7, 14 : 13-5). Hence it becomes of the utmost importance to us to find out if possible when those years ended ; when the power of the "man of sin" as a persecuting power, shall be so crippled and broken as to be no hindrance to the setting up of the kingdom of the God of Heaven, and to the progress of the truth.

Of course, if we could show when the "man of sin" *commenced* his career, it would be an easy matter to point out its ending. On this point there is great diversity of opinion, for nearly all the theories of the time of the second advent and of the millennium are based upon the supposed time of commencement and consequent ending of the 1260 years. It becomes, then, quite necessary to go back to the beginning and trace up, very briefly, the inception and birth of the Papacy.

Notwithstanding the ten successive persecutions which swept over the early Christian church—taking in their course Christian and Jew alike—the truth, as preached by the apostles and converts, prevailed so powerfully that in three hundred years pagan Rome was shattered by the "earthquake" of Rev. 8–5. Christianity rose upon the ruins: heathen temples were converted into places of Christian worship. Heathen notabilities, courtiers, and the elite of society, became eager followers of the Christian faith, apparently as a stepping-stone to the courtly favor; for Constantine had become, outwardly at least, an adherent of the despised Gallilean, and the emoluments of office were bestowed upon adherents of the new faith; time 325 A. D.

But so far removed from primitive simplicity of faith and worship had the Christian church become, that the heathen found little to humble their pride or cause material change in their manner of worship on entering the church of their adoption. The form of Christian worship was there with all its borrowed accumulations from the heathen service, but it had lost its power. The church was entering into its long night of gloom. The saints were being "sealed," and the outer court of the temple given over to the Gentiles that they might "tread the holy city forty and two months."

This general decay of the faith, incident to the cessation of persecutions, general prosperity and the Imperial favor, as well as to the admission of such vast numbers of those who had no genuine convictions and conscious experience of the truth of Christianity, led to still farther departures from the faith, and prepared the way for the development and final birth of the "man of sin"—"the false prophet," the "antichrist."

At what precise time this triple embodied monster—Rome Imperial, Rome Papa-civil, Rome Papa-ecclesiastic—may be considered to have started on its infamous career, it is impossible for mortal man to state. As early as 438 A. D. Theodosius the Great, emperor, commanded "that all nations claiming the protection of His Grace should receive the faith as propounded by St. Peter to the Romans."[1] This would not be bad if the church at Rome had not arrogated to itself the sole right in the line of succession, to act for St. Peter. But earlier even than this Valentian, emperor, forbade the bishops, whether of Gaul or of other provinces, " to depart from the received customs of the church without the sanction of that venerable man tl.e pope of the holy city"—Rome.

The code of Justinian, however, is generally held to establish the *first* historical date for the claims of the "Holy father" as the head of the church, A. D. 534.[2]

---

[1] Codex Theodos.

[2] The code was published in 533, and that is the date usually given, but the whole code was revised, corrected, emended. and finally published in Nov. 534, which should, therefore, be taken as the true date.

About the year 606 A. D. the Exarchate of Ravenna, as the constituted head of Imperial power in the now called "Western Empire of Rome," declared the validity of the Pope's claim to *universal supremacy*, and this is the basis for historical date number *two*. But not until Pepin, king of the Franks and father of Charlemagne, drove out the Lombards, subdued the Exarchate of Ravenna himself, and began to give "the beast" "his power, and his seat and great authority," did the Pope, Stephen III., consider himself firmly seated on his throne. In the year 756 A. D. (some say 750) Pepin caused the keys of the conquered towns to be placed on the altar of St. Peter, "and in this act he laid the foundations of the whole temporal power of the Pope."[1]

It will be seen from this short account how slim is the prospect of deciding upon the precise time when the 1260 years of the Papacy *commenced*. If we are fully convinced in *our own* minds of the proper date to select, can we be *sure* that is the date which the *Spirit* selected as the proper time from which to date the years? In this dilemma the scriptures themselves give us the key with which to unlock the secret. In the prediction of Daniel concerning the coming of the Messiah are these words:

"**From the going forth of the commandment to build and restore Jerusalem, unto Messiah the Prince, shall be seven weeks and three score and two weeks,**" etc. (**Dan. 9-25**).

One would think from this that the time of Messiah's

---

[1] Ranke's History of the Popes, vol. 1, page 13.

coming might have been easily found ; but it was not, because four different decrees went forth from different rulers, embracing a period of nearly one hundred years; so certain and yet so uncertain are the predictions concerning important events. God only intended the prophecy to keep alive the interest, and quicken the hopes of his true people as the time drew near, not to satisfy idle curiosity. He intended, furthermore, by the uncertainty of the time, that his people should thoroughly sift the claims of every one claiming to be the Messiah, and accept the true man on his merits and not on any popular favor or fancied date. Hence the absolute necessity of looking at the *end* of the times predicted for one who could fill all the conditions, if we would know when the order went forth.

Just so in this matter of the commencement of the Papacy, we shall be obliged to look at the *end* of the time for the character of the events and their conformity to prescribed *conditions*, if we would know of a certainty when is the true date for the beginning of the "time, times, and the dividing of time"=1260 years. Those who ignore the prescribed conditions of scripture must expect nothing short of complete failure, however ingenious their theories, in their attempts to throw light on symbolic prophecy. Order is said to be heaven's first law, and nowhere is it more conspicuous than in the prophetic record of the scriptures. The confusion lies in *man*, not in God's word.

The book of Revelations is marked by four general or

grand divisions, with minuter divisions within these four. The first part concerns the seven churches of Asia and takes up the first three chapters. The second part gives the opening scenes of the vision proper and a general summary of events connected with the career of the "man of sin," winding up in the eleventh chapter with the conditions incident to his death and judgment as a *persecuting power*. In connection with his prostration on a "death-bed," the ending of the "mystery of iniquity" and the commencement of the reign of righteousness are announced. At the nineteenth verse of this chapter a new division (the third) commences, taking up in detail (after introducing the Roman dragon and the Jewish and Christian churches in chapter twelve) the career of the Papacy in its threefold form from the beginning, and closes the waters over her in chap. 18–21. Chapter twenty of this division deals with the Roman dragon, or Imperialism, and brings him to his final doom. In chapter twenty-one—the last division—John takes up the glorious condition of the church in her new home, but only gives a gorgeous summary of her condition, because the details in amplest form were already to be found in the older prophets.

We propose now to give the conditions of chapter eleven, which mark the *commencement* of the closing days of the man of sin and his ally, Imperialism, and then place by the side of these conditions the historical facts and see if we cannot determine to an absolute certainty the *end* of the "mystery of iniquity." Then it is of little consequence to us, except as confirmatory evidence, when he began his career. Let us premise that these last days —this death blow to Rome-papal—does not necessitate his immediate dissolution, for many a man is death struck and lives some time after; and of this particular "sick man" it was declared:

"**But the judgment shall sit, and they shall take away his dominion to consume and to destroy it unto the end**" (Dan. 7-26.)

Of the ten kingdoms representing Imperialism it was said:

"**They had their dominion taken away: yet their lives were prolonged for a season and a time**" (Dan. 7-12).

Now for the conditions :—

(*a*) A condition of gloom and depression for the true church during forty two months (Rev. 11-2).

(*b*) The prophesying of the "two witnesses"—the Old and New Testaments—in "sackcloth" for 1260 days or years (ver. 3).

(*c*) The death of the "witnesses" at the hands of the "man of sin"—"the beast" (ver. 7).

(*d*) Their unburied condition in the Sodom and Egypt of the Papal dominions (ver. 9).

(*e*) Great rejoicing over their death and sending of presents and gifts (ver. 10).

(*f*) Their resurrection in a short time. said to be "three days and a half" (or years) (ver. 11).

(*g*) They ascend to heaven in a cloud and their enemies behold them (ver. 12).

(*h*) A great earthquake or political revolution (ver. 13).

(*i*) The announcement of the setting up of the kingdom of God (ver. 15).

(*j*) The judgment of destruction upon the whole crowd, and reward to the servants of God (ver. 18).

Here are ten distinct conditions or events connected with the closing days of the Papacy and Imperialism, and the setting up of the kingdom of the God of Heaven and of His Son Jesus, the Christ, which are invariably ignored and treated as separate events without cohesion or connection of any kind; whereas, they are indissolubly joined together and find their solution in one event—the death-blow to Rome's spiritual assumptions—at a definite and well established period of time, the end of the 1260 years. Now if we take the *first* of our historical dates (534 A. D.) as a supposable time (for we know nothing about it as yet and so will take the several dates in order) for the beginning of that power and add the 1260 years, we are landed right in the midst of that mightiest revolution that ever shook this earth—the French Revolution of 1793-4. But we will not anticipate, and will take up our "conditions" in order.

I suppose no one will deny for a moment that the church of true believers was in a state of gloom and depression throughout the world from 534 A. D. and onward. With the service of the churches uttered almost universally in an unknown tongue—the Latin—how could it be otherwise? With the Lamp of Life hidden under a bushel, what else could ensue but darkness? Great stress has been laid on the Reformation in Germany under Luther, but very few writers agree as to its real effects on the church of Rome or its position in prophecy. We can find no allusion to it, and therefore think is was only the "quickenings" of a pregnancy to be matured two hundred years later on, as will appear. Of that Reformation one writer says :[1]

"Though justification by faith was its dogmatic germ that great revolution took chiefly an ecclesiastical direction and became more an attempt to overthrow the organic system of popery by the reassertion of certain apostolic doctrines, than an evangelical revival of the spiritual life of the church ; hence its early loss of moral power."

" It also retained many papal errors in its doctrines of the sacraments and of the priestly offices, and erred, above all, in leaving *the church subject to the State.*" Hence its frequent lapses toward popery. The very same results followed the English Reformation, in respect to popery and the loss of spiritual power. The whole world seemed groaning under moral and spiritual darkness, and in order to show the density of this darkness as a fitting background to the light which followed it, we purpose to show the condition of the English

ns' " History of Methodism in the Eighteenth century."

Church a little more than one hundred years ago. "We see but a tithe of these things as compared with Europe, in the opening half of the last century when the human mind, pushing its inquiries in all directions, approached and entered the domain of Metaphysics in religion. The disclosure of ancient errors in natural science, as well as the falsehoods of the Papacy, had cherished a rising habit of doubt, till incredulity was regarded as a token of superior wisdom. * * * Theologians felt the influence, or yielded without consciousness. It was as if a mist had silently overspread the landscape; and neither tree nor hill, neither the house of God below nor the bright heaven above, was seen clearly. Not a land in Western Europe was exempt from that peculiar atmosphere in which all forms of speculation glided into incredulity.[1] "Never," said a writer in the *North British Review*, " has a century risen on England so void of soul and faith as that which opened with Queen Anne (1702) and reached its misty noon beneath the second George (1742-1760)—a dewless night succeeded by a sunless dawn. * * * The Puritans were buried and the Methodists were not born. * * * The world had the idle, discontented look of the morning after some mad holiday." "In 1729 the heads of Oxford University complained of the spread of open deism among the students, and Cambridge struggled with the same evil." Isaac Taylor says: At the time when Wesley was acting as moderator in the disputa-

---

[1] The Problem of Religious Progress by Dr. Dorchester.

tions at Lincoln College (1729-1734) there was no philosophy abroad in the world,—there was no *thinking*—that was not atheistic in its tone and tendency.[1] "Freethinkers were formed into clubs to propagate their sentiments, and Atheism was scattered broadcast through the kingdom." The pastoral letters of Bishop Gibson[2] show that the most pernicious efforts were put forth to undermine religion. "Some set aside all Christian ordinances, the Christian Ministry, and the Christian Church; others so allegorise Christ's miracles as to take away their reality; others display the utmost zeal for natural religion, in opposition to revealed; and all, or most, pleading for liberty, run into the wildest licentiousness. Reason is recommended as a good and sufficient guide in matters of religion, and the Scriptures are believed only so far as they agree or disagree with the light of nature.

"Now therefore what do I here, saith the Lord, seeing that my people is taken away for nought? they that rule over them do howl, saith the Lord, and my name continually all the day is blasphemed" (Isa. 52-5).

A writer in *Blackwood's Magazine* said, "Pope held his hereditary faith without the slightest appearance or pretense of any spiritual attachment to it." Sir John Barnard said, "It really seems to be the fashion for a man to declare himself of no religion." Montesquieu said, "There is no religion in England. If the subject

---

[1] "Wesley and Methodism." Am. edition, p. 33.
[2] Quoted in Tyerman's "Life of Wesley," Vol. 1, p. 219.

is mentioned in society it excites nothing but laughter. Not more than four or five members of the House of Commons are regular attendants at Church." Bishop Butler says:[1] "It is come, I know not how, to be taken for granted, by many persons, that Christianity is not so much as a subject for enquiry; but it is now, at length, discovered to be fictitious. Accordingly, they treat it as if, in the present age, this were an agreed point among all people of discernment, and nothing remained but to set it up as a principal subject of mirth and ridicule, as it were by way of reprisals for having so long interrupted the pleasures of the world."

The clergy were thoroughly infected with this tendency. Natural religion included most of their theology. The great doctrines of the Reformation were banished from the universities and pulpits. A large class of divines held to a refined system of ethics, having no connection with Christian motives and the vital principles of spiritual religion. Arianism and Socinianism were fashionable in the Established Church, and the prevailing creed of most intelligent Dissenters. Among the Presbyterians the departures from orthodoxy were very grave. Three profeesors in the University of Glasgow were Anti-trinitarians. An able school of Arian teachers arose among the Presbyterians, in Exeter,[2] about 1717. It spread through Cornwall, Devonshire, to the metropolis, and established itself in

---
[1] Preface to his "Analogy of Religion" 1736.
[2] Mr. Leckey's England in the Eighteenth Century" vol. II, p586.

Salter's Hall, in London, among the descendants of a Puritan ancestry. "Latitudinarianism spread widely through all religious bodies, and dogmatic teachings were almost excluded from the pulpit."[1]

Mr. Leckey says, "The doctrines of depravity, the vicarious atonement, the necessity of salvation, the new birth, faith, the action of the Divine Spirit in the believer's soul, during the greater part of the eighteenth century, were seldom heard from the Church-of-England pulpits. The rationalistic tendencies of the church rendered it little obnoxious to skeptics. Leslie Stephens says,[2] "Hume and Paley curiously agreed in recommending young men of free-thinking tendencies to take orders ;" and that "the skepticism of the upper classes was willing that the Church should survive, though faith might perish. Many of the clergy taught but little that might not have been taught by Socrates or Confucius." "Christianity was reduced to the lowest terms," though some gave it "a *quasi* assent, because they felt it to be essential to society."

In respect to the laboring classes a competent historian of the Church-of-England says:[3] "Throughout England the education of the laboring classes was most grievously neglected, the supineness of the clergy of that age being manifest on this point, *as on every other*. Hannah Moore tells of finding in a village near the

---

[1] Ibid. p. 341.
[2] History of English Thought in the Eighteenth Century.
[3] Earl of Stanhope.

Cathedral City of Wells "but one Bible in all the parish, and that was used to prop a flower pot." Dr. Watts declares there was "a general decay of vital religion in the hearts and lives of men," and he called upon every one to use all possible efforts for the recovery of dying religion in the world." Ministers of religion "knew nothing of the righteousness of faith in justification," and consequently cared little for the spiritual necessities of the people. They were often found in the ale houses and were not above street brawls. But this is only a small part of the testimony respecting the terrible condition of the church and of vital religion throughout Europe in the first half of the eighteenth century.

But the dawn of a better day was at hand, and the Sun of Righteousness" was about to "rise with healing in his wings." On the 9th of May, 1785, died the venerable Vincent Perronet, Vicar of Shoreham, one of Wesley's most gifted and pious helpers, whose pulpit was the only one in all England opened to him at the first. A short time before his death he wrote these memorable words to Charles Wesley,[1] "I make no doubt that Methodism, notwithstanding all the wiles of Satan, is designed by Divine Providence to introduce the approaching millennium." So says also the Divine Record :—

"**Arise, shine; for thy light is come, and the glory of the Lord is risen upon thee. For, behold, the darkness shall cover the earth, and gross darkness the people; but the Lord**

---

[1] Stevens' History of Methodism, p. 264.

shall arise upon thee, and his glory shall be seen upon thee"
(Isa. 60-1, 2).

When in 1740 the Wesley's and their co-religionists sought to lead the dissolute masses of the people to a Christian life, every pulpit in England, but the one named above, was closed against them, though they were regularly ordained ministers of the Established Church, which was declared to be an "ecclesiastical system under which the people of England had lapsed into heathenism, or a state hardly to be distinguished from it."[1] But now mark the contrast:—

Under the mighty power of the Gospel in the hands of the Wesley's and Whitefield, aided by the witnessing Spirit, there came the "Great Awakening," which rose to its full power between the years 1760 and 1776-8:— more wonderful in its effects than anything which had happened since the days of the Apostles. But the State Church would have nothing to do with it; therefore the great body of believers were *obliged* to organise themselves into distinct communities and churches, on the basis of an inner spiritual life and the assurance of a witnessing Spirit to the pardon of sin. Yet not alone in England was the effort to cleanse the existing church unsuccessful; everywhere in Europe the movement was ridiculed and persecuted. That travesty on the gospel of Christ—the Roman Catholic Church—had so debauched the minds and hearts of the people that *all*

---

[1] Ibid. p. 30.

religion was become throughout Europe, as in England, only a "fit subject of ridicule," save here and there with isolated communities as the Moravians and others.

In the providence of God it was reserved for the Church in America to receive the full effects of this tidal wave of spiritual life by which she might cleanse herself from her impurities.

"**Shake thyself from the DUST; arise, and sit down, O Jerusalem; loose thyself from the bands of thy neck, O captive daughter of Zion. Put on thy strength, O Zion; put on thy beautiful garments, O Jerusalem, the 'HOLY CITY': for henceforth there shall no more come into thee the uncircumcised and the unclean**" (Isa. 52-2, 1).

The effects of this revival of pure religion were manifested in cleansing the church of those who laid no claim to change of heart—those who had been admitted by what was known as the "half-way covenant"—in remodeling the church creeds on a simpler Christian basis, and in the adoption of a standard "*Confession of faith.*" This, the Dissenting Churches in England did not see the necessity of and have never adopted to this day. All this occurred from a few years before Whitefield's death in 1770, up to the second "Great Awakening" about the year 1800. Since that time each and every candidate for church membership has been subjected to a strict examination as to his qualifications for this sacred relation. Thus the scripture is being fulfilled: "*There shall no more come into thee the uncircumcised and the unclean.*" So far as human precaution can help, it will continue thus to the end.

"I have set watchmen upon thy walls, O Jerusalem, which shall not hold their peace day nor night; ye that make mention of the Lord keep not silence, and give him no rest, till he establish, and till he make Jerusalem a praise in the earth" (Isa. 62-6. 7).

"In THAT DAY there shall be no more the Canaanite in the house of the Lord of Hosts" (Zec. 14-21).

Let His ministers see to it then that the church is kept free, with jealous care, of unsanctified members and unholy connexions. Let a pure and spiritual membership be its crowning glory. Let the "mountain of the Lord's house," be indeed and in truth a beacon light to all nations, through all generations. We do not by any means say the church is perfect, nor indeed what she ought to be, but that she has *started* right for the first time in her history, and in the coming days and years of her glory all that is spoken of her shall be fulfilled.

"And it shall come to pass in THAT DAY, that the light shall not be clear nor dark: but it shall be one day which shall be known to the Lord, not day, nor night: but it shall come to pass that at evening time it shall be light" (Zec. 14-7).

"And to her was granted that she should be arrayed in pure linen, clean and white: for the fine linen is the righteousness of the saints" (Rev. 19-8).

We will now take up the second one of our "conditions" (*b*). The prophesying in *sackcloth* of the "Two Witnesses"[1]—the Old and New Testaments, the Bible—would signify the same condition of gloom and depression for the word of God which we have en-

---

[1] See Appendix B.

deavored to show for the church, and for the same length of time, with this explanation (given before in part). As the time of this prophesying is given by the full number of days, or years, and as the Bible was more particularly under the control of Rome and of her persecuting allies, we seem compelled to reckon by the full Roman time; this event and the setting up of the kingdom being synchronous, as before shown in chap. 8. But all this is of little consequence beside the greater fact that through all this long period of darkness, ignorance and superstition, the Bible was a sealed book to the great body of the Western Church. By the inroads of those "Northern barbarians" and from other causes, the Latin language in which the Bible was written[1] became unfamiliar to the mass of the people, while the Western or Roman Church persisted in retaining the *Vulgate version* through all its history. Translations were made, to be sure, in Germany, Bohemia and England, but always under anathema and interdict, and burned wherever found. The people of these countries sought to read the portions and paraphrases given to them by their religious teachers, Jerome of Prague, Huss, Wy-

---

[1] A clergyman lost his wife in Rome and wished to put a text of scripture on her tombstone. The Pope refused permission not only on the ground that it was unlawful to express a hope of immortality as to a heretic, but because it was "contrary to law to publish in the sight of the Roman people any portions of the word of God." Pius IX. in his Encyclical letter of 1850 speaks of Bible study as poisonous reading.

cliffe and others, and suffered great persecutions for so doing. In the Papal dominions proper, the Albigenses and Waldenses were nearly exterminated for their adherence to the truth as received from the word of God. Fully one million of them were put to death in France for their faith, during the 12th and 13th centuries. So that it may be truly said of the Bible, while it was preaching to the people the truths of God, it was doing so in "sackcloth" during all these long twelve hundred and sixty years, corresponding with the gloom and darkness which hung over the church.

But there are conditions in connection with the witnesses which do not pertain to the church. There must come a specific time when (c) the witnesses *must die*— when the Bible must be considered a thing of the past in the stronghold of Papacy. (d e) Its unburied condition, and great rejoicing at its death must appear. (f g) The Bible must suddenly come into prominence and attain a greater power than ever before, after several years of seeming death. All these things must be in connection (h) with some great political revolution which should be directed in an especial manner against papacy and imperialism or kingly power without consent of the people. To this we now turn to see how literally all these conditions were fulfilled.

The church had been arraigned for her absurd inconsistencies; for her prodigious claims upon the popular conscience and faith without giving any adequate return, and for the heavy burdens imposed upon the shoulders of the people, while she herself "would not lift them with one of her fingers." But the Bible, on the contrary, had been attacked as a myth, a fable, the work of imposters, as a lie without the shadow of proof. The popular mind was too ready to receive with eagerness the brilliant satires and witticisms of Voltaire, and to applaud his boast that he would make the Bible and Christianity a thing of the past. The polished sentences of Jean Jacques Rousseau did very much to undermine the popular faith in religion and its fountain, the Bible, and to substitute in their place among the upper classes the worship of nature, and the light of human reason. The common people saw only in the Roman Church and the privileged orders of the throne and the nobles, the cause of all their sufferings.

It is not surprising, then, when the dark scenes of the Revolution burst upon France, the faithful daughter of the Papacy, which had so often since the days of Pepin, befriended the Church, that the Assembly and the *sans-culottes* should very early turn their attention to the Church property as legitimate spoils, and to the clergy as a part and parcel of the titled aristocracy to whom the people ascribed the terrible burdens of their lives. "The lawyers had caused agitation in the country; the clergy had kindled civil war; the nobles were now about to produce foreign wars."[1] These were the charges against them. In the latter part of 1789 the Church estates, immense in extent, were confiscated by the Assembly

---

[1] Carlyle's French Revolution.

and ordered to be sold for the benefit of the State. Then followed the abolition of all Monastic vows, religious orders and confraternities, "with the exception of a few useful ones." Titles and privileges were swept out of existence, and all made to stand on a common level of equality before the law and the popular will.

Later on, the *sans-culottes* take a hand in the humiliation of the church. At Lyons an ass is dressed in priest's cloak, with a mitre on his head, and, trailing the Mass-books and a Latin Bible at his tail—for there was not a French Bible in Lyons nor in all Paris—is marched through the streets to a funeral pile where they are burned. The Christian Sabbath is abolished and the tenth day is established as a rest day instead, in the new calendar. The Decalogue seems well nigh swept out of sight and hearing. A "Feast of Reason" is appointed among the intercalary days and the work is done. No more revelation, no more divine law, men become a law unto themselves. "Professing themselves to be wise, they became fools" (Rom. 1—22). The Bishop of Paris, with his Chapter, openly appears before the Convention and declares that he has all his life been preaching a lie, and that now there is "no religion but Liberty.".

God's word is dead, virtually dead "in the streets of the great city, which spiritually is called Sodom and Egypt." Everywhere men rejoiced and embraced each other because the new and golden age of reason had come. The "Goddess of Reason—a courtesan of Paris

—is about to be worshipped, heralded by white young women girt in tri-color, and to the principal church of Notre-Dame they go to offer their homage. Her henceforth we adore." Merry making and gifts are in order; time Nov. 1793. Here we will leave the Bible in the streets of the "great city"—for the same scenes were enacted with it in Paris and all the larger cities—and give brief attention to the "great earthquake" that came with a mighty crash upon church, and throne, and nobility, and reacted upon the people themselves.

Since symbolic prophecy deals only, as heretofore observed, with moral and political events, "this earthquake" can only find its solution in the great civil, religious and political commotions of this same Revolution of France in 1793-4, which is our first supposable ending of the 1260 years. If all the conditions cluster around and find their plain solution in this date, then we are sure we have the right one and need look no further. Let us bear in mind, also, that France was the first to give the Papacy landed possessions and temporal power, and we can see the propriety of her being ordained of God the first to take them away, eat up and destroy her substance, "burn her with fire,"[1] and lead her into captivity,[2] as well as teach the other nations to do the same.

No pen can adequately depict the horrors of that unprecedented revolution when the divine right of kings,

---

[1] Rev. 17-16.
[2] Ibid. 13-10.

a titled aristocracy, and a corrupt clergy, with all their privileges and emoluments, were swept away with unexampled rage and fury. To those long ages of misrule and oppression under royalty were added, as immediate precursors of this political "earthquake," three years of famine, and the great hail storm of 1788 which destroyed all the crops just ready for the sickle, and led vast masses of people to flock from the country districts into the city of Paris. It has been said of these that they were "mostly in rags, armed with great sticks, whose very look is menacing; vagabonds, ragged fellows, many almost naked, and with appalling faces!" These, with the rabble of the city, were ready for any plots and excesses that promised them bread. The "reign of terror" had commenced.

Contending parties sought to destroy each other, and suspicion reigned everywhere. The Guillotine had already been set up. Then was passed the "Law of the Suspect" of which Carlyle says:[1] "No frightfuller law ever ruled a nation of men. All Prisons and Houses of arrest in French land are getting crowded to the ridgetile: Forty-four thousand Committees, like so many companies of reapers or gleaners, gleaning France and gathering their harvest, and storing it in these Houses— Harvest of Aristocrat tares! Nay, lest the forty-four thousand, each in its own harvest field, prove insufficient, we are to have an Ambulant Revolutionary Army; six thousand strong, under right captains; this shall

---

[1] French Revolution, Vol. 2, p. 301.

perambulate the country at large, and strike in wherever it finds such harvest work slack. So have Municipality and Mother Society petitioned ; so has Convention decreed. Let Aristocrats, Federalists, Monsieurs, vanish, and all men tremble : the Soil of Liberty shall be purged—with a vengeance !"

"Daily the great Guillotine has its due. Like a black Spectre, daily at even-tide, glides the Death-tumbril through the variegated crowd of things. The variegated street shudders at it, for the moment ; next moment forgets it: Aristocrats! They were guilty against the Republic ; their death, were it only that their goods are confiscated, will be useful to the Republic ; *vive la Republique !* "

Notwithstanding the Guillotine was doing its deadly work at the rate of more than fifty per day at Paris, suspects and condemned were accumulating in the prisons with frightful rapidity, until at one time twelve thousand were confined in them. Of these it has been said : "Perhaps no human habitation or prison ever equalled in squalor, in noisome horror, these twelve Houses of Arrest." To expedite the work four tribunals were created, each with its engine of death, till the very executioners were taxed beyond human endurance. Prisons all over France are full, and the executions by Guillotine amount to between two and three thousand daily.

Then commenced, as at Nantes, a system of "fusilading" or shooting the condemned in squads, one hundred and twenty at one time : and, O horror of horrors! barges were prepared and filled with the condemned—ninety at one time, one hundred and twenty at another—drifted to the middle of the Loire, scuttled and sunk, hatches down, *all priests of the Romish Church*. Sentence of deportation was thus, writes Carrier, "executed vertically." Many die in prison. Many thousands flee as best they may to escape the terrible vengeance that has come upon them. Suspicion reigns everywhere, and no one dares harbor a refugee lest his own head pay the penalty, and no one is safe. The Guillotine is made larger and more complete for more rapid execution : when will it cease its horrid work ?

"For her sins have reached unto heaven, and God hath remembered her iniquities. Reward her even as she rewarded you, and double unto her double according to her works: in the cup which she hath filled fill to her double" (Rev. 18-5, 6).

Surely the wind of St. Bartholomew has turned to the whirlwind of the Revolution, and "the time of her *judgment* is come that Thou shouldest give reward to thy servants and shouldest destroy them which destroy the earth" (chap. 11-18). "We are now, therefore," says Carlyle, "got to that precipitous *Abyss* whither all things have long been tending. The harvest of long centuries was ripening and whitening so rapidly of late; and now it is grown *white* and is reaped rapidly, as it were *in one day*." What a comment upon the truth of the prophetic record !

"Therefore shall her plagues come in ONE DAY, death, and mourning, and famine. Alas, alas that great city Babylon, that mighty city!" (Rev. 18-8, 10).

"For thou shalt no more be called, 'The lady of kingdoms' Therefore hear now this, thou that art given to pleasures, that dwellest carelessly, that sayest in thine heart, I am, and none else beside me; I shall not sit as a widow, neither shall I know the loss of children: but these two things shall come to thee in a moment, in one day, the loss of children, and widowhood: they shall come upon thee IN THEIR PERFECTION for the multitude of thy sorceries, and for the great abundance of thine enchantments" (Isa. 47-5, 8, 9).

The scenes of these days cannot be depicted in words. Truly her cup was being filled to her double for all the cruelties of the past, inflicted in the name of Religion. Early in this year of 1793 the King, Louis XVI., is led to the Guillotine with every indignity; and before the end of the year the Queen, Marie Antoinette, daughter of the Emperor of Austria, "is dragged on a hurdle by a circuitous route lined by thirty thousand troops and ten times that number of spectators, to the spot where Louis had died." "Shouts of joy and execration were raised on every side." By this act a blow was struck at imperialism, as well as at papacy which was to be consummated in the case of both by the "Man of destiny" before the scene closes. In this "reign of terror" it is estimated fully three millions of the best citizens of France perished by the hands of her own children. Thus there came, as it were in one day, loss of children and widowhood, ruthlessly murdered to satisfy the popular clamor. But this is not all. As if to hurl defiance in the face of everything that pertained to royalty, "the tombs of St. Denis—the holy sepulchers wherein for nearly twelve centuries, from the days of Dagobert the son of Childeric, the bodies of the kings of France had rested—were now ordered for destruction by the Convention, and rifled by a Paris mob. The bodies of kings and heroes were torn from their coffins, and their bones and dust scattered in the air, or burnt by quick-lime in a vast trench.

Nor is this all by any means, for her cup is not yet full. We have already spoken of the death of the "two witnesses"—the Bible—and the "earthquake" in which, the record says, "The tenth part of the city fell," and which caused Imperialism, in the person of the throne and the vested rights of the nobility, to topple and fall. It remains to show the spoliation visited upon the national church, and its effects outside of France upon the Papacy itself at Rome, the "seat of the beast."

On the 7th of Nov. 1793, the municipality of Paris publicly dethroned " the King of Heaven "—to use their own words—"as well as the monarchs of the earth." " From this time, day after day, men came to the bar of the Convention and abjured Christianity." What need henceforth of churches? and so there come from all parts patriotic gifts of church furniture ; "all highways jingle with metallic priest tackle beaten broad, sent to the Convention, for the poverty stricken mint." What is not of silver proves as good as a mine of lead and goes for bullets. Bells, except for tocsin, come down from ancient belfries and go to the foundries for cannon. Mass books are torn into cartridge papers, while internal decorations and sacristies are torn out for bonfires. Never was ruin so complete, for all are intent to have the churches plundered, "to have Reason adored, suspects cut down, and the Revolution triumph."

But it does not end here. In 1796 Napoleon invaded the Papal states. Thirty-five millions of francs were levied as indemnity, and some of the finest works of art confiscated and sent to Paris. In 1798 a Republic was declared, and not long after the Pope himself, Pius VI, was put in close confinement at Grenoble, and afterwards removed to Valencia and confined in the Citadel, where he died. Under Pius VII. all the Papal states belonging to the church, which constituted the "temporal sovereignty" of the Papacy, were confiscated, and in 1810 he too was carried prisoner to France and did not return until 1814. The Papal states were after a time restored, but have now again been taken by Italy *never more to be restored*, and the Pope himself, shorn of his temporal power, declares he is a prisoner in his own palace.

"**He that leadeth into captivity shall GO INTO CAPTIVITY: he that killeth with the sword must be killed with the sword. Here is the patience and the faith of the saints**" (Rev. 13-10).

"**And the ten horns which thou sawest upon the beast,**[1] **these shall hate the whore, and shall make her desolate and naked, and shall eat her flesh and burn her with fire**" (Rev. 17-16).

[1] Ten horns are ten powers or kingdoms as per verse 12, chap. 17.

There is not a power in Europe (nor for that matter in either Continent of America) which has not taken part in despoiling the Papal church of her arbitrary powers and emoluments. Her strongholds of power by which she was enabled formerly to hold undisputed sway over the minds and even the lives of the people throughout her dominions, has been taken from her *never more to be regained.* Her assumed right. alone. to celebrate the marriage sacrament has been taken from her. Her exclusive control of burial places and all church property, regardless of the rights of individuals and congregations who may have contributed towards them or invested in them, have been denied her. Her supreme control of all institutions of learning. as well as of education itself, has been taken from her and in one form or another has been given to the State. Her right to appoint and displace priests and bishops at her own sweet will, has been greatly modified and curtailed in almost all the kingdoms of Europe ; and last but by no means least, her diplomatic relations with all the world have been completely severed, and she has now no resident ministers and agents to and from her former willing vassals.

We left our "two witnesses"—the Bible—dead in the streets of the "great city which is called Sodom and Egypt where also our Lord was crucified"; *i. e.*, his gospel and himself are rejected, and an infamous prostitute substituted in his place—"away with him" and give us "Barrabas." When the three years and a half were ended according to the mind of the Spirit, it is impossible to tell, no clue is given. All we are told is this :—

"**And after three days and a half the Spirit of life from God entered into them, and they stood upon their feet; and great fear fell upon them which saw them. And they heard a great voice, saying unto them, Come up hither. And they ascended up to heaven in a cloud; and their enemies beheld them**" (Rev. 11-11, 12).

One of the chief causes which led to a love for and unwonted activity respecting the Bible in connection with the new spiritual life of the Church, already described, lies in the reaction which took place when a better reading of the "Dendera Tables"—which at first were popularly believed to have overturned the Mosaic account of creation and connecting events—led to renewed and greatly increased faith in the divine record as the true word of God, and that it would surely "accomplish that whereunto it is sent."

This new confidence in the Bible gave a wonderful impetus to efforts for the spreading of the Word without note or comment. Bible societies began to be organised for more thorough work than had heretofore been undertaken; notably, the British and Foreign Bible Society in 1804; two in America in 1809, afterwards merged in the American Bible Society. At this present time there are more than eighty societies and auxiliaries for the printing of God's word. Even Voltaire's old printing press is said to have done duty in the same line, while the very house where he lived is now a depot for the Geneva Bible Soc. publications, and packed with Bibles. His prediction that one hundred years would witness the Bible and Christianity a thing of the past, is the very opposite of the truth. To-day "the good old Book" stands on a height it never reached before, from which there is no receding. 165,000,000 of Bibles, Testaments, and portions of Scripture, in two hundred and six languages and dialects, tell of the wonderful activity that has sprung into being for the spread and study of God's word since the creation of the societies. Is it possible that all these scenes and events necessary to the filling of the conditions, shall ever be *re-enacted?* If not, then they are in truth things of the past and the prophecy is fulfilled.

Now let us stand for a moment in the midst of the scenes of this mightiest revolution that ever shook the world, both in its scope and its results. Let us catch the spirit of the events we have so briefly and so feebly narrated in connection with the symbolisms of the eleventh chapter of Rev., which may not inaptly be termed death bed scenes of the Papacy. Look *back* over the dark ages of the past under the domination of the beast and his rider—the "woman arrayed in purple and scarlet," "mother of harlots and abominations of the earth." Listen to the prayer of her slain, "How long, O Lord, holy and true, dost thou not judge and avenge our blood on them that dwell on the earth" (6–10).

Now turn and consider the events which started out from this dark background into new life and prominence—the birth in *one day* of the latter day kingdom;

the re-awakening of the modern Church, the resurrection of the Word of God from the *sackcloth* cerements of a death without sepulture—and tell me if the Angels who saw these facts of the past and the future more clearly than you or I can, were not right in exclaiming with exultant voices :—

"**The kingdom of this world is become the kingdom of our Lord and of his Christ**".

Moved by this exultant song of victory, the four and twenty elders take up the theme and ring it out through Heaven's high arches :—

" **We give thee thanks. O Lord God Almighty, which art, and wast, and art to come; because thou hast taken to thee thy great power AND HAST BEGUN TO REIGN**" (11-17).

To all intents and purposes the Papacy is dead, and its persecuting power is gone forever. Her Imperial ally, the real executor of all the cruel orders of the Papacy, is too near his own end to be longer feared; while their united efforts, just now intensely active, to restore the temporal power of the Pope, will involve both in irremedial ruin and a common grave in the "sea" and the "Abyss" from which they came. (Rev. 18-21 and 20-3). For this happy event the world is ready to exclaim, Amen! and Amen!

Let us now come back to events in the New World and see what progress our young nation is making towards manhood.

CHAPTER XI.

FIERY TRIALS AND JUDGMENTS FOR CLEANSING THE KINGDOM.

"Hear the word of the Lord ye children : for the Lord hath a controversy with the inhabitants of the land because there is no truth, nor mercy, nor knowledge of God in the land. By swearing, and lying, and killing, and stealing, and committing adultery, they break out and blood toucheth blood ; *therefore shall the land mourn*" (Hosea 4-1, 2).

"In thee have they set *light by father and mother*: in the midst of thee have they dealt by oppression with the *stranger*; in thee have they wronged the *fatherless and the widow;* thou hast despised mine holy things, and hast *profaned my Sabbaths;* in thee have they taken gifts to shed blood ; thou hast *taken usury* and increase, and thou hast greedily gained of thy neighbor *by extortion*, and hast forgotten me, saith the Lord" (Eze. 22-7, 8).

"As a cage is full of birds, so are their houses full of deceit: therefore they are become great and waxen rich ; they are waxen fat, they shine : yea, they overpass the deeds of the wicked ; they judge not the cause, the cause of the fatherless, yet they prosper and the right of the needy do they not judge. Shall I not visit for these things ? saith the Lord: shall not my soul be avenged on such a nation as this ?" (Jer. 5-27 to 29).

"Therefore thus saith the Lord: ye have not hearkened unto me, in proclaiming liberty, every man to his neighbor, and every one to his brother ; behold, I proclaim a *liberty for you*, saith the Lord, to the sword, to the pestilence, and to the famine" (Jer. 34-17).

"If thou wilt not observe to do all the words of this law that are written in this book, that thou mayest fear this glorious and fearful name, The Lord Thy God; then the Lord will *make thy plagues wonderful*, and the plagues of thy seed, even great plagues, and of long continuance, and sore sickness and of long continuance" (Deut. 28-58, 59).

Although these sins are charged against Israel of old and they have suffered the predetermined penalty, inflicted as we have seen with terrible severity, yet there is nothing to prevent a repetition of like judgments for like offenses. This appears to be assured from the fact that history is constantly repeating itself, and (since "all judgment has been committed to the Son") his coming in judgment upon the ungodly for the idolatry of this age—whose harvests of crime are a fac-simile of the ancient crop—is now at our very doors and ready to burst upon us.

It seems strange that one hundred years of national life under such great mercies should have produced such a crop of "tares" as here enumerated by the prophets, yet we cannot deny the truthfulness of the picture. But even this was foretold by Christ in the parable alluded to. In the parable of "The Sower" (Matt. 13-4, 8), the seed is the *word* of the kingdom, and the product are the followers of Christ—Christians. In the parable of "The Tares," on the contrary, the seed sown are the *children of the kingdom* (ver. 38), and the resultant harvest is the kingdom of Christ on earth.

But the tares are the children of the wicked one— wicked men, anarchists, atheists, and the like—and the harvest is at the "consummation of the age" when the kingdom is to be cleansed of them by pestilence, which answers to fire for the natural product.

"The field is the world": but which world? Evidently not the old world, for that was nearly *all tares* when the gospel of the kingdom was first proclaimed. Clearly, then, the New World is meant, and this answers to both the prophetic and historic record, as we have shown. Hence the parable can find its solution nowhere else. The last of the seven parables (ver. 47) continues the same idea and shows the necessity, as well as the justice, of the judgment which shall separate the bad from the good, and prefigures the absolute certainty of the final judgment and separation of the wicked from the good at the end of the world.

"But every man shall die for **HIS OWN INIQUITY**: every man that eateth the sour grape, his teeth shall be set on edge" (Jer. 31-30).

We have not the slightest foundation for believing that the days of vengeance for offended law are over, but every assurance for the reverse. As in Egypt the death of the first-born was, in the cumulative judgments, the heaviest of all preceding the deliverance of God's people, so we may fairly infer that the last crowning judgments of God upon a guilty world before the kingdom is voluntarily given into the hands of the Son of David for an everlasting kingdom, will be of the most stupendous character and most decisive in their results. But we are not left to inference alone for our conclusions respecting the terrible nature and near approach of these judgments. Let us for a moment consider the *time* of the harvest.

Whatever may be our individual belief respecting the peculiar character and the time of each of the seven plagues or vials of wrath, to be poured out upon those twin brothers of iniquity—Imperialism and Papacy—there can be now but one intelligent and well grounded opinion as to their commencement at the time of the French Revolution, substantiated as it has been by the mighty events which have transpired within the pale of those ten kingdoms since that time[1]

But if there lingers doubt in any mind respecting these statements, the character of the *sixth* plague[2] and the present signs of the times ought certainly to set it at rest at once. Expositors of note agree that Euphrates is used in the Apocalypse as a symbol of the Turkish power, and its drying up is intended to indicate the gradual yet speedy decay of that once formidable empire. "Two woes are past; behold, the *third* woe cometh *quickly*," said the angel at the sounding of the seventh trumpet when the "mystery of God" was finished. Consequently we find that power gradually losing its hold upon its vassal states and kingdoms. First, Egypt gained many concessions; then Greece set up for herself in 1828; and in the last Russo-Turkish war all her provinces north of the Balkan mountains

---

[1] Appendix C.
Rev. 16–12.

gained their autonomy or right to govern themselves.
with hardly a blow struck on their own account, simply
by the acquiescence of Germany and Russia.

This war of three years duration was one of the most
singular on record; for, while Turkey had an army of
two hundred and fifty thousand men constantly in the
field at various points eating out her substance, not a
notable or decisive battle was fought in all that time, so
literally are the words of scripture fulfilled. The London *Times* gave emphasis to this when it declared,
" Turkey appears to be dying of *dry rot*." Even at that
time Bismarck openly invited Austria to help herself to
turkey, but her time had not come.

It cannot now be long delayed when Austria and Russia will divide between themselves all that is left of
Turkey in Europe. When this takes place England
will certainly foreclose her "protectorate" mortgage on
what is left of Turkey in Asia, to protect her Suez canal
against the designs of Russia, which she will do at all
hazards[1] Germany will be remunerated for assent to
these sweeping "reforms" by taking the German half
of Austria, and so all parties will be compelled to be
satisfied, save Russia, who will find in England's share
of the spoils in Asia a sure cause of complaint and war.
But Turkey will disappear quietly, vanishing out of sight
forever like the drying up of a river, and the way will
be prepared for the seventh angel to "pour out his vial
into the air" (chap. 16-17). Immediately following

---
[1] Please read Isa. 19-20.

this notable event the following declaration is made:

"And there came out of the temple of heaven, a great voice from the throne, saying, IT IS DONE. And there were voices, and thunderings, and lightnings; and there was a great earthquake, such as was not since men were upon the earth, so mighty an earthquake, and so great" (Rev. 16-17. 18).

The tremendous preparations in Europe for a conflict in the near future of which they have no certain knowledge, ought to have great significance with us and cause us to ponder well the "signs of the times," for we are assured by the above quotation that nothing like it has ever been seen on this earth since man was upon it. Mighty and terrific as the French Revolution was, this one shall be so great that the former shall sink into insignificance beside it. That was but the after pangs of the birth of a nation; this shall be the convulsive throes of the dissolution of hoary headed kingdoms. Russia has constituted herself the head of Imperialism, and, in some way, will enter into the scheme of the Papacy and the border States for the restoration of the temporal power of the Pope, and to further her own schemes of aggrandisement through the Greek Church. Perhaps the "deadly wound" of the beast will be healed. Who knows? Of one thing we are certain. Russia and all who are joined with her will have an opponent of whom they little dream, who will sink them out of sight, as saith the prophet Ezekiel:

"Thus saith the Lord God: Behold, I am against thee O Gog, prince of ROSH, Meshech and Tubal; and I will plead against him with pestilence and with blood: and I will rain upon him, and upon his hordes, and upon the many people that are with him, an overflowing shower, and great hail stones, fire, and brimstone" (Chap. 38-3, 22).

Now if these events are to take place in the Old World upon the enemies of God and political Israel, preparatory to the reign of universal peace, we may fairly infer that simultaneous with these stupendous events will be the destruction of the wicked on this side of the water, and the cleansing of this God-given land—this sanctuary of spiritual Israel—at, or prior to, the taking of the kingdom by Christ, the son of David. The cleansing of the Temple in the olden time was but a type of this; yet how insignificant was that event compared with this later cleansing. That was with a whip of cords; this will be by the inexorable, relentless, operation of law, every man dying for his own iniquity. As that was introductory to his public ministry as the Messiah, so this cleansing of the human fabric of the divine government—the truer temple of the indwelling presence—will be preparatory to his taking the throne as the true and only successor of his father David. Of this cleansing in respect of time and necessity Christ has given fair warning.

"The tares are the sons of the evil one: and the enemy that sowed them is the devil: and the harvest is the consummation of the age, and the reapers are angels; and they shall gather out of his kingdom all things that cause stumbling, and them that do iniquity, and shall cast them into the furnace of fire" (Matt. 13-38, 41).

"But take heed to yourselves, lest at any time your hearts

be overcharged with surfeiting, and drunkenness, and cares of this life, and so that day come upon you unawares: for as a **SNARE** shall it come on all them that dwell on the face of the whole earth" (Luke 21-34, 35).

"For the upright shall **DWELL IN THE LAND**, and the perfect shall **REMAIN** in it: but the wicked shall be cut off from the earth, and the **TRANSGRESSORS** shall be **ROOTED OUT OF IT**" (Prov. 2-21, 22).

The whole tenor of scripture points the same way, that the wicked in the latter day shall suffer the consequence of their doings, and the righteous shall reap the reward of theirs. The one class shall miserably perish, while the other shall long live to "enjoy the work of their hands." In the olden time the sins of the wicked brought ruin upon all, good and bad alike. In the latter day "*every man shall die for his own iniquity.*" Then the righteous were carried into captivity in the common calamity for the common good. In these days it will be a "survival of the fittest," that they may "dwell in a place of their own," with their enemies far removed from them. Those who *smell fire* wherever they see the *word*, are, we fear, too much of the spirit of those "sons of thunder" who desired to call down fire from heaven to consume them who would not receive Christ. His answer ought to silence us: "Ye know not what manner of spirit ye are of. For the Son of Man is not come to destroy men's lives but to save them" (Luke 9-54). In the next chapter we shall show the character of Christ's coming. At present let us look for a moment and see if fire can be mentioned and have no reference to the end of the world. Hear what Malachi says :

"But who may abide the day of His coming? and who shall stand when He appeareth? * * * For, behold, the day cometh that shall burn as an oven; and all that do wickedly shall be stubble; and the day that cometh shall burn them up, saith the Lord of Hosts, that it shall leave them neither root nor branch" (Chap. 3-2 and 4-1).

Now these terrible denunciations of Malachi have generally been held to refer to the days of Christ's first advent, and had special reference to the purity of his teachings, the exactitude of his requirements, and the all consuming nature of his love as compared with the formalism of the times and the hypocrisy of the Pharisees. Just so these latter-day judgments will be the natural outcome of the moral turpitude and corruption seen in these days in defiance of all the lessons of the past, which cannot abide the purity of "the perfect law of liberty," nor stand the test of His all absorbing zeal and love. He says, therefore, that He will come by the *sword* and by *flood* and by *pestilence* to execute judgments upon them who despise his law and trample on his sabbaths.

We have already suffered the judgment of the *sword* which for five years was bathed in fratricidal blood because of our refusal to hear the cry of the *stranger* and "let the oppressed go free." For fifty years the opportunity was offered to the people and the Christian Church "to deal justly, love mercy, and walk humbly with thy God" in respect of the slaves of this land, and we refused to do it. We selfishly said, If the Southern people want slaves let them have them, but we do not want them in the North. Those who sought to defend their cause or labored for their release from the cruel bonds of unremunerated toil were ridiculed, abused and oftentimes assailed.

Christians kept on praying, "Thy kingdom come," but they never lifted a finger to carry out one of the chief purposes for which the Son of Man came to the earth, "to open the prison doors and let the oppressed go free." Nor would they until doomsday, if God had not taken the cause of the oppressed in hand and delivered them by a "mighty hand and an outstretched arm." But He laid more than the full price of their ransom upon the shoulders of the North. In nearly every household in the land, north and south, the avenging angel entered and, failing to see the blood of the covenant taken from the bleeding wounds of Calvary, but, rather, the blood of poor enslaved Africa, from the cruel lash of the slave driver's whip, took the first-born and, often, more as the terrible penalty of *complicity* with wrong doing and crime.

In the providence of God another question of far deeper import, in its terrific results upon the homes of the people and upon the moral character of the youth of the land, is presented to us for our suffrages. We are tampering with it very much the same as we did with the question of human slavery, though this enslavement of which we speak begets a servitude more damning by a thousand fold, than the worst forms of human slavery ever were. Slavery left a man's soul unfettered, though his body was loaded with chains, and free for a hope of eternal life and joy beyond the grave; but the slave of the cup is doomed for time and for eternity. His home on earth becomes a hell, and his future life is hell intensified.

Thousands of professing Christians are saying, "We don't like the *methods* of those who propose to annihilate this evil *at once ;* it is altogether too *sudden ;* the thing *can't be done.*" Just what you or your fathers said about slavery, until God got tired of waiting for your slow movements and *compelled* you to "undo the heavy burdens and let the oppressed go free."

But for God's abounding mercy in raising up a noble company of Christian women, burning with love for Christ and for human souls, who have set their hearts and hands to the work of cleansing the land of this foul blot, we should find ourselves very shortly paying a severer penalty for our indifference, and *high license complicity* with this abominable curse, by so much as the slave of the cup is more unutterably cursed than the slave of the lash. They come to the Christian people of this land and ask us for our help by giving them the franchise, or for our votes against the evil--*either or both*—for its utter annihilation. If you will not give either, but choose rather to be reckoned among the great army of saloon keepers, atheists and socialists as one of themselves—as a church elder found himself recently after a vote for high license—the curse of God will certainly rest upon you and yours, and you will pay the penalty sooner or later with fearful interest. Remember the judgment of the *sword*.

"If thou hast run with the footmen and they wearied thee, then how wilt thou contend with horses? and if in the land of peace wherein thou trustedst, they wearied thee, then how wilt thou do in the swelling of Jordan?" (Jer. 12-5).

"Go through, go through the gates; prepare ye the way of the people; cast up, cast up the highway; gather out the stones; lift up a standard for the people. Take up the stumbling-block out of the way of my people" (Isa. 62-10; 57-14).

We have already given in the first chapter some little idea of the enormity of this crime of crimes. But it needs to be impressed on every reader in every possible way what an immense stumbling-block is this hell-born traffic to the progress of the truth and the establishment of Christ's kingdom on the earth. It is impossible that His kingdom and one of Satan's mightiest agencies, if not the very throne of the arch fiend himself, should exist in the same realm together; one or the other must go down. If you are a follower of Christ you ought to know which will be the conqueror. If you do know, how can you say, "It can't be done," and because you *think* it can't be done you will help to *continue* its foul and slimy existence by licensing and giving it legitimacy and respectability. Nineteen millions of communicants at the Lord's table in this land, male and female, ought to furnish a sufficient number of brave, earnest, souls to drive out this monster. But for the deadened consciences and pusillanimous members of the Church of Christ it would be done immediately.

It is not a question for the reader to ask whether one or another is the better way for controlling and regulating the business; it is only a question of right or wrong. If it is right, good, and wholesome, then vote to continue it. But if it is wrong, an evil, and a curse, then help to stamp it out at once. The experience of two hundred years shows conclusively that the business is not one to be controlled or kept within safe limits. The cold-blooded murder of at least four persons. and now the beating of another one nearly to death for daring to enforce the laws for the regulation of this business. shows the desperate character of those engaged in the sale of the poison. For this opposition to law is not the act of one or two men whose business might be injured or interfered with, but the deliberate and concerted action of a whole community of saloon keepers and liquor men. Every man, therefore, who votes to continue this business by high license or otherwise for the revenue it brings to the corporation treasury. becomes a participator in the *crimes* as well as the *profits* of the business. Flee from the unholy copartnership, as you would the fangs of the Cobra.

Yet not alone to the crime of drink are all the judgments to be charged, for its twin sister, covetousness, comes in for a full share of the rewards of unrighteousness, since Paul declares it to be idolatry. If it can be judged by its effects, truly Paul was not far out of the way, for debauchery, licentiousness, perversion of justice, and blood, would seem to brand it as equal in its influence to any effects of idol worship ever practiced by ancient Israel. We have no need to dwell long on this part of our theme, for the rumbling of the chariot wheels of coming vengeance is heard from every quarter of the land. Though the demon of drink lies in great measure at the bottom of the discontent and poverty of the laboring classes, yet it cannot be denied that the inordinate greed of gain which seems to possess all classes, as if that alone was the chief end of man here and hereafter, gives just ground of complaint and affords these blatant orators the staple subject for all their harangues·

If men were not dead to all sense of shame and self-respect; if the love of gain had not blinded men to the miseries of others; if their consciences had not become seared as with an hot iron, and their eyes covered with golden scales, they would be able to see the disreputable nature of this business of dealing out death and eternal damnation to those who otherwise would have adorned some home and been a helper and not a besotted drone in the human hive. More than seven hundred millions of dollars pass over the counters of these men in the dishonest desire to transfer without proper equivalent to their own corrupt pockets, the hard earned wages of honest toil. These millions are taken from fourteen million five hundred thousand men and women who are either confirmed drinkers of alcoholic and malt liquors or are traveling that road with sure and speedy steps, of whom sixty thousand drop annually into a drunkard's grave. Surely there is need to take the stumbling blocks out of the way, for out of these two offenses spring all the minor crimes charged upon Israel of old, for which they were driven out from their beautiful vineyards and homes to become wanderers in the earth.

Nor are these the full measure of our guilt in imitation of the sins of olden time, however much we may boast of ourselves as belonging to an advanced civilisation. The slightest causes are now, as of old, made the excuse for divorce and desertion from those whom we have promised before God to love and cherish until death comes to sever the connection. The Courts are filled with these constantly increasing cases of heartless and cruel desertions which include all classes, high and low, rich and poor, christian and infidel. To her shame, be it said, the Church has winked at this state of things by giving to such persons recommendations to sister churches, and receiving the same from others.

But, thanks be to God, a different sentiment is beginning to prevail, which gives promise of better things to come, and it cannot come any too soon, for Christ denominates those who are guilty of it without proper ground, as adulterers. Yet in an Eastern church recently a minister was compelled to resign his pastorate because he had spoken plainly of this great and growing sin, a leading member of whose congregation had not only been himself divorced, but had then recently married a divorced woman. Ministers of the pure and holy Jesus, lift up your voices with one accord against this crime against nature and refuse to high and low, rich and poor, the banns of marriage where either party has been divorced save for the one crime of adultery.

Another relict of the olden crimes is found under the garb of religion in the plurality of wives as practiced in Utah. Unless christian ministers and others are active and vigorous in their opposition, the hope of gain to either political party may lead to the reception of Utah as a State, when she must of necessity be left to regulate her own internal affairs according to her own liking. Just here comes in the necessity of an amendment to the Constitution which shall make the word of God the basis of all moral legislation, and not the customs or sentiment of the people. By such a change polygamy becomes a crime against God and not against laws for social order. Under such a law no State could enter the Union, whatever the advantage might be to parties, with such a record as that of Utah. But as we have already spoken of this evil in the first chapter, we will pass on without further comment.

The last in the list of sins which characterised Israel of old, which threatens to engulf us as a nation is, pollution of the Sabbath by devoting it to unholy purposes of gain and pleasure. In the Report of the Sabbath Commission in Massachusetts, it is stated that the first Sunday trains in this country were run into Boston for the convenience of church members residing in the country, who desired to attend the ministry of their regular pastors in the city, and who had sufficient influence to have an accommodation train run for their especial advantage. From this small beginning have come the running of Sunday trains all over the country for all sorts of purposes.

Our chief rulers and our legislators in too many instances, like the princes of Israel, have little regard for the sanctities of the Sabbath, and are unmindful of the example they set to the people and of the risks incurred in their disregard of God's righteous law. Even Congress in the last hours of its sessions has not scrupled to encroach on the sacred hours of the Sabbath, with all the turmoil of closing scenes. But above all, the Government has become a desecrator of the Sabbath— one of colossal proportions—in carrying and distributing the mails in all the large cities and towns of the land which contain some 60,000 offices whereby the employees are compelled, to a greater or less extent, to forego the restful, freshening and elevating influences of that holy day, and are as it were forced to assist in calling down the penalties of an outraged law of God.

The running of the mail trains for the Government furnishes the R. R. officials an all powerful excuse for the continuance of the Sunday trains for other purposes by which hundreds of thousands, mostly young men, are compelled to become violators of God's law, to their own moral and physical debasement. " Shall I not visit for these things, saith the Lord ? Most assuredly He will, and that right early, for, as events are now occurring, the days of trial cannot be far off. European statesmen seem to have a precience of the coming doom of nations, and are preparing for it as best they may under the *inspiration* of the spirit of all evil, but under the *directing* "hands of the mighty God of Jacob." We too are preparing for it under the same directing hand but with not half vigor enough.

> "A noise shall come even to the ends of the earth; for the Lord hath a controversy with the nations, he will plead with all flesh; he will give them that are wicked to the sword, saith the Lord. Thus saith the Lord of hosts, Behold, evil shall go forth from nation to nation, and a great whirlwind shall be raised up from the coasts of the earth" * * * (Jer. 25-31, 32).

But the "weapons of *our* warfare are not carnal but spiritual" and moral, and "mighty through God to the pulling down of strong holds." We have no need of armies but we have need of *men*, Christian men; men true to their convictions of *right* and fearless in proclaiming them; men who love the truth rather than the praise of men, who esteem "the reproach of Christ greater riches than the treasures of Egypt." Who of such "will come up to the help of the Lord against the mighty?" peradventure we may greatly modify and lessen the calamities that are surely coming to cleanse this God-given land of "all things that offend, and of them which do iniquity."

Are you aware, dear reader, that infidels, atheists, socialists, and nihilists, are organised and organising all over the country in city, town and village, for the express purpose of removing by legislation every distinctively christian usage of the Government ? Such is the fact, and they are confident of success, basing their "demands" on the fact that God is not recognised in the Constitution. Hence, they argue, the Government has no right to recognise in any form whatever, the usages of the Christian religion above the Muhamadan, Parsee, Heathen or any other religions. Their "demands" occupy a prominent place in their leading papers and are of this sort. (1) "We demand that churches and all other ecclesiastical property shall no longer be exempt from taxation. (2) The employment of chaplains in all institutions supported by public money, shall be discontinued. (3) That all religious services now sustained by the Government shall be abolished, and especially that the Bible in the public schools, whether as a text-book or for religious worship, shall be prohibited. (4) That the appointment by the President or by the Governors of states, of religious festivals, or fasts, shall wholly cease. (5) That all laws directly enforcing the observance of Sunday as the Sabbath shall be repealed. (6) That judicial oaths shall be abolished, and simple affirmation under penalties be substituted. (7) That all laws looking to the enforcement of "Christian" morality be abrogated. (8) That in all Government and State action no preference shall be given the Christian religion. (9) That the whole political system shall be founded on a purely secular basis.

Christian men have seen this threatened danger and have felt compelled to organise themselves into "The Moral Reform Association" for the purpose of arousing the christian public on this great question by the circulation of information by pamphlets, by lectures, and by the publication of a paper devoted to this and kindred subjects.[1] They had been satisfied, but for this organisation of infidels, to let truth make its own way, being sure of the final result. The "Liberal League" compelled organisation on the part of the friends of God for the purpose of saving what He has given to us of free institutions.

Coincident with this movement, appears this mighty "Crusade" against the saloon, championed by the Christian women of the land under a divine inspiration, to avert if possible some portion of the overflowing storm of retribution that is surely coming to sweep over the land for its cleansing. We have already had the *sword* as heretofore stated. We have had a foretaste of what the *fire* can do in two of the largest fires of modern times. We have but snuffed the breeze of the coming tempest in the terrible tornadoes of the western plains. Water-clouds, phenomenal tides, tidal waves and bursting waters from pent up floods have told in some slight degree what may be expected "when the overflowing scourge shall pass through" upon a sin laden and God-defying people.

Even old earth herself has staggered under the great

---
[1] The Christian Statesman, 1520 Chestnut st., Philadelphia, Pa.

load of inquity resting upon her breast and has "reeled to and fro like a drunken man," carrying dismay unutterable to thousands of brave hearts. "Even the pestilence that walketh in darkness, and the destruction that wasteth at noon-day," have not left us without a foretaste of coming doom. Though these are but *premonitions*, they call upon us with no uncertain voice to "Cleanse the land and remove the stumbling blocks out of the way:"

"**For the Lord shall make a consumption, even determined, in the midst of the land**" (Isa. 10-23).
"**THAT DAY is a day of wrath, a day of trouble and distress, a day of clouds and thick darkness, and their blood shall be poured out as dust, and their flesh as dung: for he shall make a speedy riddance of all them (sinners) that dwell in the land**" (Zeph. 1-15, 17 18).

"For, behold, the Lord cometh out of his place to punish the inhabitants of the earth for their iniquity: the earth also shall disclose her blood, and shall no more cover her slain" (Isa. 26-21). God's people are told to rejoice when they see all these things coming to pass: "for lo, your redemption draweth nigh" and there need be no fear. He will provide a place of refuge as he has said:

"**Come, my people, enter thou into thy chambers, and shut thy doors about thee; hide thyself as it were for a little moment, until the indignation be overpast**" (Isa. 26-20).

We are no alarmists, sounding the "tocsin" without sufficient occasion. Through all this coming trouble we can see the silver lining to the cloud, and that it is but the ushering in of a better day, a day of triumph for those whose faith can ride the storm and whose bodies are clean enough and pure enough to withstand the pestilence. But, christian reader, how will you cleanse your skirts of the blood of those with whom you daily walk and converse, and never warn by pleading words of tenderness of the danger they are courting by a life of sin and open neglect of the great offer of love and mercy? Are there not some whom you can "pluck as brands from the burning?" Some whom you may help to protect by the blood of the covenant "sprinkled on the door-posts and lintels" when the avenging angel passes through?

God is laying "judgment to the line and righteousness to the plummet" in these three questions now placed by His marvelous providence before the American Christian public for their earnest consideration, *Yes or no.* First, shall this fair land be any longer fouled and cursed by the saloon with its slimy trail of sixty thousand yearly victims? or shall the land be cleansed and made the happiest and most prosperous on the earth for ages to come? Second, shall the Sabbath be any longer polluted and thereby cursed, by the greed of gain and lust of pleasure? or shall it be lifted again to its divine pedestal as an institution of God for man's spiritual profit and endowment? Third, shall the Word of God be taken as a basis of national legislation, and Christ, the son of David, be acknowledged—as was God at Sinai—

as the rightful sovereign of this nation? or shall this Government be simply a civil compact of the sovereign people for the common good, without personality or moral obligation?

On these questions you are asked, nay, you will be compelled, to give an answer one way or the other by *stepping over the line.* Either *with* the foul crew who are running the saloon, together with all those who are seeking to prolong its existence by giving it a lease of life and respectability, or *against* it and on the side of "God, and home, and native land." "Ye can discern the face of the sky, how is it ye cannot discern the signs of the times"?

CHAPTER XII.

BINDING OF THE DRAGON FOR A THOUSAND YEARS.

"And I saw an angel coming down out of heaven, having the key of the abyss and a great chain in his hand : and he laid hold on the *Dragon* the old serpent which is the devil and satan—and bound him for a thousand years, and cast him into the abyss, and shut it, and sealed it over him, that he should deceive the *nations* no more, until the thousand years should be finished ; after this he must be loosed for a little time" (Rev. 20–1, 2, 3).

There is perhaps no prominent topic of the Apocalypse upon which there has been less difference of opinion and controversy than this of the binding of Satan. All seem to concur in this one thought, the old enemy of man is some day to be shut up and bound in chains in his own place for at least a thousand years and, perhaps, a great deal longer time, which latter is their devout wish. Their thoughts have dwelt with delight on that coming day—"the good time coming"—when the world will become the abode of the saints "with none to molest or make them afraid." No temptations, no inducements to fly the track, a happy, rolicking time in a sea of bliss, or in the midst of the sedater pleasures of an eternal Sabbath of rest.

It seems a pity to waken one from such pleasant dreams, even though they be delusive. But truth is truth, and if these beautiful figments of the imagination have not a solid foundation in truth, the sooner they tumble the better. The Spirit says it is high time they tumbled.

It is a well established rule of interpretation that where the scriptures give an explanation of their teachings in any department, as they do in numerous cases, that explanation is to be taken as authoritative as the Word itself and holds good throughout. Proceeding on this self-evident rule let us look a little carefully at this passage, apparently so plain.

There are six factors mentioned in this part of the vision; two of them living agents, three material, and one, duration; to wit, the angel and the dragon, the key, chain and abyss, and the thousand years. We have put our own punctuation in the quotation for greater clearness, since punctuation is at best an arbitrary arrangement simply for convenience, and have left out the "*pit*" as being no part of the text, while *abyss* is the exact correlative of *abussos* (the Greek word). It is also the equivalent of "*the deep*" when reference is had to the sea, which we can all readily understand. Here let us emphasise what we have said before and what must be apparent to everyone, that the Bible is essentially one book, written by one person—the Holy Spirit—by the hands of many amanuenses, and must therefore, of necessity, be one and indivisible, with unity of design, method in arrangement of its symbolisms, and determinate values throughout. Anyone who ignores this truth will make "confusion worse confounded" in the interpretation of prophecy.

There are two master minds and but two in the field for the control of this world—Christ and Satan (presupposing of course that God and Christ and the Holy Spirit are essentially one person. On the one side as *invisible* agents, are the Son of God, the angelic host and the saints in Paradise. On the other are Satan, the fallen angels and the spirits of the damned in Tartarus. As *visible* agents are spiritual and political Israel on the one side, and on the other the anti-Christian kingdoms and forces of this world. As the heavenly, spiritual, forces are not seen save as they are represented on this panoramic canvas which John saw passing before him, so the forces of Satan are seen only in the same way.

Neither Christ nor Satan are introduced anywhere throughout the Apocalypse save by symbolic persons and agencies. In the fifth chapter Christ is represented by " a Lamb as it had been slain," and in Chap 19-11 by one on a white horse called Faithful and True; pure symbols and nothing else. So throughout the bcok, Satan himself is never once introduced save by his *agents*—Imperial and Papal Rome—and these are symbolised by the Dragon and the beast, which represent state and church governments, so that poor Satan has not even a symbol to show what he is.

Again, if we can determine the value of any symbol in the earlier books of the Bible, we may be sure the same value attaches to the same symbol wherever found; for, otherwise, there would be confusion in determining what is meant, and the revelation would be useless and no revelation at all. This ought to be self-evident, yet the great body of expositors, with two or three exceptions, have attempted solutions on the assumption, as one of their number has so innocently expressed it,[1] "That each prophecy is to be explained by itself, and no interpretation is to be derived from a supposed uniform meaning of symbols." "If the blind lead the blind, shall they not both fall into the ditch?" That is groping in the Catacombs without the guiding string. Is it any wonder that such are lost in a labyrinth of doubt and perplexity and give up in despair?

The prophet himself all through the book gives us

---

[1] Dr. Butler's Lectures on the Apocalypse.

plainly to understand by the use of the very language of symbols that his real meaning lies in the opposite direction from that which he says. Remember that John was writing under the direction of the Spirit about matters which it was His evident intention to *reveal* and at the same time to *hide*, so that the utmost ingenuity of man could not penetrate the secrets any further than He chose to reveal them, and yet keep alive a strong desire to know the hidden meaning of the whole.

From an acknowledged rule of interpretation, that parts of a vision being symbolic and political necessitates the whole to be symbolic and political, we are warranted in assuming the whole book to be symbolic, and the burden of proof rests wtih those who would have a literal reading, to show otherwise.

In Daniel 7-3 we find four *beasts* coming out of the sea at the call of the *four winds* which act in Satan's dominions as the four living creatures act in John's vision —as ushers to introduce the various agents and actors (see chap. 6). Now the last beast was declared to be (Dan. 7-23) "the fourth kingdom upon the earth" "diverse from all the beasts that were before it," "and it had ten horns" (ver. 7). Thus we know to an absolute certainty that all beasts coming out of the sea are, in symbolic prophecy, the representatives of wicked, political kingdoms: that is settled once and for all. In Rev. 13-2 we have another beast coming out of the sea having all the characteristics of the first three beasts of Daniel's vision: viz., the leopard, the bear, and the lion. Thus we are able to connect the two visions by a link of no mean proportions, and this is further strengthened by the interpretation which the angel gives in Rev. 17 chap.; all which points unmistakably to the Roman, political, kingdom in one form or other.

Now John does not say where his Dragon came from nor, definitely. what power it represents. But in chap. 13-2 he is represented as giving " his power and his seat and great authority" to the *beast* which is very plainly connected with Rome in chap. 17 and Dan. 7-23, 24. Thus we know that the Dragon of John's vision and the fourth beast of Daniel's, are symbols of the Roman, imperial power in different stages. In chap. 12-7 we find "there was war in heaven; Michael and his angels fought against the Dragon; and the Dragon and his angels fought, and prevailed not; neither was their place found any more in Heaven."

Now does anyone for a moment suppose there was in Heaven an actual battle, as represented, between the pure spirits of Heaven and the degenerate spirits of hell? for, observe, the same terms are used in ver. 9 as in chap. 20-2. Or was there even a battle between the angels and the power on earth represented by the Dragon? Nothing of the kind in either case. How much more reasonable to suppose—what all the circumstances of the case warrant us in doing—that it was simply a painting on heavenly canvas, unreal and visionary, yet standing out as a living picture to John of some of the mighty realisms of earth which should transpire centuries after John and the stage trappings had ceased to be. Undoubtedly, Michael and his angels represent Israel and his hosts as the exponents on earth of God's appointed forms of government, whether spiritual or political; and the Dragon and his angels, as well, represent all political dominions opposed to God, of which Roman Imperialism and the Papacy stand at the head.

In the vision of Zechariah. chap. 3. we have another instance in the same line of symbolism, where Joshua represents spiritual Israel returning from Babylon and attempting to restore the worship of God at Jerusalem under great trials and difficulties. Opposed to him stands Satan representing Babylon. and hindering in every possible way not only their return but the rebuilding of Jerusalem. But in all cases it is through living agents, and, no matter what the language may be. Satan never appears in person or is recognised in the language of symbols otherwise than as himself a symbol of something "earthly, sensual. devilish."

So in the passage under consideration. The angel or messenger is one of Michael's angels which stand for Israel in one form or other, who lays hold of the Dragon of Imperialism in whatever kingdom or set of kingdoms it may present itself in opposition to Israel, and puts him "*hors du combat*"—"lays him out," as the phrase is. for a "thousand years, so that he will not be able to offer resistance to representative government or Republicanism for ages to come. Doubtless, a definite time is here put for an indefinite, and simply means a very long time.

In connection, we have the key and the chain. If they are unreal and only symbolic—as common sense, sanctified or unsanctified, must admit—by what rule of interpretation is one part of the vision, to say nothing of the same verse, to be taken as literal and the rest as symbolic? Dear reader, it won't do; better let the old shanty tumble and build a new house on God's word and common sense.

So of the *abyss*, translated in the authorised version "bottomless pit." The dragon and the beast, we have seen, came out of the sea; yet in chap. 11–7 the beast is said to have come out of the abyss, thus making the sea and the abyss interchangeable terms, both being the home of monsters. Thus they became the symbols of vast multitudes of wicked and corrupt people out of whom came kings asserting their right to rule by force and might rather than by justice and truth, and then claiming that they ruled by *divine right*.

That the sea has this meaning is apparent from chap. 17–15 where it is said to John in explanation, "The waters which thou sawest"—the sea out of which the Dragon and the beast rose—"where the whore sitteth, are peoples, and multitudes, and nations, and tongues." Thus we are not left in doubt as to the meaning of both sea and abyss. Now since both the Dragon and the beast came out of the sea and the abyss, what more natural thing in the world than when they are no longer

CLEANSING THE KINGDOM. 275

needed in the drama. that they should return to the sea and the abyss which gave them birth.

We have then as the substance of all this discussion these several truths as symbolised by the angel. the Dragon. the chain. and the abyss. These wicked, anti-Christian. powers, represented in the New Testament by Rome—the successor to Babylon of old as the foe of Israel—are surely coming to a time, now but a short way off, when they will be utterly destroyed and put out of the way in such a manner as to be harmless, like a caged and bound prisoner, for long ages to come.

That this blow will be given by Israel. spiritual and political, there cannot be a doubt. The one, operating by the quiet and imperceptible influences of religion and free institutions. has already caused the European world to deny this shameless assumption of the divine right of kings to rule without the consent of the people and without representation. The other, by a war with the whole host of those opposing kingdoms which represent, substantially, the old ten kingdoms of Papal Rome and her ally of the civil power—at whose head stands Russia. self constituted champion of Imperialism and the Church—will be the agent under God for their complete overthrow.

Into this war will be gathered all the long standing feuds, animosities, disputed boundaries, and wounded pride of centuries for a final adjudication by the sword. "But they that take the sword shall perish by the sword." and there can be but one opinion with careful Bible students as to the side on which victory will perch. For this final struggle of the ages we have already shown they are preparing on the other side of the water with superhuman energy. But the struggle cannot come one whit sooner than God shall permit, for it must not only be a devastating war but an exhaustive one. To this end it will be delayed, notwithstanding all rumors from time to time to the contrary, until the terrible burden of expense shall so thoroughly exhaust the nations that when the struggle comes, which cannot be averted by turning to the right hand or to the left, they will be utterly ruined as opposing, war-like, governments. The "peace of Europe" will be assured.

Already the annual deficit of France is two hundred millions of francs, and her public debt is stated to be seven billions of dollars. The tremendous burden of taxation necessary to support such vast armies of nonproducers, will have a tendency to send thousands and millions to this country for relief, especially the Jews who are still God's people for a final purpose. Be it understood when we speak of the utter destruction of these kingdoms and of the Papacy we only speak of them as opposing *principles* of government and church polity. God's controversy is not so much with the peoples of those kingdoms as with the rulers and the ideas they represent. The people will indeed suffer much, but Imperialism and the Papacy will go down with a crash. The Papal church will no longer be Roman, for it will have no Head and no College of

Cardinals to elect and consecrate one. The church in this country will become the American Catholic Church with all its vast properties and benevolent institutions ready, by wonderful outpourings of the Holy Spirit, to take its place with all other denominations of the Christian church for the furtherance of the kingdom of Christ on earth.

Let those who are fearful of the ascendancy of that Church as a foreign, dictating, political intriguing church, quiet their fears, for God has wonderful things in store for us as a homogeneous people intent on doing his will in cleansing the land of the foul blot of whisky drinking and Sabbath desecration.

The duration of the thousand years is entirely problematical, since this term was one in common use by rabinical as well as classic writers, and is generally used as a round number for a long time. From the fact that there is no evening nor morning mentioned in connection with God's seventh day rest, it has been thought by some, as the work of creation ceased then and God's Sabbath has continued since that time, that the seventh age of the world into which we are about entering, will be the commencement of a Sabbath of peace and rest for the world—as compared with the past— which shall extend far beyond the definite term of a thousand years, into the longer term represented by a year of days and a day for a year in prophetic time ; equal to three hundred and sixty-five thousand years as the full term of the blessed reign of Christ on earth.

Thus we have given what we fully believe to be a natural, scriptural and common sense interpretation of these much abused texts, and trust we have not done it so rudely or hastily as to leave a bad wound or an aching void. The salve of divine grace, and quickened movements for the rescue of the perishing in anticipation of the " crowning day of glory by and by," ought to work in us a healthy condition of mind for a better perception of the truths of God's word respecting the coming kingdom. "*Search* the scriptures, for in them ye think ye have eternal life." We will now turn our attention to the long expected event—the coming of Christ in the clouds of heaven, which will be given in the next chapter.

CHAPTER XIII.

BEHOLD, HE COMETH WITH CLOUDS TO TAKE THE KINGDOM.

"And then shall appear the sign of the Son of man in heaven: and then shall all the tribes of the earth mourn, and shall see the Son of man coming in the clouds of heaven with power and great glory. And he shall send his angels with a great sound of a trumpet, and they shall gather together his elect from the four winds from one end of heaven to the other" (Matt. 24-30, 31: Mark 13-26: Lu. 21-27).

"Behold he cometh with clouds; and every eye shall see him, and they also which pierced him: and all kindreds of the earth shall mourn because of him" (Rev. 1-7).

"I saw in the night visions and, behold, one like the Son of man came with the clouds of heaven and came to the Ancient of days, and they brought him near before him: and there was given him dominion, and glory, and a kingdom, that all people, nations and languages, should serve him: his dominion is an everlasting dominion which shall not pass away, and his kingdom that which shall not be destroyed" (Dan. 7-13).

The graphic descriptions in the first two quotations of Christ's coming in the clouds have so long been held to refer to the end of the world and the judgment of the wicked, that it may seem to partake of temerity to entertain a different opinion and run counter to the well established opinion of good and learned men for generations past. But truth is truth and must prevail though the heavens fall. Let us look at these strange declarations and gather if we can their full import, with this premise:

We need often to be reminded of what we have heretofore stated, that the Bible is an Oriental book, full of Oriental expressions and modes of thought which cannot be measured, without great care, by our English idioms and precise modes of speaking. Add to this a language of symbols with which we Occidentals are unfamiliar, and we must not be surprised if many of the expressions of the prophetic parts of the Bible are of the most startling character to us and not easily comprehended, though the real meaning is as simple as the alphabet. Witness Joel 2-30, 31 quoted by Peter on the day of Pentecost as applicable to that day; and yet, literally, nothing of the kind was seen.

Now, while the Bible is so plain in its general teachings that a "wayfaring man though a fool may not err therein," there are parts of it so intentionally hidden in symbolism that the most pious, learned, and acute, scholars, have been unable hitherto to give us any intelligible interpretation that would harmonise all parts of the scriptures and agree with God's expressed plan for the government of the world. Especially is this true of the great epochs of the Church's history, and the culminating epoch of Christ's advent to take the proffered kingdom. When Daniel asked, What shall be the end of these strange disclosures made to him he was told, "Go thy way, Daniel, for the words are closed up and sealed till the time of the end" (chap. 12-9). On the contrary, John was told not to seal his vision " for the time is at hand," already begun to be. Yet good men and true have been puzzling their heads from that day to this to find out the secrets of John's vision, and of Daniel's also, and are as wide of the mark as ever because, simply, God's time for making known his secrets had not come.

All of these good and wise men have, however, answered God's purpose and have kept alive an interest in these things, and have furnished much food for thought and—work for the printers. The intent of scripture prophecy has never been to satisfy the idle curiosity of saint or sinner. Otherwise, wicked men would conspire to overthrow God's plans. Nor has God intended that any man, however wise, should find out the secrets of the future one moment sooner than suited His own wise purposes.

The real intent of prophecy has been rather (*a*), by writing history *beforehand* to give an unanswerable argument through all time for the divine origin of the Bible ; (*b*), to give such a vision of the future glory of the Church and the reign of Christ on earth as would give the recipients of the vision—and the Church as well, under the inspiration of an assurance of final victory—great encouragement and strength under severe trials and obstacles. Thus Elijah had visions of God which greatly strengthened him under terrible depression of spirits. Daniel had wonderful visions of the coming Messiah and the latter day glory, to encourage the returning exiles amid their trials. Paul had unutterable visions to encourage him amid his severe hardships, which lifted his soul so far above all his trials that he could even *glory* in tribulations, but his vision was of *heavenly* scenes and subjects—*the only one recorded*—and he was not able to say a word about it because it was incommunicable to mortal ears.

John's vision was intended to encourage and elevate his soul in his lonely banishment in the isle of Patmos, where a minute description of the "mystery of iniquity" was revealed to him in its rise, its duration, and its miserable doom. It was intended also to portray the glory to which the Church should attain, upon the destruction of this anti-Christian power, in her final victory over all enemies without and within.

God has seen fit to hold the key to this "mystery" until close to the time of the end, when events have too far transpired to be affected one way or the other by wicked men; while, by opening the mystery now, it may help thousands of God's people to clearer views of their God-given inheritance and lead them to greater exertions for the cleansing of the land.

I have already shown that any hypothesis which proposes to limit or cut short the work of grace at this stage of the world's progress and Christian development, bears on the face of it serious evidences of not being the true one; for if it is a judgment which includes a world in flames and a *personal* coming, which that event necessitates, then the work of redemption ends, leaving the work which Christ has undertaken to do not only not finished, but hardly begun. If we suppose a moral judgment—not a judicial one as at the end of the world—under the operation of a law which in itself is love, that shall enforce its penalties on every corrupt and obdurate soul with inexorable and relentless rigor, then we have a judgment in harmony with every principle of the divine government as revealed, and in accordance with sanctified common sense.

By such a judgment as this the tables would be completely turned upon Satan and his kingdom, virtually making *him* the destroyer of his own legions, a turn of affairs which would go far to open the eyes of surviving sinners to the "true inwardness" of his designs, and lead millions to the cross. Thus they will be able to see what they never could see before, that it has all along been only by the *restraining* power of Christ's love that such wholesale destruction has been hitherto delayed. By the other mode there is an acknowledgment of defeat by leaving the world, the grand battle field of the ages, even though it be in flames, to the possession of Satan before the work of recovery is fairly begun.

It is a miserable subterfuge and a begging of the argument to claim that the infants are to be reckoned to swell the numbers of the saved. They are no trophies of redeeming grace. If they are, it were better far that we all died in infancy. The real victory lies in the grace that enables us in the strength of redeemed *manhood* to subdue the arch enemy and tread him under our feet. Glory be to His dear name! But is there any other judgment spoken of in the scriptures, other than the final one, when the doom of the material world is finally come? We think there is.

In Daniel 7-10 it is declared, after describing the four beasts which rose out of the sea, the last of which represented the Roman power with its little horn of the papacy, that the "*judgment* was set and the books were opened." Nearly all expositors agree that this refers strictly to the judgment respecting these powers in their temporal kingdoms, and to nothing else. John, in Rev. 11-18, referring to these same powers and to the time when the fourth beast or power should receive its death blow, says:

> "And thy wrath is come and the time of the dead[1] that they should be JUDGED, and that thou shouldest give reward to thy servants the prophets, and to the saints, and them that fear thy name, small and great; and shouldest destroy them which destroy the earth."

Yet the world stands and is likely to stand for untold ages to come. If John's vision and Daniel's relate to the same subject, as no one can deny, then the judgment referred to is the same in both cases and already passed.

That these predictions refer exclusively to the temporal affairs of these kingdoms and to their destruction as forms of government hateful to God and inimical to the best interests of men, ought to be apparent to every candid mind and lover of the truth. God wages relentless war against all who oppose the kingdom of his dear Son, which seeks to give the highest liberty to all, but is willing to sacrifice the life of that Son to save the *subjects* of wicked kingdoms to a better life and a better form of government. Wicked governments, like corporations, have no souls that can be judged in any other place but this world and on this present plane of conditions. To this judgment, sanctified common sense says, Amen!

What the "sign of the Son of man" is we do not pretend to know, and it is useless to guess about it, since the scriptures give no intimation of its character in any

---

[1] Dead in trespasses and sins?

way, and being yet future it will probably be revealed in due time to all patient souls who are "waiting for the consolation of Israel". Matthew is the only one who speaks of it, and other scriptures make no allusion to anything of the kind.

Not so however with the "trumpet of a great sound," for it is written in Isa. 27-13:

"And it shall come to pass in THAT DAY, that the great TRUMPET shall be blown, and they shall come which were lost in the land of Assyria and the outcasts in the land of Egypt, and shall worship the Lord in the holy mountain at Jerusalem."

"Cry aloud, spare not, lift thy voice like a trumpet, and show my people their transgression, and the house of Jacob their sins" (Isa. 48-1).

Christ also says to his disciples, "When thou doest thine alms, do not sound a trumpet before thee." In Rev. 8-6 it is said: "And the seven angels which had the seven trumpets prepared themselves to sound." Now it is evident from all these passages that no material trumpet is in anywise intended, notwithstanding the fanciful interpretations which have been given by learned exegetes respecting Matt. 6-2. But what we do gather is this: any events, however trivial they may at the time appear to us, which have the effect of bringing about the predicted results, may be termed a trumpet and fills all the requirements of the case.

Furthermore, we are absolutely certain beyond all successful contradiction, that the seven trumpets had finished their sounding at the time of the French Revolution. But who has heard their mighty reverberations along the sounding board of time, or given any special heed to the terrible appeals of that reeling, crashing earthquake? From all this we gather that no other trumpets will sound than those which have already sounded, and that all these marvelous events will culminate at the end of this dispensation—"the consummation of the age"[1]—when Christ will take his kingdom, through spiritual Israel at the hands of God the Father, for a reign on earth of unexampled prosperity.

Of the same general character are the terms used for the gathering of "his elect from the four winds, from one end of heaven to the other," for the older prophets are full of the theme and sound it out in most explicit terms.

"I will bring thy seed from the east and gather thee from the west; I will say to the north, give up; and to the south, keep not back; bring my sons from far and my daughters from the ends of the earth, even every one that is called by my name" (Isa. 43-6).

God be praised for the luxury of living in this day when we see it come to pass that spiritual Israel is at last, at the end of the ages, occupying the "place of her own" in the New World, created and kept in store for her, and that she has created for herself, under the guiding hand of God, "a new heaven" and "habitations of peace" upon the mountains of Israel, "*the high mountain*" of our God. The "trumpet" has indeed sounded,

---

[1] Matt. 13-39, 40: 24-3.

and Israel in all lands and Judah also, with the oppressed of all nations, are listening to the sound and are flocking "as clouds and as doves to their windows" to this New World.

Yet the Church of Christ has not heard the sound, though moved by a mighty, divine, impulse since the French Revolution, to enter upon her Christ-appointed mission for the recovery of the world. Is it because "your hearts are overcharged with surfeiting and drunkenness, and cares of this life"? We plead with our readers to look into this matter, "lest that day come upon you unawares, for as a *snare* shall it come upon all them that dwell upon the face of the whole earth." We plead with you for redoubled exertions for those who are living carelessly and dwelling at ease; friends, neighbors, relatives and dear ones, who will be opposed to his coming and exposed to the coming storm, for the kingdom must be cleansed of "all things that cause stumbling, and of them that do wickedly" (Matt. 13–41). Be yourself a trumpet. "Cry aloud! spare not; lift up thy voice with strength; say to the cities of Israel, 'Behold your King,' the Prince of Judah, Son of David."

"*And every eye shall see him and they also that pierced him!*" If no one has ever heard with mortal ear the "great sound of the trumpet," neither is there any reason to believe that any mortal eye will see Him until the final judgment. Certainly not at the end of this dispensation or "consummation of the age" when he is coming "to be admired in all them who believe," whose coming and whose "glory shall be revealed in us." We shall see Him for whom our souls have longed in his love and by his indwelling presence; and even in the "overflowing scourge" we shall see abounding love in protection to his own true disciples, for the "*Consumption decreed shall overflow with righteousness.*" But there shall be confusion and dismay to all those who have been reckoned from the day of his crucifixion to this present, as "they who pierced him."

If a closer connection than this is desired, we reply: if the high priest could, from the world of spirits, see the "Son of man on the right hand of power," as Christ said he should, until He comes to take the proffered kingdom, surely he can see Him from the same place "coming in the clouds"—and so also can "they which pierced him"—without supposing a personal, visible, coming. As to those who shall "mourn" because of him, we have sufficiently indicated in this and previous chapters what will be the cause of their mourning. But Zechariah speaks of a class who "shall look on me whom they have pierced, and shall mourn for him as a father mourneth for his only son" (chap. 12-10). Of these it may be said that our interpretations give abundant scope for the realisation of all such promises, in the wonderful outpourings of the Spirit upon the house of Judah, now very near at hand, upon whom is coming a "spirit of prayer and supplication," with the above result.

HE COMETH WITH CLOUDS. 289

"In THAT DAY there shall be a fountain opened to the house of David and to the inhabitants of Jerusalem for sin and uncleanness. And it shall come to pass that in all the land, saith the Lord, TWO PARTS therein shall be cut off and die; but the THIRD PART shall be left therein. And I will bring the third part through the fire, and will refine them as silver is refined, and will try them as gold is tried: they shall call on my name, and I will hear them: I will say, 'It is my people': and they shall say, 'The Lord is my God'" (Zec. 13-1, 8, 9).

Here is no indication of a burning world, but there is abundant evidence and cause for great mourning, with the happiest results to follow:—We will now take up the main point.

"*Behold, he cometh with clouds, in power and great glory.*" There are a number of these passages which speak of His coming in the clouds, which have taken their coloring and interpretation from the scene at the ascension of our Lord from Olivet, and from our constant tendency to attach a literal meaning where nothing of the kind is intended. We can readily understand by long usage what Christ means when he says, "I am the *vine*, ye are the branches"; "I am the good *Shepherd*"; "This is my body broken for you, and my blood shed for you"; yet we are unable to understand when he says, "Ye shall see the Son of man coming in the clouds of heaven with power and great glory," because of the declaration of the angels as recorded in Acts 1-11. Let us look at it a moment and see if we can make out what it really means.

There is evidently no symbolism or metaphor about

the statement, simply a plain matter of fact that, "while they beheld, he was taken up and *a cloud* received him out of their sight"; a very natural circumstance indeed, and one very likely to happen to anyone rising far above the earth, especially in a cloudy day. Observe, it is merely an adventitious circumstance which none of the evangelists thought worthy of record if, indeed, they saw either the cloud or heard the voice of the angels. The great fact to them was, that He whom they loved was taken from them bodily and "carried up into heaven." Their tearful eyes saw nothing further. Other accessories were of small importance, not even the declaration of the angels. Whether they all saw and heard or not matters little. Luke records it, probably, from their lips and that is sufficient, but what do the angels say?

"**This same Jesus who is taken up from you into heaven, shall so come in like manner as ye have seen him go into heaven**" (Acts 1-11).

Which simply means, that as he ascended and was lost to view *in* a cloud, so, when "the Lord *himself* shall descend from heaven with a shout" (2 Thess. 4-16), he will in all probability appear to sight coming *out* of a cloud, especially if, as we have said, it shall be a cloudy day; and inasmuch as no time is set for this occurrence, the whole trend of scripture puts it at the final winding up of the affairs of this world. If anything more can be made out of this oft-quoted and misapplied passage, our readers are welcome to it.

If, on the other hand, we can show any passage or passages where symbolism is evidently used, which give a natural interpretation for clouds other than as objects of nature, we have proven our position in all the passages relating to his coming in the clouds, for *all* these passages are in connection with other evident symbolisms. As heretofore remarked, it is a rule of interpretation that the same symbol, whose value is once determined. bears the same character throughout all prophecy. We have already shown the moral character of the trumpet and the call of the elect from the four winds. which place the passage in Matthew at once in the category of symbolic prophecy with those of John and Daniel which are confessedly so.

Now in Rev. 11-12 it is said of the two witnesses, "They ascended up to heaven in a cloud, and their enemies beheld them." Will it for a moment be believed that the Bible or the Church or any line of witnesses were taken up bodily to heaven in a cloud and seen by their enemies? Of course not. It means that the Bible, as the true witness of God against an ungodly world, was suddenly lifted from its dead condition in the Papal world, as we have already shown. to new life and prominence and great vigor amongst men, and advanced rapidly in favor and circulation; which is precisely what we have seen since the Papacy and Imperialism received their death-blow in the Revolution of 1794.

In speaking of those who should come from all quarters of the globe to this latter-day home of Israel. Isaiah says, "*Who are these that fly as a cloud and as doves to their windows*" (60–8). So in Ezekiel's vision, as we have shown, he uses a vast cloud to signify the great Scythian horde of people who entered Asia and environed Israel. In Xenophon's Anabasis is a very fine description of the approach of an army of horsemen across the plains, under the figure of vast rolling clouds. They are of frequent use by classic writers, as typical of vast bodies of men. Paul says, "seeing then that we are compassed about with so great a cloud of witnesses," etc. From all this we gather that his "coming in the clouds" is unmistakably connected with large bodies of people who will be intensely interested in his coming, through whom and by whom it will undoubtedly be brought about.

There are several passages where it is positively asserted, without symbolism or circumlocution, that Christ will come and do a definite work, and yet no one thinks of attributing a *personal* coming to the language. To the churches of Asia, John was instructed to write the warnings of God against the gross errors and worldliness which were gradually creeping into them and threatening to undermine their faith and vital connection with Christ. These warnings are most explicit, and couched in such terms as these:—

"Repent, and do the first works or else I will come unto thee quickly and will remove thy candlestick out of his place" (Rev. 2-5).

Nearly the same words were addressed to the churches

of Pergamos and Philadelphia; while to the church of Sardis he wrote thus:—

"**If therefore thou shalt not watch I will come on thee as a thief, and thou shalt not know what hour I will come upon thee.**"

After the sounding of the seventh trumpet (1794), and commencing from that point the pouring out of the six vials of wrath (but before the seventh is poured out) John says of Christ:—

"**Behold, I come as a thief. Blessed is he that watcheth and keepeth his garments, lest he walk naked, and they see his shame**" (Rev. 16-15).

There is no shout, no "clouds," nothing to distinguish this last coming from the visitations to the seven churches, yet in point of time it is evidently connected very closely with the "coming in the clouds" in Matt. 24-30.

It is clear enough to us now that this "coming" to the churches of Asia was no personal coming at all, but, rather, that he would come upon them in *judgment* and would wipe them out of existence unless they repented. Furthermore, though the language was so explicit that he would "come quickly," we know as a historical fact that there was not only no personal coming, but that it was more than five hundred years before nearly all of them were finally destroyed by the Saracens whose shibboleth was, "The Koran or the Sword." If there is no personal coming intended in these explicit statements, then we may fairly assume that there is no personal coming intended in the passages quoted at the head of this chapter and similar ones, in the absence of any direct statement to the contrary, with other accessories such as appertain to his final coming to judge the world.

Another consideration lies in the fact that all of God's great moral epochs are of a quiet, unostentatious character, of no great significance to the world at large at the time of their occurrence, but mighty in their results upon the destinies of men as we look at them now from the standpoint of God's word and history. Political epochs of history have always been marked by tumult, revolution, blood and suffering, to a greater or less extent, and will continue to be so marked until the last great battle for supremacy shall result in the extinction of Imperialism and the Papacy before the reign of "peace on earth, good will to men."

Not so is it with the great moral epochs of God-in-Christ's government. The call of Abraham; the founding of the royal line of David for an eternal kingship and kingdom; the advent of Christ as a "root out of dry ground," and the second coming of Christ, the hope of the ages, to take the voluntary offering of the kingdom which the "God of Heaven" has already set up, may all be classed as great moral epochs whose character and advent are marked by quiet, unostentatious, tread, unnoticed by the great mass of the people, but whose results are mighty and far reaching for the good of men.

"*None of the wicked shall understand, but the wise shall understand*" (Dan. 12-10).

We are now prepared to take up the quotation from Daniel, at the head of this chapter. Here we see the same metaphor or symbol "of clouds" used as in the other instances, and He is coming to take "glory and dominion and a kingdom." But who accompany him and bring him before "one of ancient days"? Evidently the people represented by the "clouds." But who gives him the kingdom? This is not so apparent until we have considered for a moment who is meant by "one of ancient days." From the description given in verses 9 and 10 it has been for a long time held by many good and learned expositors that the Almighty is meant. Yet if we look back to the vision of Ezekiel (chap. I) we shall see a striking likeness between the two visions in several particulars.

In the vision of Daniel we see "one of ancient days" seated, evidently, on His throne, with the fiery flame about him and "his *wheels* as burning *fire;* thousand thousands ministered unto him, and ten thousand times ten thousand stood before him." In Ezekiel (verses 26-27) we have the throne

"As the appearance of a sapphire stone, and upon the throne the appearance of A MAN above upon it: and I saw as the color of amber, as the appearance of FIRE round about within it, from the appearance of his loins even upward, and from the appearance of his loins even downwards, I saw as it were the appearance of FIRE, and it had brightness round about."

From the fifteenth verse we have a description of the *wheels* and their peculiar manner of moving. The living creatures are wanting in Daniel's vision for the reason that in Ezekiel's vision they stood as the symbols of Israel, as heretofore shown, but at that time *rebellious* Israel as we learn from chap. 2–3. In Daniel's vision the time is carried forward to the latter days when rebellious Israel has become spiritual Israel and obedient to the Divine will to such an extent that God can work through them to the accomplishment of his purposes respecting the seating of Christ on the throne of his father David, as it is written :

"Thy people offer themselves willingly in the days of thy power, in the beauties of holiness, from the womb of the morning. The Lord at thy right hand hath striken through kings in the day of his wrath. The places are full of dead bodies. He shall strike through the head over a wide land" (Ps. 110-3).

Consequently we find the "living creatures" of Ezekiel reproduced in Daniel, no longer as a symbol but by Israel herself, a great and mighty host, "ten thousand times ten thousand," under the synonym of "one of ancient days" which, in a slightly different form, was a favorite expression of the older prophets when speaking of the early days of Israel's devotion to God. See Isa. 51-9: 44-7: 24-23; Ps. 44-1. There can be no question but that God is the "power behind the throne," but the agent through whom He works in all the ages on this earth is his own beloved Israel under her pet name, "one of ancient days." The scriptures are filled with tender expressions of God's love and tender regard for his "ancient" people.

It is to be remarked that Christ himself does not appear in the vision at all but by the simile of "one *like* a son of man." Neither one nor the other of the Godhead ever appears in person in symbolic prophecy, as we have before shown, so that it is absurd to take this vision of Daniel's as representing a personal coming of Christ "in the clouds of heaven."

Simply stated, then, the vision stands thus: Christ, seated at the right hand of the Father, is induced by the voluntary choice of the people under the special leadings of the Father, to become a candidate for the earthly throne of David, precisely as God was chosen in "ancient days" to be king over Israel. though afterwards rejected for Saul, according to the manner of the nations about them. When thus presented to the people, just as he is being presented to-day, there will be given to him in the near future:

"Dominion. and glory. and a kingdom. that all people. nations. and languages. should serve him: his dominion is an everlasting dominion. which shall not pass away. and his kingdom that which shall not be destroyed."

This harmonises all parts of the vision and agrees perfectly with events which are transpiring to-day in a most remarkable manner, as we pointed out in the last chapter. On which side of the line are you going to be, my brother, when this question is put to you ? Dare you say by your vote, " Away with him ! away with him!" * * * "We will not have this man to rule over us"? As you vote to-day on the question of the cleansing of the land, so the chances are that you will vote on the higher questions of the Sabbath, and Christ in the organic law.

The error of the commonly received interpretation which represents God as having already given Christ his spiritual kingdom at his first advent, is seen in several particulars. It places the giving of the kingdom *before* any of the important events of the vision had begun to transpire, while this presentation to "one like a son of man" is *after* all preceding kingdoms had been cast down, which is just the direction in which events are now moving with sure and swift steps. Again, any kingdom to be acceptable to Christ must be a voluntary offering of loving, obedient, subjects or people, and he will have no other. He was offered a kingdom at his first advent, but it was not the kind he wanted and he refused it.

We have already seen that God, the Judge and Executor, lost the allegiance of the world at the beginning and, consequently, has no spiritual dominion to give, while it is the special province of *Christ* to win the kingdoms to himself and present them to the *Father*, "that God may be all in all." God is at liberty to work by all material and political forces to make Christ's people—already won as individual subjects—"to offer themselves willingly in the day of thy power." All the actual events, as far as they have transpired and seem on the eve of being realised, fit so completely the conditions of the vision throughout, that the conclusion is inevitable for the above interpretation and for no other. There is no sort of appropriateness in styling God the Father as "one of ancient days," since he is a spirit "without beginning of days or end of years," while in respect of Israel the term is exceeding appropriate and warranted by scripture.

This "coming in the clouds of heaven" refers, then, in no instance to a personal coming with natural clouds, but to a spiritual coming to take especial charge of this God-given land and government through his servants, men fearing God, loving righteousness and hating iniquity. It will be a coming so quiet and in the common course of events as to require the utmost watchfulness to perceive its true significance.

Among the causes which have led to wide spread apathy on this subject—although we rejoice to know that vast numbers are giving earnest heed to it—may be mentioned the extravagant calculations which began to be made by Wm. Miller forty-three years ago, and which were continued by others for some years after. The unwarranted and unscriptural accompaniments of those predicted times had a very lively tendency to throw the whole subject into disrepute and contempt. That was indeed a "midnight cry" eminently adapted to rouse the attention of the whole land to the all important theme, and was evidently so intended of God. He sent it forth in just that shape for good and wise reasons, leaving us to detect the fallacies and heed the call. That was more of a "blast of Gabriel's horn" than we will ever hear again, unless this unpretentious book shall serve as a "*last call*" to many.

Another reason is found in the excessive spirit of worldliness which has crept over the Church "as a snare," which has led to the commonly expressed thought, "If we are prepared for death we are prepared for his coming," when the probability is that we are really prepared for neither. The two events have not the remotest connection. Another reason is found in a general expectation of something *marvelous* in connection with the return of the Jews to Palestine, such as a complete topographical and geologic change in that land preparatory thereto. By these and other causes we are likely to cheat ourselves out of a realising sense of the glorious patrimony which our Heavenly Father has provided for us. The prophets of twenty-five centuries ago saw it and were glad. Yet millions of Christians will continue to look for something marvelous in the dim future, so near and yet so far.

"O Zion, that bringest good tidings, get thee up into the high mountain: O Jerusalem, that bringest good tidings, lift up thy voice with strength; lift it up, be not afraid; say unto the cities of Judah, Behold your God" (Isa. 40-9).

"For the government shall be upon his shoulder: and his name shall be called * * * Prince of Peace; of the increase of his government and of peace there shall be no end, upon the throne of David, and upon his kingdom, to order it, and to establish it with judgment and with justice from henceforth even forever. The zeal of the Lord of Hosts will perform this" (Isa. 9-6, 7; see also Jer. 23-3 to 6; Luke 22-29, 30).

"The Lord hath taken away thy judgments, he hath cast out thine enemy: the king of Israel, even the Lord, is in the midst of thee: thou shalt not see evil any more" (Zeph. 3-15).

The joyous festivities of the marriage supper for which the "midnight cry" was uttered, call for *life* not death, and the above quotations and hundreds of others tell the same story. But as we have much more to say on this same line of thought we reserve it for the next chapter on the millennial glory.

CHAPTER XIV.

THE MILLENNIAL GLORY.

"In *that day* there shall be a root of Jesse which shall stand for an ensign of the people: to it shall the Gentiles seek, and his *rest shall be glorious*" (Isa. 11-10).

"And ye shall serve the Lord your God, and he shall bless thy bread and thy water; and I will take sickness away from the midst of thee" (Ex. 23-25).

"And the inhabitant shall not say, I am sick: the people that dwell therein shall be forgiven their iniquity" (Isa. 23-24).

"He will swallow up death in victory; and the Lord God shall wipe away tears from all faces; and the rebuke of his people shall he take away from off all the earth: for the Lord hath spoken it." "And I will rejoice in Jerusalem"—habitations of peace—"and joy in my people: and the voice of weeping shall be no more heard in her, nor the voice of crying" (Isa. 25-8: 65-19; see also Rev. 7-17: 21-14).

'For since the beginning of the world men have not heard, nor perceived by the ear, neither hath the eye seen, O God, beside thee, what he hath prepared for him that waiteth for him" (Isa. 64-4).

"There shall be no more thence an infant of days, nor an old man that hath not filled his days: for the child shall die an hundred years old; but the sinner being a hundred years old shall be accursed." (Isa. 65-20.)

"I will also make thine officers peace and thine exactors righteousness" (Isa. 60-17).

Having by anticipation seated Christ on the throne of David to continue a King forever, it becomes our pleasant privilege to gather from the scriptures some of the beneficent results to be derived from his reign. Happily, God has not left us entirely to faith and imagination respecting the things of the kingdom, but has filled the scriptures to overflowing with portraitures of the mansions of rest which he has prepared for his people in the purified earthly kingdom. On the other hand, nothing at all has been said of Heaven, save an occasional reference to it as a place of holy angels and perfect bliss. Certainly no symbol could illustrate it, and no language could intelligibly portray it.

Paul had a look into it and heard unutterable things which he says it was "not possible for a man to utter," and we are satisfied to let it alone, since the Father has revealed nothing definite respecting it. If we can live to see the installation of the glorious reign of Christ on earth, and witness but the *commencement* of the wonderful things which are written concerning the "place of their own" from which Israel shall "move no more," we shall certainly think that Heaven has begun here below and say, " Lord, now lettest thou thy servant depart in peace, for mine eyes have seen thy salvation, which thou hast prepared before the face of all people" (Luke 2-30).

Hitherto the world has been filled with misery and woe growing out of wars, oppression and bloodshed, as the result of man's willful disobedience and constant refusal to submit himself to rightful authority, and, believing himself able to remedy all evils by offering to God sacrifices of his own choosing, he has gone about seeking his own pleasure in his own way rather than in God's way. Not only did man find unhappiness, sorrow, and death, as the result of his willful and wicked course, but the good old age of the patriarchs, reaching to nearly a thousand years, was gradually reduced until God stayed the unnatural and premature decay and limited man's life in its downward tendency to three score years and ten; otherwise, I doubt if there would have been any left to-day to tell the tale of man's fall.

With man's reduced physical powers from those of a giant to almost a dwarf; with his intellectual powers, capable of grappling with the mightiest problems of physical science, darkened and contracted to a minimum ; with all his instincts and appetites brutalised, how could it be otherwise but that the seeds of disease should bring a full harvest of all kinds of sickness, and that tears, not joy, should reign through the ages.

To save the race of men from utter annihilation and lift them to a higher plane of living, God removed Abraham from among his kindred of Mesopotamia into Canaan, whence we have followed his descendants, in previous chapters, until one of their number, God-born, is seated on the throne. The command had already gone forth for the cleansing of the land of all those who had caused the people to stumble and of all that did iniquity, and now, at his coming or just before it, the judgment had been given for law to take its course among the wicked and incorrigible, which results in a "survival of the fittest." They had laid themselves open to pestilence by their corrupt lives, and now, obstinate to the last, they are swept away as with the besom of destruction, and their record is left to "point a moral or adorn a tale." Let us by anticipation stand in that day, now but a few years away, and note just a few of the results.

A race of people fittest to live are in possession of the land after its cleansing. Not all are saints by any means, as the usual hypothesis of the new heavens and the new earth necessitates, but they are Christian men and women whose faith has lifted them above the waves, and enabled them to ride the storm into calm waters. Others are there who, by Christian education and the prayers of Christian parents, had kept themselves free from the grosser sins, and in whom a conviction of the terrible nature of sin has been produced by the solemn scenes through which they have passed, and they are now ready to lay themselves and their all upon the altar and enter the service of the King. Wonderful outpourings of the Spirit have been witnessed during the process of cleansing the land, and the Church has been quickened into a new life, so that it is not difficult now to hear the voice of the Spirit, saying, "This is the way, walk ye in it."

The smiles of Heaven and the benediction of the Father, and of the Son, and of the Holy Spirit, are upon all those who have come through the fiery ordeal, blood washed and cleansed, or prepared for cleansing, in the "fountain opened to the house of David and to the inhabitants of Jerusalem for sin and uncleanness." Is it to be wondered at, then, that Christians have clearer views of God's protecting care of his people, or that their faith and trust are greatly strengthened, and that they have come into closer relations with Him whom their souls love, and that there comes into the soul such experiences of nearness and hiding in Him, that they realise now as never before that "his rest is glorious?"

A different atmosphere is about them on every side. The themes of Christ and his kingdom are now the subjects of conversation rather than the gossip of society, or about the last play at the theater, or the last prima donna at the opera. The sublime prophecies of God's Word, which have found such wonderful fulfillment in their day, illustrating God's loving care through all the centuries, excite in them the deepest love and reverence, and become without effort the topic of every gathering by the wayside, in the home, and at the public assembly. All are eager to learn of some larger experience, some deeper insight into the hidden mysteries of God's love as revealed in Christ. None is unwilling now to talk with the unconverted, or to plead with them to yield at once to the blessed invitation, but each will vie with the other in hastening to tell the glad story of a Saviour's love, and " *all* thy children shall be taught of the Lord."

There is little need of detailing to any extent the happy results which will flow, from the very commencement of the reign of righteousness on the earth. The scriptures are filled to overflowing with the blessed pictures of joy, peace, and happiness, which cluster around this objective point of all revelation—the taking of the kingdom by the Son of David. We may be sure that a different moral atmosphere will prevail throughout the land. No more shall we hear of the dastardly attack, or the vile intrigue for entrapping the unsuspecting and the innocent, "for there shall nothing hurt nor destroy in all my holy mountain." The voice of cursing will no more be heard in the streets. The hot words, the angry blow and the deadly bullet, will be things of the past "because the accuser of our brethren is cast down," and the saloon, his greatest earthly agency, is relegated to hell from whence it came. What a history it will be when written out! What loathing of sin and of all that pertains to the service of Satan, by whose inspiration and agency the horrible work of the past has been wrought out!

But why repeat the story which everyone's memory will be able to supply of this terrible nightmare of war and raids on defenceless villages; of murders and robberies; of cruel desertions and suicides, and the almost innumerable crimes with which the daily papers all over the country are now filled?

It is not worth the while to stop and show the utter fallacy of the theories which have heretofore been broached by pious, acute, and learned men, respecting the "new heavens and the new earth" and the reign of righteousness without temptation, that is promised to follow. It has been, perhaps, not their fault that they saw no clearer the secrets of revelation, for, doubtless, God "hid these things from the wise and prudent that he might reveal them unto babes." They did the best they could and that was all God wanted, and just what he wanted through all the ages, and it was for just such results that the predictions were put in the enigmatic or symbolic form.

Our fault will be if we continue to take these blind efforts for a *conclusion*, and refuse to accept a plain, common sense solution which fills *all* the required conditions of prophetic record. We propose, therefore, to show from *present* developments of the grace of Christ, that all the requirements contained in the scripture quotations at the head of this chapter, with all others not quoted and pertaining to this subject are, *even now*, an accomplished fact, or in easy process of fulfillment. Glory be to the name of Jesus! If we can show that these things are *commenced* in any small degree, we have God's authority and mode of speaking for saying the thing *is done.* Please remember that. If it is true now, some years before Christ actually takes the throne, what may we not expect when that happy event transpires.

Before entering directly on the subject proposed, let me say that all of God's relations with this world in its physical and moral advancement have ever been on the progressive plan of gradual development, and we have not the shadow of proof that He will not continue on the same plan for ages upon ages to come. No one now believes that this world was made in six literal days, but that it was in process of development through countless ages. In fact, we now see that the Bible itself shows the same fact, and states three things only to have been an actual creation, viz., matter, life, and man. Matter and life were in their lowest original forms, and the world and everything in it were wrought out from these by the law of development, or evolution, if you please, to their present form and conditions, save man, who was unique in his creation, being made in the image and likeness of the three persons of the Godhead, and placed upon the earth, when it was fitted for him, as the last crowning act of creation.

There is nothing generally irruptive and sudden in the whole development of creation; only in the finality of a world may we make a possible exception. What is true in the physical world is true also in the moral world, as we have abundant reason to know. We may rest assured, then, that the present order of natural and moral law will be observed throughout. Any victories gained over sin and natural propensities, over Satan and his works, over bodily infirmities and disease, over reduced vitality in the ages of men and even over the terrors of death, will be wholly and unmistakably by the faith of the Lord Jesus, on this present plane of conditions.

"**And this is the victory that overcometh the world, even our faith**" (**John 5-4**).

No Christian man or woman will deny that lack of faith is the great and essential need of the Church to-day, for we hear continually this prayer, "O Lord, increase our faith." How often are we met by requests for prayer for those who have lost their faith. often coming from the persons themselves, while thousands have made shipwreck of their faith and have gone back to the world. Well may we ask, what is the cause of this, and where lies the difficulty?

In great measure. doubtless, this state of thing has grown out of the teachings of the Church herself, strange as it may appear. So much stress has been laid upon works as a necessary adjunct of faith, that it has grown almost into an axiom, "If you want anything done, go and *do it.* If you wish your prayer answered, answer it *yourself.*" Is a church in need of a pastor, a committee is chosen to canvass the country and the candidates, and on their own judgment a " call" is given, and almost superhuman exertions are immediately commenced to accomplish the desired purpose. Does the church need funds for any enterprise of mission work, immediately a Fair is called for with all its concomitants of a post-office, a fish pond, a grab-bag, and, perhaps, a lottery out and out; or a cake, sugared over with frosting and a ring inside, for which shares are sold in the interest of the pastor or some favorite elder or deacon.

Is anyone sick among you, let him send for — the elders? Oh, no; that would be the heighth of presumption and the man might die. Send for the physician; that is help that can be seen and felt. The maxims of the world have also been largely adopted by Christians, which seem to have wrought a complete change in the simplicity of the "faith once delivered to the saints" to such an extent that little is left in the Church, save in one's own exertions, by which to overcome the world.

Now, in these closing hours of this sixth age of the world, God is bringing back the old-time faith in such men as George Muller, Dr. Cullis, D. L. Moody, William Quarrier of Glasgow, and a host of others who have determined to take God at his word and stand out upon his promise, come life or come death. As a result of this confidence, God is answering their prayers in a most remarkable manner and giving all needed funds for great benevolent work, health and strength to the sick and diseased. souls to those who are searching for them, and to all who thus trust Him such a divine influx of joy and love and forgetfulness of self as baffles all description.

Christians are being led to realise as never before that the past of their lives has been spent in wanderings in the wilderness of Sinai, and that they have never yet entered into the promised land of rest, but are hoping for that good time in the dim future "on the other side of Jordan." But many are beginning to realise that the real Jordan, as well as the Red Sea, exist in the midst of this present plane of conditions, and *not* at the *close* of life; that the land of promise is just before each one and may be entered by faith at any time when we are ready to cut away from our visible "base of supplies" and enter the enemies' country to clean them out, root and branch, with a promise and a "ram's horn."

No more than with Israel of old is it a folding of hands in the enjoyment of God-given homes and vineyards and fruitful fields, for as they of the olden time did some of their hardest fighting after they entered the land of rest, so modern Israel of the "advance guard" have their conflicts and struggles with Satan and his hosts. But the victory is an easy one now, because they overcome "by the blood of the Lamb and by the word of their testimony." By unmistakable signs God is calling his people to a higher plane of living than ever before, and demanding of us a complete consecration of self and all that we have to his service. "He that seeketh to save his life shall lose it, but he that will lose his life for my sake shall find it."

The number of those who are thus willing to step out on the promises of God and cut loose from all that binds them to the world, is becoming more and more numerous every day, and, as the years roll on, the number will be swelled to "an innumerable company which no man could number." This movement of "Holiness unto the Lord" is of the Spirit, preparatory to the time of trial that is certainly coming upon the earth to "try every man's work of what sort it is." If, hereafter, "holiness unto the Lord" is to "be written upon the bells of the horses," we must certainly begin by writing it upon our own hearts and lives.

Let us rejoice that the dawning of a better day is at hand. Already the chariot wheels of the Almighty are faintly heard speeding over the plain for the "manifestation of the sons of God." A shaking among the "dry bones" of the valley is heard; the faint rumblings of the "first resurrection" are in the air; the graves of those old martyrs for the truth, those who counted not their lives dear to them for the testimony of Jesus, *and those only*, are beginning to crackle under the mighty impending voice of the Son of God when he shall cry with a loud voice, " Elijah, Daniel, Jeremiah. Paul, Peter, John, and the rest of the martyrs, *come forth!* Enter into my people and revive in them the old-time faith that would brave a kingdom; enter the lion's den; endure indignities, and go to a martyr's doom in defence of the truth;

go to the mouth of the fiery furnace, yea, *into* it for the testimony of Jesus."

This is the faith we want, and this is the faith we are to have by the first resurrection, for which Christ himself has given us the key of interpretation in that memorable conversation with his disciples respecting the mission of John, and the general expectation of Elijah to precede the coming of Messiah. Speaking of John, Christ says, "And if ye can receive it, this is *Elijah* that was for to come." In the Apocalypse, John says. "I saw the *souls* of them that were beheaded" (or had the martyr's crown) "for the witness of Jesus and they" —*and none other*—"lived and reigned with Christ," etc. "This is the first resurrection." No bodies are seen, and no intimation that they walk the earth in their proper person, so that we are forced to the conclusion that if Christ's reign is a spiritual one in and through his people, this resurrection must be a spiritual one also. To this the Spirit gives most hearty assent.

Who shall tell me, then, that these commanding figures in the line of faith in these days, are not in themselves the impersonation of the old heroes, as John was of Elijah? "If ye can receive it," yes, "if ye can receive it," they are the pioneers of a great company yet to come at the crowning of the King. God speed that day, and to Christ be all the glory, now and forever. The premonitory symptoms of such a revival may be gathered not only from these pioneers of a living faith, but in the wonderful increase in late years of the number of Christ's followers. In the four years preceding the census of 1880 the net gain over losses by death, discipline and other causes, was 1,631,799, or more than four hundred thousand each year, while the increase in churches has been more than ten for every working day of ten hours for the whole four years. The increase in ordained ministers has been in the same time nearly ten thousand, to say nothing of the army of evangelists and Christian workers who have gone into the "fields already white unto harvest." The late movement among the students of the land is most surprising, for quite two thousand of them stand pledged to the mission fields in foreign lands. "For the law shall go forth from Mount Zion, and the word of the Lord from Jerusalem."

" I will take sickness away from the midst of thee " is our second quotation; and for this assurance we have the promise of the Omnipotent God which cannot fail. Has this promise been, hitherto, fulfilled? Has there been any time in the world's history when we can say it has been realised? Of course not. There it still remains to be fulfilled in all its fullness in the near future, for the gentle steppings of the Spirit are *even now* felt in the hearts of many who are taking God at his word, and claiming relief from bodily infirmities and sicknesses far beyond the skill of earthly physicians. That the promise is not run out is fully established by Christ's own assurances. If we want proof as to the *time* when it should begin to be fulfilled, we have it in the words communicated to John (Rev. 22-2) as the peculiar heritage of spiritual Israel, or the Church in the new dispensation : "*The leaves of the tree shall be for the healing of the nation.*" Do you say this finds its fulfillment in the gospel of Christ working in the heart and life of his followers and gradually overcoming sin, the cause of disease ? It does more than this, for it gives promise of the life that *now is*, as well as of that which is to come.

The cause of all the trouble in Eden was that the woman believed the assurances of Satan rather than the word of God, and every child born into the world since that day has re-enacted the same scene, and with the same identical results. It is for *us* to "bruise the serpent's head" when by the faith of Christ, or *Christ's faith in us*, we shall implicitly step out on the promises of God and "*ask* that ye may *receive*, that your joy may be full." The only conditions imposed are these:

"If ye abide in me and my words abide in you, ye shall ask what ye will and it shall be done for you."

If the reader is looking for a happy time *here or hereafter*, when Satan shall be *bound* and cease his troubling, he will be most woefully mistaken.[1] The scriptures teach no such doctrine. The *wicked* may "cease from troubling," but Satan *never*, unless you have learned to hate all his works and tread him under your feet here in the flesh by the power of love in Christ Jesus.

---

[1] Rom. 8-14; Job 1-6; Cor. 11-14.

"For we know that the whole creation groaneth and travaileth in pain until now * * * waiting for the manifestation of the sons of God, and the adoption, to wit, the redemption of our body into the glorious **LIBERTY** of the sons of God" (Rom. 8-22, 19, 23).

Now, if we can truly say, "The law of the spirit of life in Christ Jesus hath made us *free* from the law of sin and death, then we are taken out of the clutches of the law of sin which worketh disease and death, into freedom and heirship, yea, and even *kingship* with Christ, for it is written:—

"Thou hast made us unto our God kings and priests; and we shall reign on the earth" (Rev. 5-10).
"And I appoint unto YOU a kingdom, as my Father hath appointed unto ME. that ye may eat and drink at my table in my kingdom, and sit on thrones judging the twelve tribes of Israel" (Lu. 22-29, 30).

This is in perfect harmony with Christ's declaration, which very properly introduces our third topic: "He that keepeth my sayings shall *never see death.*" Of the truth of this there are numerous examples in these days. In the days to come they will be wonderfully increased as disciples come into the full liberty of the Gospel. Death will become like a gentle sleep, so peaceful and quiet, without an anxious thought, even among those who before have had great fear of death, without a sigh for earth, but a glorious expectancy of stepping over the line into sweet companionship and eternal bliss "with Him whom my soul loveth." "Death is swallowed up in victory: O Grave, where is thy sting! O Death, where is thy victory!" And if we have such victory *even now*, what shall it be in the years and ages to come, after Christ has begun to reign.

Nor is it difficult to imagine, with such power over sin, disease and the grave; with the reign of "peace on earth, good will unto men"; with the land weeded of the incorrigible foes of Christ—atheists, infidels, socialists, nihilists, and the like—that the cause of all trouble departs. Sorrow and sighing shall flee away and tears, save tears of joy, "shall be wiped away from off all faces." This is become literally true in thousands of cases to-day, giving glorious promise of what shall be when the kingdom shall be given into the hands of the Son. "For it doth not yet appear what we shall be, but we know that when He shall appear we shall be like him"—if we have cultivated his spirit of love and forgiveness—"for we shall see him as he is." We shall understand, as never before, what redemption means, and see ourselves reflected in his image, being transfigured into his likeness,[1] to whom be glory forever.

Neither will we have to strain our eyes to get a foreglimpse of the vast treasure house of material blessings in store for God's people in the ages to come, standing as we do on its very threshold and hardly able as yet to look beyond the vestibule; but we can see enough to excite the wildest hopes. What secrets of wonderful power and magnificence Nature shall yet be forced to disclose in the years to come, no mortal may as yet

---
[1] 1 Jno. 3-2.

know. Enough is known already, above all conceptions of the past, that we may rest assured the prophet was right and saw marvelous sights when he wrote:

"**Since the beginning of the world men have not heard, nor perceived by the ear, neither hath the eye seen. O God, beside thee, what he hath prepared for him that waiteth for him.**"

The experience of eminent scientists shows that there is no known limit to the possibilities which are open to inventive genius. Experience shows that the progress of discovery becomes more and more rapid as it advances. Each discovery reveals some new truth which prepares the way for another step in advance. Often, indeed, the investigation of an apparently insignificant matter will lead to very great results by removing some obstacle which has blocked previous progress. Dr. Werner Siemens has pointed out in a recent lecture in Berlin, how all these developments of science will tend to bring many things within the reach of all classes, which have until now been enjoyed by the rich only; that shorter hours of labor will be the rule, and a more even distribution of the comforts of life, as well as of the profits of labor.

A glorious prospect thus opens for the development of God's bounties out of this grand storehouse of his, kept intact for so many generations. We have come to take these things so naturally and in the course of events, tkat we have no realising sense of the blessings we enjoy, even in the peace and security of the land, with complete freedom to come and to go, anywhere, everywhere, with none to molest or to make us afraid. Carriages are ready at all hours of the day for the humblest citizen, in all the cities of the land. at the merest trifle of cost. For long distances that formerly would have taken many weary months to travel. the swift railroad car with its luxurious apartments "fit for a king," is within reach of all. if necessity calls, bringing us to our destination in a most rapid manner.

If we desire to walk or to ride in our own conveyance, the land is free from ravenous beasts and reptiles, because it is written. "No lion shall be there, nor any ravenous beast." How different is this from most other countries. I think I have already stated that more than twenty-five thousand people are destroyed annually in India, the greater part being by poisonous serpents. Yet a little while and the land will be cleansed of ravenous human beasts, so that "*nothing* shall hurt or destroy in all my holy mountains, saith the Lord."

Our tables are supplied with the delicacies of this and every other land and within the reach of all. but for the foul curse of drink. It has been said by foreigners that we waste enough to support a European population equal to our own. What a comment on the prodigality of our resources! We should be surprised beyond measure to know the details of the daily living of the world outside of Israel. But the comforts of this God-given land of spiritual Israel surpass everything conceived of in Christ's time, save by inspiration, yet how little we realise the extent of our blessings, even now.

In the furnishing of our houses it is the same, and luxuriousness prevails to an extent that could not have been dreamed of in the wildest flights of the imagination. With the cheapening of every kind of embellishment necessary to an elegant appearance in the home, the wage of labor has increased fifteen fold, so that these things are within easy reach of every industrious and frugal man. But how many there are who, as boys, started from the lowest walks of life, without influence or friends, born perhaps across the water in a foreign land, have risen so rapidly in wealth and position as to become merchant princes, and to enjoy palaces beyond the ability of the mightiest monarchs of olden time. Not because they may have more money, for that cannot be said, but because the products of this age are beyond those of any other age of the world.

The message of a President is flashed across the continent and reaches its destination hours—by the clock—before it is delivered, though it be taken from his lips as he reads it. It is cabled under the ocean to Europe, printed and commented upon, cabled back again, and the comments are in the papers of the principal cities of our own land the next morning. Men sit in their offices and call a friend fifty or a hundred miles away, or in a factory but a few miles away, with whom they wish to converse on matters of business or pleasure, and immediately they are in communication with him.

Our newspapers come to us in rain or shine, filled with news from every quarter of the civilised globe, and the poor man would think himself undergoing great privation if he could not look at the daily paper, though it be filled, all too often, with details of bloodshed and oppression. How long will it be ere these swift messengers of a world's development shall contain only cheering news of Christ's onward march to victory? The glad harbinger of a better day is already dawning. The Sun of Righteousness is now tipping the "high mountain" of the Lord with shimmerings of golden light, and "with healing in his beams." "Even so, Lord Jesus, come quickly."

With a cleansing of the land and a survival of those best fitted to live; with the Sabbath a delightsome day and his courts a pleasure; with a people fearing God. loving righteousness and walking as little children free from carking cares. doubts. and fears: with the leaves of the tree of life for the healing of the nations. what wonder that men are speedily regaining lost vitality and age. and rapidly coming to the time when "the child dying shall be an hundred years old: but the sinner being an hundred years old shall be accursed." As it is now, with all the elements of evil about us and antecedent to us; with the terribly depleting effects of modern drinking habits upon us, and the disastrous effects of the crowded and sin-laden condition of all large cities. the average of human life is said to have advanced nineteen years in the last one hundred, where Life Insurance statistics have been kept. These companies in England are beginning to make a distinction in rates for those who are considered "first-class," and a corresponding advance for those who are considered as "second-class" by reason of loose habits of life. When such classification is completed in Europe and this country, I think the average of life with the better class will be found so far in advance of the sinners as to astonish us.

The gospel is not yet doing its best for men because we have not yet learned to cast our burdens on the Lord, and to be "anxious for nothing; but *in everything*, by prayer and supplications, with thanksgiving, make known your requests unto God." Care, anxiety, and *overfeeding*, make terrible inroads on our vitality, and not until we can fully understand the "liberty wherewith Christ shall make us free," can we reap its full benefits. Thus we can readily perceive an easy and natural solution respecting the returning age of men which can be had in no other way; and this is the only interpretation that commends itself to sanctified common sense.

This passage has always been a great stumbling-block to the ordinary pre-millennial theory, and any amount of ingenious conjecture has been expended in its solution, but all to no purpose; for how the sinners were to survive the general conflagration, and sneak past the first resurrection into the abode of the saints, has been a problem past finding out. The interpretation here given under the teaching of the Spirit, is the only reasonable one that can be given to it, namely, that the victories of Christ are to be won on this present plane of conditions and in present spheres of action. With present agencies intensified and enlarged under the operation of the Spirit, we shall yet find that sinners, while yielding themselves to the outward observances of religion and good morals, though withholding the inner service of the heart, will reap all the physical benefits of pious, ancestral, parentage, and their own moral lives. If they resist all the beneficent influences of the Spirit and godly surroundings until death comes at the age of one hundred, their condition will certainly be "accursed."

It is a very simple conclusion from the premises; if man lost his strength of body and mind by reason of sin, then, certainly, a life of righteousness ought to have its beneficent effects and produce constantly increasing years, with corresponding joy in life, happiness in the bounties of heaven, and such nearness of access to the Father and communion with the Lord Jesus, as to make a very heaven upon earth. To this view the scriptures throughout agree, and to no other. Hundreds of passages could be cited which fall into this line of thought as naturally as the air we breathe. Instead of being interpreted with a spiritual meaning and pertaining to a celestial life beyond the grave, or even upon a renewed earth, they are to be taken in all their literalness to the fullest extent, which should certainly have the effect of producing in the heart of the believer the liveliest enthusiasm and intense interest in the "things of the kingdom," as an offset to the cares and perplexities of the material life offered to us by the god of this world. This was God's intention in giving these portraitures of the coming kingdom, but how sadly have we failed to perceive their true meaning and have even gone so far, as some are doing, as to cast aside the Old Testament scriptures as pertaining to a past age and people with which we have nothing special to do. Let us not thus throw away the richest part of our inheritance, but rejoice in it as a free gift of God for countless ages to come.

CHAPTER XV.

THE HEAVENLY JERUSALEM.

"And he carried me away in the spirit to a great and high mountain and showed me that great city, the holy Jerusalem, descending out of heaven from God, having the glory of God; and her light was like unto a stone most precious, even like a jasper stone, clear as crystal" (Rev. 21-11).

It is probably seen by this time that we have very little faith in any interpretation which makes the last three chapters of the Apocalypse to portray the end of the world, the general judgment, and the heavenly estate on a renewed earth. Nor have we faith in any interpretation which calls for a literal reading of any part of these chapters where a symbolic rendering can make sense. The verse which we have quoted above is another very strong proof of the symbolic character of the whole chapter. As a *literal* reading there is neither sense nor reason in it, while as a sybolism it is in the highest degree both reason and sense. Let us try it first as a literal reading.

John is carried in spirit, or imagination, to a great and high mountain to see the descent of a city, complete with walls, streets, and mansions, capable of containing *all* the nations of the redeemed. The whole city is adorned with the most precious stones in the *foundations* of the walls, the wall itself being of jasper *fifteen hundred miles* on each side. The gates of this immense city, three on each side, are each of one single pearl, while the city itself, with its palaces and mansions of rest and all the streets, is of pure gold. There is no night in this celestial city, and no need of the sun nor of the moon ; consequently it could not be on this earth, for so long as this earth contains the same essential elements as at present, the presumption is it will stand in very nearly the same relation to the sun and moon as at present.

John says he saw this immense city descending out of heaven upon the earth. If this huge city was in right earnest descending out of heaven, where was the necessity of his being taken to a high mountain to see it ? One place would be as a good as another. But why continue this most rediculous supposition? The whole story as an actual occurrence is as senseless as the story of Aladdin's Lamp. Yet we once heard an intelligent Christian lawyer attempt to calculate in round numbers the value of such a city.

If, on the other hand, we take the verse as a symbolism—as the entire character of the book warrants us in doing—we are able to determine at once from other parts of scripture, the value of each symbol and get an intelligible idea from it. We have had occasion to observe before that a mountain, as a symbol, is intended to mean a prominent nation or kingdom. The only apparent deviation from this well established value was in the case of the frequent use of the term "high mountain" as an actual designation of the place where God intended to found a great nation and kingdom, and to that "high mountain"[1] John was very probably taken, as will more fully appear as we proceed.

The very general equivalent of a symbolic city as given by the best expositors, is a church, and a "great city" would indicate a very large body of worshippers; so that we have here the very sensible idea of a very great nation or kingdom in which the Christian Church is to be an all important and essential element as an institution. Its descent out of heaven would indicate that the holiness and purity of Heaven were becoming an essential feature of its earthly condition to such an

[1] See chap. 6.

extent that the most precious stones are needed to convey an adequate idea of its glory.

It is quite unfortunate for us that we have lost the language of colors as represented in gems, and thus we lose the important lessons to be gained by this very unique description of the new Jerusalem. This language of gems was well understood by the ancients, and fairly preserved to us down to the Middle Ages, when we gradually lost the meaning of the colors so conspicuously and tenaciously emblazoned on crests, shields, and heraldic devices in the old world. In cathedral windows we still see our Lord and the Apostles clothed with garments of conventional color, significant of individual character. But what that character is we can only judge by what we know of each individual person, which at best would be only a guess for all the light the artists themselves could give us in regard to their own work. Yet they continue in the same old routine to paint as did their masters of the olden time.

We can, however, gather enough from ancient writers to know that all the colors of light were to them expressive of spiritual truths. The Israelites certainly knew the value of these renderings of light in the gemmed breastplate of the High Priest. Even the forms, sizes, arrangement and adornment of every part of the Tabernacle and the Temple were to them emblems of truths, and spake with intelligence to them. In Huck's translation of the Chinese records of Christianity we read of religion being conveyed in the *blue* chariot, and its doctrine being a *blue* cloud because it is truth from heaven. We read also of the *vermilion* palace and the adornments of all colors. The Brahmins associated the days of the week by colors, with Divine qualities. Thus, Sunday is pure sunlight; Monday is moonday, since its reflection is white and indicative of purity; Tuesday is represented by the flame-colored coral, or love and hope in action; Wednesday is emerald, kindliness and accommodation; Thursday, the topaz, holy knowledge; Friday, the diamond, light embodied in teachable truths; Saturday, the sapphire, truth, slow and sure. "The seven precious things honored by Buddhists in China and elsewhere are gems or other substances of various colors. These are used to express virtues, and are accordingly found in the tombs of Buddhist notables in India.[1]

From these slight evidences it must be apparent to any one that the adornments of the Heavenly Jerusalem were expressive to Orientals of spiritual beauty and truth pertaining to the Church of God in the new dispensation; not by any means a description of any real city in Heaven or on the earth. This view is corroborated by what follows:

"And I saw no temple therein; for the Lord God Almighty and the Lamb are the temple of it. And the nations of them which are saved shall walk in the light of it, and the kings of the earth do bring their glory and honor into it" (Vers. 22, 24).

---

[1] Mythology of India.

From this last verse it is very evident that God and the Lamb are not in any literal sense the temple, but the persons worshiped. The worshipers themselves are the temple, as we gather from other parts of scripture not symbolic. Thus the Apostle writes under direction of the Spirit:

"**Know ye not that YE are the temple of God, and that the Spirit of God dwelleth in you?**" (1 Cor. 3-16).
"**What! know ye not that your body is the temple of the Holy Ghost which is in you, which ye have of God, and ye are not your own?**" (1 Cor. 6-19).

Here we have the body of every true believer to be the temple of God, and the inner sanctuary of the heart —the seat of the affections and will—as the true home of the invisible presence of the Lamb of God. How beautiful, and in perfect harmony with all scripture, is this plain view of our theme. To this Church of God on earth in this God-given land of Israel, all eyes are turned in all quarters of the globe. "The nations of them which are saved (will) walk in the light of it; and the kings of the earth (will) bring their glory and honor into it." They will then have learned to rule in the fear of God, after beholding the doom of those kings who presumed to rule in a manner displeasing to Him, and contrary to the best interests of their subjects. If the nations *now*, under the quiet, enlightening, upheaving, influences of this God-given Republic, are getting clearer perceptions of the wrongs of ages in connection with the "divine rights of kings," think you not after the last great battle they will have still clearer perceptions of the source of their awakened energies and quickened convictions? Most assuredly they will, for God himself has said respecting this very conflict:

"**Thus will I magnify myself, and sanctify myself; and I will be known in the eyes of many nations, and they shall know that I am the Lord**" (Eze. 38-23).

More especially will all this be true in respect to the relations which will hereafter exist between the State and the Church. The one sad relic of Imperialism and the Papacy is the union of these two, to the great damage of the Church and hindrance of the truth. To the astonishment of the world we have severed forever this connection, and the unprecedented growth of the Church in this country gives unmistakable evidence of God's superintending care. There is then "no more need of the sun nor of the moon" (symbols of rulers and mighty kings) "to shine in it, for the glory of God *doth* (now) lighten it, and the Lamb *is* (*now*) the light thereof" (ver. 23). Nor will it take long for the nations of the Old World to learn the lesson and follow our example when the churches themselves have become imbued with the spirit of Christ, and then most truly can it be said "they walk in the light of it."

On any other hypothesis than the above there is neither sense nor reason in respect of this much abused text. But with the one here advanced under the teaching of the Spirit, all scripture falls into line in its appointed place. adding new beauty and luster with each new accession. until the whole chapter is surrounded with a halo of glory equal to the very highest flight of the prophet's art of delineation.

"In THAT DAY shall the branch [1] of the Lord be beautiful and glorious, and the fruit of the earth shall be excellent and comely for them that are escaped of Israel. For though thy people Israel be as the sand of the sea. ONLY A REMNANT shall return: a consumption is decreed, OVERFLOWING with righteousness" (Isa. 4-2; 10-22).

We have seen in a previous chapter how literally these verses have found their fulfillment in the return of spiritual Israel to her God-appointed land. while several passages show clearly that Israel is to be preferred before Judah in the distribution of blessings, both spiritual and material, and will be the medium by which Judah shall come to know the truth as it is in Christ. God speed the day which is even now dawning upon us![2] By all that has transpired we have an assurance that all the promises respecting the reign of righteousness on the earth, will be fulfilled without the intervention of a burning world or a judgment day other than the natural and self-courted judgment which every sin-

---

[1] The "topmost branch of the high cedar"?

[2] A wonderful movement seems at present to be going on among European Jews, in a readiness to read the New Testament without strong prejudice. A second edition of 120,000 copies, printed in Vienna, was recently sent to England for distribution. 100,000 of which were paid for by one wealthy Scotchman. An eminent

ner lays himself liable to when he deliberately enters the service of Satan.

A glorious prospect is opened to us for continued and doubly energised activity in the service of our blessed Lord, while the Holy Spirit is being given in large and ever larger and more abounding measure as the years roll on, "until every knee shall bow and every tongue confess to the glory of God the Father." A great victory will be gained for Christ, when even the "wrath of man shall praise him," when the tables shall be so completely turned upon Satan that even his profoundest scheme for the destruction of Christ's kingdom shall have proved a very means of aiding that kingdom, by cultivating such a reverence for his name and person, that the Holy Spirit will find the easiest converts of the future among the Catholics of this land and of the world. "Thy kingdom come *on earth*, O Lord, thy will be done."

The whole creation groaneth and is waiting for this manifestation of the sons of God, and for the restitution of all things to original purity and happiness; for the time when men, redeemed by the precious blood of Christ, shall walk with God in Eden restored, in the

---

Hungarian Rabbi, Dr. J. Lichtenstein, has greatly surprised his co-religionists by publishing, recently, two very able tracts affirming the divinity of Jesus, though still remaining obedient to the Mosaic dispensation. Jews in many places of Asiatic Turkey, as well as in Russia and Poland, are extremely desirous, privately, to know more about the Messiah.

consciousness of a complete victory over sin; a re-investment of kingly dignity over the creation of God; a reinstatement into physical and intellectual vigor and an uninterrupted intercourse

"*With beings wrought of finer mold than we.*"

With a clearer vision we shall be able, like Jacob, to see "angels ascending and descending" on the heavenly ladder, and this earth will be to us indeed "the Holy City, the New Jerusalem, prepared as a bride adorned for her husband." Thanks be to God, we have not to wait for a definite time in the dim future for the appearance of this golden city. To some it has already appeared, and they are walking its golden streets and resting in its blissful mansions. Each night its gates are closed upon them for quiet, peaceful slumbers. Each morning its gates of pearl are swung open by angelic porters, and heavenly music fills the air while praise is on the lips. Few, comparatively, are the inhabitants of this great city at the present, but these rejoice in the assurance of increased numbers day by day; quickened movements in the direction of "the kingdom" when "judgments in the earth" lead men to seek a "covert from the storm," and a "*boom*" when the Son of David takes the throne. The Spirit and the Bride say, come into the city *now* and take your choice of its mansions of rest. And let him that heareth this invitation re-echo the voice and say, " Come : and whosoever will, let him come and drink of the water of life freely."

CHAPTER XVI.

THE RELEASE OF THE DRAGON, AND THE PERSONAL COMING OF CHRIST.

"And when the thousand years are expired, Satan shall be loosed out of his prison, and shall go out to deceive the nations which are in the four quarters of the earth, Gog and Magog, to gather them together to battle; the number of whom is as the sand of the sea: And they went up on the breadth of the earth, and compassed the camp of the saints about, and the beloved city; and fire came down from God out of heaven and devoured them" (Rev. 20-7, 8, 9).

"For the Lord *himself* shall descend from heaven with a shout with the voice of the archangel and with the trump of God; and the dead in Christ shall rise first: then we which are alive and remain shall be caught up together with him in the clouds, to meet the Lord in the air; and so shall we ever be with the Lord" (2 Thess. 4-16, 17).

"We shall not all sleep, but we shall all be changed in the twinkling of an eye, at the last trump: for the trumpet shall sound, and the *dead* shall be raised incorruptible, and we shall be changed" (1 Cor. 15-51, 52).

"But the heavens and the earth which are now, by the same word are kept in store reserved unto *fire* against the day of judgment and perdition of ungodly men. But the day of the Lord will come as a thief in the night; in the which the heavens shall pass away with a great noise, and the elements shall melt with fervent heat, the earth also and the works that are therein shall be *burned up*" (2 Peter. 3-7, 10).

We have connected these symbolic verses of Revelation with those of direct prophecy from the epistles of Paul and Peter because they *seem* to be connected by the one judgment of *fire*, which is the peculiar feature of the last judgment, the resurrection, and the personal appearing of our Lord. They seem also to stand in chronological order, though not by any means necessarily synchronous events but rather the contrary, for there is no special reason to suppose that the millennial kingdom must cease because the Dragon is destroyed by a judgment of fire at the time he is suffered to go up and down in the earth to deceive the nations. But there is every reason to believe from very many passages, that this kingdom will continue on in increasing splendor until the resources of the earth are exhausted. As there is no positive clue by which to determine those events, we shall be obliged to gather the truth from the general tenor of scripture as we proceed.

Satan is no more Satan now than when, under his proper name of Dragon, he waged war with political Israel and, with the judgments of God upon him, got terribly defeated. The nature of the beast never changes though his names may. Nor is there the slightest evidence, but rather the contrary, that the next chapter (21st) is a continuation of the story immediately following the events of the 20th chapter. We have seen that the first three chapters give the counsel to the churches, and then from the fourth to the eleventh the history, in a general way, of the imperio-papal powers, and the death-blow that was given to them, with the moral phenomena which accompanied that memorable time. From the twelfth chapter John goes back to the point of beginning and takes up the papal-ecclesiastical power in minute detail. He gives all her peculiar features, color of her garments, place of her abode, and name of the people with whom she dwells, with many other items, until the final battle results (chap. 20) in the *suppression* of the Dragon of Imperialism for a very long time—put in round numbers at a thousand years—and the utter *annihilation* of the Papal *Hierarchy* (chap. 18-21), but does not destroy the Catholic Church by any means, nor indeed the *spirit* of imperialism.

At the end of the thousand years, whatever time that may be, there are found those who have a lurking desire for the old regime of imperial power, perhaps scions of royalty, who consider themselves to have been cheated out of their divine (?) rights, and are determined to regain them if possible. It is very significant that the effort begins among the people of that nation which assumes, to day, to stand as the head and front of imperialism ; viz., Gog and Magog. From the fact stated of their encompassing "the camp of the saints," it would seem that the powers opposed to political Israel in the last great battle, have attributed their terrible defeat to the Church of Christ—perhaps under the general term of Protestantism, which certainly is well known to be an opponent of all forms of error in faith and church forms.

In these long years of peace and consequent prosperity the powers of the Old World will have had ample time to recuperate their fortunes so terribly dissipated by the last disastrous conflict, and have come to imagine they can now wage successful war against their former conquerors and establish again the old Imperial regime. Under the instigation of Satan, the arch-enemy, they account for their defeat on some plausible grounds and forget the judgments that came upon their hosts, and they will not be lacking in pretexts for re-opening the war for supremacy in the government of the world. It is but the renewal of the same old war that began in Heaven for supremacy there, only now the battle-field and the living actors are changed to this earth. As in the last conflict, so now, they have "counted without their host," for this time the judgment from heaven is final and conclusive. Imperialism is doomed to utter and complete destruction, for the record is, "Fire came down from heaven and devoured them."

On looking at the tenth verse (chap. 20) we find that the Dragon. under his alias of the devil, is "cast into the lake of fire and brimstone, where the *beast* and the *false prophet* are." We learn from chap. 18-21 that these, under the symbol of Babylon (which stands for the whole hierarchy of Rome, civil and ecclesiastic), were cast with great violence into the *sea* from whence the beast and the Dragon came. We may fairly conclude, then, since there can be no conflict in the record, that the term "lake of fire and brimstone" is used to signify the extreme penalty imposed for this *second* attempt to usurp unwarranted power and to enslave the people. To suppose that a principle of government and a false system of religious teaching, as the symbols of the Dragon and the beasts undoubtedly represent, can be cast into hell, is simply absurd and admits of no argument. We may consider it settled, then, that the whole system of falsehood instigated by Satan in government and religion, is gone forever under the terrific assaults of that mighty Conqueror—"The Word of God."[1]

This term of a thousand years as a definite number of years during which false systems of government and religion are to remain inactive and dormant on account of their crushing defeat, appears improbable on the face of it. Doubt is fixed to something like certainty when it appears from all reliable sources that the term is purely a rabinical one indicating a long period of time. By them the days of the Messiah on the earth were reckoned to be a thousand years. Clark says, "Both the Greeks and Latins have the same form of speech in speaking on the state of the righteous and wicked after death." He also quotes from classic writers to show in what sense it was used, from which we gather that the term was singularly indefinite, according to the subject or persons to whom it was applied, very much as we use it now in random remarks and calculations. That John used it as a common form

---

[1] Read carefully chap. 19-11 to the end.

of speech borrowed from others, the whole construction of the book implies. We may conclude then that it means simply a long time, without doing violence or injustice to the language used.

On the other hand, it is in the highest degree improbable that the very numerous and emphatic utterances of prophecy respecting the continuation of the throne of David "throughout all generations," "an everlasting dominion which shall not pass away, and his kingdom that which shall not be destroyed," shall be *limited* by a thousand years. The term should be used in the ordinary sense in respect of imperialism, and in a prophetic sense of a year of days and a day for a year in respect of Israel; which would give us a period somewhat commensurate with the above promises, or three hundred and sixty-five thousand years. For this transposition we have a warrant in the declaration of God that "one day with the Lord is as a thousand years and a thousand years as one day." It is intimated also in the Decalogue in these words: "Visiting the iniquity of the fathers upon the children unto the *third* and *fourth* generations of them that hate me, but showing mercy unto *thousands*" (of generations) "of them that love me and keep my commandments" (see also Deut. 7-9).

If we look at the context a little more closely we shall see that this phrase of "a thousand years" was spoken of those only who were *beheaded* for the witness of Jesus "and such as worshiped not the beast," who constituted the first resurrection, and they alone lived and reigned with Christ; while none of the rest of the righteous dead lived and reigned with him until *after* the thousand years were ended. How long after we are not told, so that we are left perfectly free to adopt the more probable interpretation given above of an immensely long period, without doing any violence to the text, and really in keeping with numerous passages which favor the longer term.

This seems the more probable when we consider that after this rebellion, the kingdom will be so completely sifted of all malcontents that only the true and consecrated followers of Christ will be left, and the *special* mission of the martyr spirit of the first resurrection will have ceased.

With the accretions of population by those "fittest to live" it would not take long to fill the earth with a busy, prosperous, and happy people, with renewed strength and prolonged lives far beyond anything the world has ever dreamed of. From this we might judge that the above long period of time would amply suffice to exhaust the resources of old earth and give good excuse for winding up its affairs, since it will be no longer needed. It will have proved to be the moral battle-field for a universe—a "test case" for eternity. Men, angels and all created intelligencies have been the spectators and part participants, and our Christ has won the victory, and "thy people shall long live to enjoy the work of their hands" (Isa. 65-22: 60-21).

THE NEW JERUSALEM. 341

"In his days shall the righteous flourish;
And abundance of peace, till the moon be no more"
—(Psa. 72-7).

"THEN cometh the END when he shall have delivered up the kingdom to God, even the Father: when he shall have put down all rule and all authority and power: for he must reign till he hath put all enemies under his feet. And when all things shall be subdued unto him, then shall the Son also himself be subject unto Him that put all things under him, that God may be all in all" (Cor. 15-24. 25. 28).

Here then we have something definite respecting the *time* of the end, in harmony with all scripture, with this discussion from beginning to end, and with common sense. As we have had occasion already to say in a former chapter, if it took four thousand years for man to run to his lowest point under the leading of Satan, do give the gospel of our Christ an equal length of time at least to recover man from his lost condition. It must also prove its power to keep him from *again* falling under the dominion of sin, or what shall hinder another defection in heaven itself, as before. Finally, it must show a *profitable* investment of intelligence, power, and skill, or the plan and the investment are a failure if more are *lost* by the plan than will eventually be saved by it, as would be the case if the work of redemption is cut short now. All this takes time on the part of man, but the victory will be so complete that the number of those who shall be saved as compared with the lost will be as an ocean to a bucketful.

If there shall be found any at the end of these long ages of happy government under the benignant rule of

Christ, who shall say in their hearts—though their outward lives may profess conformity to his laws and rule—it will certainly be justifiable on the part of the King to execute judgment upon them at once, as past all reasonable hopes of redemption.

"When the Lord Jesus shall be revealed from heaven with his mighty angels, in FLAMING FIRE taking vengeance on them that know not God, and that obey not the gospel of our Lord Jesus Christ" (2 Thess. 1-7, 8).

"For the Lord *himself* shall descend from heaven with a *shout*, with the voice of the archangel, and with the trump of God: and the dead in Christ shall rise first. Then we which are alive shall be caught up together with them in the clouds, to meet the Lord in the air: and so shall we *ever be* with the Lord" (1 Thess. 4-16, 17).

"But the heavens and the earth, which are now, by the same word are kept in store, reserved unto fire against the day of JUDGMENT and perdition of ungodly men" (2 Peter. 3-7; also ver. 10).

These passages declare unmistakably, without symbolism or circumlocution, that the judgment of the ungodly at the last is to be by *fire*, and the destruction of the world by the same element. Not the slightest clue is given as to the *time* of this event, and there is only one passage in the whole Bible that is able to determine it, and that is the one we have quoted above from 1 Cor. 15 chapter, which speaks of his finished work and the character of it. That governs the whole subject in unmistakable language, and any attempt to evolve or construct a personal coming before that time by an unwarranted combination of "crazy quilt" passages gathered here and there, will only meet with disappointment and failure.

In connection with this judgment of fire and a world in flames we have the first intimation of any *personal* appearance of our Lord. This also is equally uncertain as to time, but, like the other event, it naturally connects itself with his finished work as "Mediator between God and man." We learn, moreover, that when this personal appearance takes place, there is a full and complete resurrection of *all* the redeemed dead of all the ages, and a quickening of all those who are living on the earth at the time. It is no resurrection of a certain class to the exclusion of the great body of believers—as in the case of the "first resurrection" if we believe that to be a literal rising from the grave—but a resurrection and a quickening for *all* of the followers of Christ under the old and the new covenants, without any distinction whatever.

Nor should we fail to notice that the character of the former coming to take the kingdom is marked in a majority of cases by the phrase, "I come as a thief," which at once connects it with similar phrases in relation to Christ's coming to the churches of Asia in judgment for their defection from the faith, which we know to have been an impersonal coming, and completely in the line of natural and ordinary events.

But the character of Christ's final and *personal* coming as revealed in this the only passage where that event is mentioned, is characterised by "*a shout*, and the voice of the archangel," which removes it at once from all connection with the thief-like character of his coming to cleanse the land "of all that offend, and all that do iniquity," before assuming his rightful crown as the Son of David.

It is to be observed also that when this judgment of fire, the resurrection, and this change, are effected "in a moment, in the twinkling of an eye, at the *last trump*,"[1] that the saints are to "meet the Lord *in the air.*" So shall we *ever be with the Lord.*" Not the slightest intimation is given that there is to be a return to this earth as the abode of the saints, so that we are forced to the conclusion, so plainly given throughout the scriptures, that this earth is to be the abode of the poeple of God to the end of time under *present conditions*, until a complete and thorough victory is won for Christ, and the *entire* church in this land and throughout the world has become pure and holy, "without spot or wrinkle or any such thing"—fit Bride of Christ, the conquering Son of God.

It is to be noted also that these events in connection with "the end" and the "last trump" are indissolubly joined to the giving of an incorruptible body to *all* the saints, which still further connects the various passages together in natural order as accompaniments of one and

---

[1] 1 Cor. 15-52.

the same event, viz., the closing up of the affairs of this world and relegating all power and authority to God the Father and Creator of all things.

Much more might be gathered from the scriptures to prove these various statements, but we have already transgressed the intended bounds of this book and must leave them in their suggestive condition. We urge our readers not to be satisfied with the mere reading of this book, but to search the scriptures for further proofs of their title to the boundless patrimony provided for them by their Heavenly Father, of whom you are the heir, even a joint heir with Jesus Christ your elder brother. We desire to impress upon each one his responsibility in this matter. If the Spirit has convinced you of the truth of these revelations of the Word, then proclaim your convictions on every fitting occasion, that the hearts of God's people may be comforted and settled in the truth, and that all right minded people may be enabled to "step over the line" on the side of God and home and native land, for its cleansing from the foul sins that are so likely to bring judgments upon us, peradventure we may mitigate their severity.

FINIS.

APPENDIX A.

THE TIMES OF THE GENTILES.

(Page 178.)

When Nebuchadnezzar is told by Daniel in the interpretation of the king's wonderful dream that *seven times* should pass over him, and a beast's heart should be given to him until he should learn that the Most High ruleth in the heavens and on earth, we judge that seven literal years are intended, and so it is generally held. But when God declares in respect to the national life of Israel that He would punish them yet *seven times* if they continued to disregard his will, we judge that a much longer time is intended, by so much as the life of a nation is longer than that of an individual, extending even to a cycle of seven years of years or 2520 years.

This view is wonderfully sustained when we come to apply the facts of history to the career of Israel; for, if we take 1776 as the close of her long life of captivity and oppression in one form or another under the iron heel of the Gentiles, we find that the commencement of this cycle carries us back to 744, B. C., the very time when Israel began to be carried captive by the Assyrians under Pul and Tiglath-pileser, and their places supplied by a foreign population.

Again, in Daniel's interpretation of the king's dream respecting the image. as recorded in chap. 2–31, which relates to four great kingdoms which should dominate the world to the time of the end (which is more fully set forth in another vision in chap. 7 under the symbols of four great beasts rising out of the sea), Nebuchadnezzar is represented by the head of gold of this great image; in other words, that the Babylonian kingdom was the first of these four kingdoms, the last of which should be the Roman, represented by the feet and toes of the image.

If we are right in supposing this larger cycle expresses the duration of the oppressions of Israel, there is additional reason for applying these same "seven times" in their larger range to the duration of the four kingdoms symbolised by the image, at the head of which stood the Babylonian kingdom ; and if we apply the facts of history as before, we have another wonderful confirmation of our supposition that the "times of the Gentiles" covers a like larger cycle of years of years.

Now, if we reckon back from 1794, which we have assumed to be the end of the 1260 years of the Roman domination of the saints, we are led back to 726, B. C., the very year in which Nabopolassar, the satrap of Babylon and father of Nebuchadnezzar, threw off the yoke of Assyria and established the kingdom of Babylon on a sure basis.

We also see in this larger cycle of 2520 years just the other half of "time, times, and the dividing of time"— the 1260 years of Daniel and the Apocalypse—which limit the duration of the "man of sin" as the last expiring relic of Gentile oppression over spiritual Israel. Thus we behold the hand of God reaching back into the dim ages of the past and pointing out on the dial plate of time the sure fate of nations for thousands of years.

APPENDIX B.

THE TWO WITNESSES.

(Page 229.)

Having never seen in print this interpretation of the witnesses, though it is incredible to us that no expositor of note has thought of this, the plainest and easiest of all solutions, we think it proper to give our reasons for saying that they symbolise the Bible and *nothing else*. Yet the latest book out says, "The Spirit and Prayer" are meant, and these are thought to be by the author profoundly new and original, and *not one* of the conditions of scripture are met by his interpretation.[1] Older expositors have thought with much more reason that two lines of witnesses for the truth are meant, who in all these years have stood up for the truth in various parts: notably the Albigenses and Waldenses in France, Bohemians, Lollards, and others. But they do not meet the conditions, and at best can only be held as mouthpieces for the Bible—the *fountain* of truth. In verse three the "two witnesses" are defined to be "the two

---

[1] Bishop McIlvaine's Wisdom of the Apocalypse.

olive trees *and* the two candlesticks standing before the God of the earth." We have no difficulty in defining the metaphorical "candlesticks," for Rev. 1-20 defines them to be the churches, without any chance for argument. But the two olive trees are a vital part of the symbolism and determine its character, and the scripture as usual gives the true solution. In Zec. 4-3, after giving a description of the candlesticks in verse two, the prophet goes on to describe, as an inherent and principal part of the candlestick, "Two olive trees by it, one upon the right side of the bowl, and the other upon the left side thereof." After asking, " What are these, my lord?" he is answered:—"This is the word of the Lord unto Zerubbabel. saying. 'not by might, nor by power, but by *my spirit*, saith the Lord'" (ver. 6). Twice again he asks, "What be these two olive branches which through the two golden pipes empty the golden oil out of themselves?" Then the angel replies. "These are the *two anointed ones*"— shining ones—"that stand by the Lord of the whole earth" (ver. 14). From this scripture it is evident that the "two olive trees" are superior to the candlesticks since they supply the oil without which the candlesticks cannot shine or give light, and if these represent the Church as shown, then the "olive trees" must of necessity be that which supplies the Church with its life and power, and that is none other than the Word of God— the Old and New Testaments—without which the Church is shorn of its power and gives no light to the world.

This is still further evident from the reply of the angel in verse 6: "Not by might, nor by power, but by *my spirit*, saith the Lord." As the Word of God supplies the Church with its means of light and strength and life, so the Spirit of God works through the Word and makes it "sharper than a two-edged sword" and is, moreover, itself the creator of the Word through which it works. This solution meets all the conditions, as we shall see.

APPENDIX C.

THE VIALS OF WRATH—REV. 16–1.

(Page 248.)

Much discussion has been indulged in respecting these last "plagues," and what facts of history answer to each separate "vial." As they were of no special importance to our main subject we embody our opinions of these plagues in this place simply as confirmatory evidence of the truth of our conclusions respecting the death blow to the Papacy and evidence of the truth of scripture prophecy.

It is to be noticed that the first vial was poured out "*upon the earth*," from which arose the "beast" of Rev. 13–11 which has generally been held to be a symbol of the ecclesiastical branch of the Papacy.

Hence the "noisome and grievous sore" indicates a pestilential moral atmosphere, and a foul spirit of opposition and infidelity among the adherents of the Church, which could only find its counterpart in the demoniac rage of the Catholic people of France and even the defection of the bishops and clergy, as stated in chap. 10.

The second vial was poured out "*upon the sea,*" which as a symbol we have shown to denote vast masses of corrupt people, from the midst of whom corrupt and wicked rulers might arise, as monsters from the sea. This was most emphatically realised during this same Revolution of '93-4 when Royalty was dethroned, and the ruling powers were taken from the ranks of the people, and often from the lowest classes during that terrible "reign of terror," " and it (the sea) became as the blood of a dead man." About one-tenth of the population of France (3,000,000) were ruthlessly murdered in this " great earthquake, and the *tenth part* of the city fell" (Rev. 11-13).

The third vial was poured out "upon the rivers and fountains of waters: and they became as blood." These, according to the explanation of the angel in Rev. 17-15, indicate states and communities of people as distinguished from kingdoms, and is only a restricted duplicate of the last vial, to show the widespread cry for blood in this time when every man's hand was against his neighbor. The sixth verse very plainly indicates the reason of this terrible retribution, and who should be the victims of it, as a fitting reward for the St. Bartholomew massacre and for the Albigenses and Waldenses who were ruthlessly slain by the people and soldiers of France at the bidding of the Pope.

"The fourth angel poured out his vial upon the Sun," which is a symbol of the highest dignitary in Church or State. The judicial murder of the King and Queen of France, and the terrific indignities heaped upon Pius VI. and Pius VII. by Napoleon, will fill all the requirements of this vial. Some of these have been shown in chap. 10, but a tithe was not told. The Catholic religion had been completely overthrown by the Assembly and the people of France, and when for political reasons Napoleon re-instated it, it was degraded in the eyes of the Church dignitaries by being put on a level with all other religions, and not the slightest sign of its former power was allowed or even hinted at.

Napoleon compelled the attendance of Pope Pius VII. at his coronation, "not to confer a crown but to adorn a ceremony." Could humiliation be more complete! Yes, for the fifth vial was poured out "upon the *seat of the beast*, and his kingdom was full of darkness." This limits the *time* and *place* of these events with unmistakable certainty, for no facts of history so completely fill the conditions of the prophecy as the spoliation of the Vatican treasures, the heavy indemnity levied, the dismemberment of the States of the Church, and the Pope's power declared to be ended. Napoleon further degraded him by making him a French subject and a salaried dependant of the French Court, with an annual income of £80,000.

The sixth vial we have already spoken of as relating to the quiet drying up of Turkey. The seventh vial is yet to be poured out and is near at hand.

The revolutions of 1848, when every throne in the Latin World "reeled to and fro like a drunken man," gave evidence of their tottering condition, while the closing scenes of the Œcumenical Council and the preparations to deify the Pope, became the occasion of other misfortunes "to consume and destroy his kingdom unto the end."

www.ingramcontent.com/pod-product-compliance
Lightning Source LLC
Chambersburg PA
CBHW020302240426
43673CB00039B/679